THE GOOD GUIDE TO THE LAKES

HUNTER DAVIES

Chief Researcher — Colin Shelbourn

Published by Forster Davies Ltd. Loweswater and London

The Good Guide to the Lakes by Hunter Davies
Chief Researcher, Colin Shelbourn
Published by Forster Davies Ltd., Loweswater and London.

1st edition, 1984 (white cover) 11,000 copies;
2nd printing, 1984, 15,000 copies; 3rd printing, 1985, 5,000 copies.

2nd edition, 1986 (blue cover) 15,000 copies.

This is the third, revised edition, 1989, 15,000 copies.
ISBN 0 9509190 6 3

Created, printed and published in Cumbria, of course.
Typeset by Cardtoons Publications Ltd., Windermere.
Printed and bound by Titus Wilson & Sons Ltd., Stricklandgate, Kendal.

STAR RATINGS
☆☆☆ Not to be missed
☆☆ Highly recommended
☆   Interesting

Throughout this book, we have used star ratings for almost everything, from mountains to restaurants, as a way of indicating those places or services which we think are worth experiencing. Listings with no stars at all are there mainly for reference.

Telephone numbers At the time of writing this edition, British Telecom were changing STD codes for a number of exchanges in Cumbria. In some cases a prefix is also added to the number. As no one at Telecom could tell us exactly *when* each change would take place, we've left off most of the STD codes. Sorry about that. In most cases, if the number has changed, you'll get a voice telling you the new number. In some, you just get the number unobtainable tone, in which case try directory enquiries. Thanks BT.

CONTENTS

Introduction

Welcome to the third version of this book. I thought about saying third 'edition', but the word edition can give the impression that we just pressed a button and did no new work. Goodness, have we worked, checking and chucking out, adding and subtracting, re-searching and re-writing, to make it a totally revised and updated version of a guide book which we like to consider a modern classic, judging by its sales and friends, and one which we hope will come out, in future updated versions, for ever and ever. Thank you.

Publishers do boast blithely about new 'editions' when they are often nothing of the sort. There's a new 'edition' of Peter Rabbit almost every year, despite the fact that not a word has changed since 1902. Wainwright's Fell Guides have had umpteen 'new' editions, but have remained totally unaltered since they first started to come out in 1955. 'New' very often means new, improved price, rather than new, improved content. This is just jealousy of course. Wish I was the publisher of either of those classics.

With *The Good Guide*, the sections on things like mountains and lakes have stayed much the same, as one might expect, but almost everything else had to be re-assessed and re-done. In the end, we decided to re-set and re-print the whole lot from scratch. This time, modern magic being what it is, Colin Shelbourn has done the typesetting himself, sitting at home in Windermere in front of his little machine (an Apple Macintosh). I now hope in future it will prove easier and cheaper to update. Note, all the same, that the price has not changed since the 1986 edition, sorry, 1986 version.

Once again, it is an all Cumbrian production, written and researched in Lakeland, and printed there. Still in Kendal, but not the same printer as the first two books. Well, we like to spread our huge orders around, keeping as many local printers off the streets as possible. And once again, we have taken no bribes, accepted no fees or treats, hidden or otherwise, nor charged anything for inclusion or accepted advertising. I never bothered to make that really clear in the first two editions, but it has recently been revealed how one well known guide book lady charges a 'sponsorship fee' to appear and another, nationally known firm, includes adverts from places mentioned. End of my boasting, except to say the object of the whole exercise is the same as it was in the beginning - to guide you to all that is BEST in Lakeland.

The first version came out in 1984. You must remember it, white cover, rotten maps, rather fell to pieces if ill treated. I re-printed that version twice, and in all we but then I don't live near any of them. They will find their market, and the boom will fade, just as in the last 200 years of Lakeland tourism we have had other fads and fashions.

Only one minor aspect irks me. How come these massive new complexes, costing millions, so often manage to get planning permission, when if I want to put a new window in my Lakeland barn I will be stopped, good and sharpish?

Low Flying Planes

I can see nothing in favour of this, though defenders do exist. In fact I have regular arguments with one, a retired Lakeland vicar, a good neighbour and friend, except when the dreaded planes swoop over our heads and I scream in fury and he beams with pride. He is an ex RAF man and maintains we need our brave pilots to be trained in this way to save our future lives. I say not here mate, go somewhere else and practise.

The whole problems is now a tragedy, not just an annoyance for all Lakeland walkers. There have been eight serious accidents in just ten years. In August 1988, the worst incident so far, four pilots were killed near Penrith, when low flying planes collided. The costs in man power, quite apart from the billions of pounds these planes cost, is a scandal. One day, it will happen right over a village or town. I wish Dale Campbell-Savours, MP for Workington, the best of luck in his campaign to keep all low flying fighter jets out of Lakeland.

Sellafield

This in a way is good news, if you are considering British Nuclear Fuel's processing plant as a tourist attraction, which it has suddenly become. Sellafield is the biggest success story in Cumbrian tourism in the last five years.

In our 1984 edition, it did not even make it into the Top Twenty List of most visited places. In the 1986 edition, it crept in at number 16, with 25,000 annual visitors. Now, as you will see, if you hurry to the latest available list (page 246) it has become, with 148,000 annual visitors, the most popular building in all Cumbria.

Sellafield has therefore beaten all other houses and buildings where heads are counted, leaving Dove Cottage and Hill Top miles behind, and even exceeding the previous number one favourite, Brockhole, the National Park Visitor Centre. It makes one wonder if all these years we have been wasting our time, waxing lyrically about Wordsworth, or purring over Miss Potter's charming watercolours. Could it be that the great unwashed, as well as the fragrantly washed, don't really want literature or art, or even Nature, but prefer to gape at a nuclear plant?

Sellafield has of course been rather cheating, in the

tourism stakes, letting the public in for free and spending a fortune on national TV and press advertising, which no other Cumbria tourist attraction can afford. And we all suspect that it's simply part of some devious PR plot to change the whole image of the nuclear industry. All the same, you can't force people to go where they don't want to go. Sellafield is not handy, but they've certainly trailed out there in their thousands.

The bad news, on the nuclear front, is not just the ever present danger of things going wrong at Sellafield, several of which have been exposed in recent years, but Chernobyl. Who would have thought that a Russian nuclear station, thousands of miles away, could possibly have any effects on little old Cumbria. But that's what happened in 1986, with disastrous effects on our sheep farming. It was not until late 1988 that the Government withdrew the last restrictions on certain hill farmers, when it was felt that local lamb was no longer being contaminated.

Farming

Hill farmers generally have had a bad five years. Not just because of Chernobyl, but land economy generally, plus EEC competition and regulations. You can see the effects clearly in the drastic drop in land prices in some areas. (Though not in house prices.) Around Caldbeck, as I know to my cost when I sold a few fields recently, land which was around £2,000 an acre ten years ago, fell to £1,000. Outlying pasture, fairly rough, has gone for as little as £500 an acre. No wonder so many hill farmers threaten to pack up. Beatrix Potter was thought to be engagingly eccentric, when she decided to devote the last thirty years of her life to Herdwick sheep. Now she would be presumed to be potty. The breed has been on the verge of becoming an endangered species, though it now seems safe, thanks to the protection work of the National Trust, but economically the future of all hill sheep farming is far from secure.

There was a suggestion, perfectly serious, put forward at a National Park meeting that farmers should be disbanded in Cumbria. The present Government, little interested in rural economic moans, wants farmers generally to look for alternative incomes, such as building houses on their unwanted land, which of course is not possible in Lakeland, as the National Park planners would certainly not allow that. In Lakeland, therefore, one solution would be to leave the farmers in their farm houses and cottages, but take away their stock and call them Nature Wardens. They would open their gates for us, doffing their caps for any pennies, keep the fields neat and pretty, using none of those nasty fertilisers, knock down and then build up dry stone walls, purely for our amusement, then perhaps herd back and forth a few Herdwicks, kept for entertainment, not to be bought and sold. Then it's all back to the farmhouse, for a Cumbrian tatie pot supper. It could well happen.

Weather

Hmm, more bad news. The brilliant summers of 1983 and 84 gave us all a good time, and the most marvellous swimming in Lakeland becks and lakes I have ever had, but also had a nice knock-on effect for tourism generally. Memories lingered on, repeat bookings were made for the following year. Alas, 1985, 86, 87 and 88 turned out to be rotten summers, here and throughout Britain. Figures for even the most popular Lakeland places dropped. I was in one Tourist centre when there was a call from a very well known hotel, usually permanently booked up three months ahead, to say huh, we do have a few vacancies, can you send any punters.

The worst aspect of these four poor summers is that bad memories will take some shaking. Many people will have vowed never to come again. You and I know that there is no such thing as bad weather in Lakeland, only bad clothing. The ever changing weather is one of the attractions, but there are those people, I'm told, who don't like getting wet, especially in a caravan or a tent. Let's hope, for all our sakes, the coming summers will be better.

World Heritage

It's hard to decide how bad the news was, or just a minor humiliation, when in December, 1987, a meeting in Paris decided not to recommend the English Lakeland as a World Heritage site. What does it mean anyway? Search me.

I happened by chance to be in a hotel near Kendal, researching for this book, when I found myself at breakfast with another single bloke, who turned out to be an inspector for the World Heritage Committee. He seemed to be obsessed by strange things, such as quarries, the way AA inspectors used to be more interested in the ratio of lavatories to bedrooms, rather than whether a hotel was nice or not. I also failed to get out of him what the advantages would be, should Lakeland be deemed a World Heritage site. There seemed to be no money in it, no direct development aid, but ah, think of the honour.

However, it was a disappointment, when the news was released. I suspect that some of the problems I have mentioned above, such as the rash of Timeshare developments, the low flying planes, have not helped our cause. Then there is the over use of roads, too many motor boats on Windermere, insensitive farming, alien forestry, lakes turned into reservoirs, all of which would appear to have let us down.

The only excuse, for our apparent failure, is that we were entered in the wrong competition, as if we were some sort of wilderness. Two hundred years ago, when Wordsworth was young, we might easily have persuaded any group of pernickity international bureaucrats that we were truly at one with Nature. We still like to think this is so, at least in our hearts and minds, and we genuinely believe that it is the wonder of Nature which attract us to Lakeland. But if we look honestly and coldly around, so much of what we see is not 'natural' any more. Perhaps it never has been, in the last 200 years, since the trippers first arrived, or even 2,000 years, since the first settlers. Lakeland is now a mixed site, not a pure child of nature. Next time, apparently, we will enter another category. It probably is better to boast that we combine the best of Nature and of Culture, of man and the environment, living in harmony, for us all to enjoy. All Lakeland lovers would agree with that.

Lake District Protection Bill

As I write, this looks like being the Big One, a topic which will run and run for the next two years at least, before it finally becomes translated into law.

It's now exactly forty years ago, in 1949, that the original National Park legislation went onto the statute books. Naturally, quite a lot has happened since then, new problems have arisen, different sorts of pressures have appeared. There are new creations to worry about, from Timeshares to Sodium Street Lights, windsurfing to wet bikes, plus the old problems of erosion and conservation.

The Lake District Special Planning Board has taken some stick, these last few years, by apparently doing little to cope or counter the new problems, such as, for example, the low flying jets. Turns out it's not been through lack of interest, so they now tell us, but lack of muscle. Under John Toothill, the National Park Officer, a very bold campaign has now got under way to get a Bill through Parliament which will give the LDSPB greatly increased powers to restrict all development in the Park and control lake usage.

It remains to be seen how all this will effect you and me, as all the details will take time to emerge. Some of the big aims sound good, such as making all National Park land 'inalienable', which means it can never be developed. They don't in fact own a lot, compared with the National Trust, but it will affect some well known stretches, such as the Caldbeck Fells. Coming down the scale, I'm not sure I'll be all that thrilled to have their officers telling me what colour I can or can not paint my Lakeland house.

So who pays for all this? Ah ha. That's where the fun will lie, and the feathers will get ruffled. Several million pounds will be needed to implement their new powers, if and when they get them. The Government, any Government, is usually mean and short sighted when it comes to conservation. National Appeals have in the past not been very successful. So the current plan is to build in powers for the LDSPB to raise local taxes. Mr Toothill has already suggested, for example, that all visitors might pay an extra 50p. per bed night, just for the pleasure of sleeping in the Lake District. Just imagine how all the Lakeland hoteliers will react to that. Apoplexy, I should think. (But it can be made to work - the French have been successfully operating such a scheme for years.)

I look forward to all the discussions and the debates, the rumblings and the rows. If nothing else, it should give every Cumbrian newspaper an easy leader column topic for the next two years.

Good News

I don't think things are getting worse, despite the fact that for almost the last 200 years moanie minnies have been saying Lakeland has been ruined. Since mass tourism began in Lakeland in the 1840's, with the arrival of the railways, ripping up the landscape for bridges and stations, there have always been some people bewailing the crowds, the new developments, the ugly hotels, the grandiose country homes of rich industrialists. By comparison, the present rash of Timeshares is hardly visible. Nature conservation has always been necessary, as certain walks and popular fells will always become worn, but this can be regulated and damage repaired. Goodness knows, we have enough authorities in Lakeland these days, doing what they think is best for us. As for vandals, so what's new. Wordsworth took Coleridge on a walk round Keswick in 1799 and when they came to the Castlerigg stones, already famous, some yobs had already been there - and daubed them with whitewash.

Manmade things have definitely improved. While Keswick, Windermere and Grasmere still suffer and can be insufferable in summer, the peripheral towns grow better all the time, especially places like Cockermouth, Penrith, Maryport and Whitehaven. You can actually see the improvements, appreciate the architecture, now that little lanes, shop fronts, public buildings and private houses are being restored and revitalised. Hotels and restaurants continue to get better, as more and more enthusiasts follow the path laid down forty years ago by Sharrow Bay and offer personal and distinctive hospitality. We have discovered several new places for this edition, but know there must be dozens of little establishments, small restaurants or six bedroom hotels, begun by amateurs, usually just one couple, which will already have regulars raving, yet are still struggling because they are not generally known. So write and tell us, please. And any other discoveries you make, or mistakes you have found here. It can happen, as places close.

Since our last edition, we must bid a Sad Goodbye to the Dolls Museum in Ambleside and to Jack Hadwin's motor cycle collection in Broughton-in-Furness. Closed, alas. Not such a sad farewell to the Lake District Heritage Centre in Ambleside, which I never liked. Meanwhile, it's a Big Hello to the Keswick Railway Museum (with the possibility of a Motor Museum also being opened in Keswick), to the Hall House Collection, in Kendal, and to Hawkshead's new Beatrix Potter Gallery. And of course a hesitant hi to all those sumptuous Timeshares.

On a personal note, I have to record that the Lake District Book of the Year Award is now established, usually with a post-award luncheon to celebrate, all proceeds going to charity. *The Good Guide*, or other similar marvels from the little Lakeland publishing firm of Forster Davies Ltd, can never win, as the prize began with the help of some of the proceeds from the first edition of the Guide. I'm also a judge. That does make things rather awkward.

It's also nice to record that Colin Shelbourn, hardly out of university when this Guide began, and still this book's Chief Researcher, has blossomed into a full time Lakeland author, artist and all round entrepreneur. Apart from three Lakeland books to his credit, his firm is responsible for those funny postcards and little maps you now see all over Lakeland. He's also cartoonist for the *Westmorland Gazette*. I do like it when local people manage to create and carve out a career for themselves, without ever having to go and work in the sorry South. There will always be opportunities for people, locals or outsiders, to make a living for themselves in Lakeland, if you look carefully at the market, and don't expect to make your fortune. After all, living up here is what matters most.

In my case, it comes nearer all the time. For ten years, we had a holiday cottage at Caldbeck, spending three months a year there. Since the last edition, we have bought a house at Loweswater. What joy, what bliss. We found it at last. And very soon, it will be our true home.

Finally, till the next edition, when I hope we'll meet here once again, I wish you as much pleasure out of reading and using this guide as we had in researching and compiling it.

Hunter Davies,
Loweswater, 1989.

Chapter One

Planning

Things to do or know or consider before leaving home - or to bear in mind when you have just arrived.

Location Is that all it is, that little hilly region up in the top left hand corner of the map of England? How can so much fuss have been made for the last 200 years over such a small area? Ah, but in that pocket handkerchief are all nature's delights, plus quite a few man-made wonders. As you will quickly discover.

The Lake District is all in the County of Cumbria, (once Cumberland, Westmorland and part of Lancashire) England's second largest county in terms of acreage. There is a large circle inside the county which is called the Lake District National Park, a boundary line which at times appears perverse, cutting out some parts of Cumbria which are equally beautiful, but this inner circle contains the jewels in the crown. The National Park area is only thirty miles across, not much bigger than Greater London. Compared with national parks in America or in Australia, its size is insignificant.

It is bordered today on its east side by the M6 motorway. If you were driving fast, you could pass the Lake District in half an hour and never know it was there. What a tragedy that would be.

What is it? It's a load of very old lakes and mountains covering an area of some 880 square miles. The mountains are high compared with other British mountains, and there are four over 3,000 feet, and the lakes are big in British terms, with one being 10 miles long, but as far as the world's biggest mountains and the largest lakes are concerned, they are but pimples and puddles.

It has been called lots of things. The Cumbria Tourist Board, having billed it for years as "English Lakeland - the

Most Beautiful Corner of England" then changed it, according to the slogan on their envelopes, "Lakeland - the Roots of Heaven". It is also known as the English Lakes, The Lakes, Lakeland. You can use a permutation of several words. We intend to call it the Lake District, or sometimes LD if space is short, meaning that part of Cumbria designated as the Lake District National Park.

How to Get There

Road   Most visitors zoom up the M6 by car from the South. As Motorways go, it can be surprisingly attractive, far less crowded than those horrible race-track stretches further South, around Manchester and Birmingham. After Lancaster, you begin to see real scenery, then once into Cumbria, hurrah, there are real mountains. Watch out for the police. Empty stretches of Cumbrian Motorway can make the mind wander, the heart soar, and the speedometer rise above 70mph.

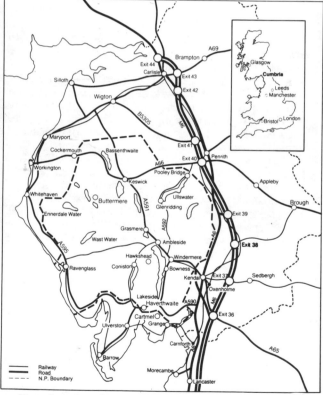

From London, the distance by Motorway to Kendal, the Southern gateway to the Lakes, is about 260 miles. Turn left at Junctions 36 or 37. For the Northern Lakes, heads down for Penrith, another 20 or so miles, then turn left at

Junction 40 for Ullswater or Keswick. Mad drivers can get to the Lakes in four hours from London. We generally take six hours on family trips, with two stops, one for a picnic and one for watering the animals.

The M6 proper peters out just north of Carlisle, but those coming down from Scotland, from Glasgow or Edinburgh, do have reasonably good dual carriageways most of the way till they reach the Motorway. There are two useful Tourist Information Centres on the Motorway, when you're heading to the Lakes. On the northern stretch, just south of Carlisle, there's one at Southwaite Service Station. From the south, drivers can stock up on free literature at Forton Service Station, just south of Lancaster.

If you're approaching the Lake District from the East, then it's hard cheese. The roads over the Pennines are pretty, and the one over Hartside Pass, via Alston, is sensational, but they can take forever as they are narrow and twisty, even some of the so-called main or A roads. First timers should never try a short cut or attempt a minor road. You might never be seen again.

Rail There is no direct train into the Lakes. You have to change at Oxenholme, and even then you can only travel as far as Windermere, the only railway line inside the Lakes. There were others, but they have all gone. It means that Oxenholme, a toy town station, hardly more than a halt, becomes in the summer a meeting place for all the rucksacks in the Western World. But Oxenholme is on the main intercity route, from Euston up to Carlisle and Scotland, and you can get there by train from most British cities, far quicker than by roads. Best train times:

> **London** - 3 hours 38 minutes
> **Birmingham** - 2 hours 24 minutes
> **Manchester** - 1 hour 25 minutes
> **Liverpool** - 1 hour 45 minutes
> **Glasgow** - 2 hours 8 minutes
> **Edinburgh** - 2 hours 20 minutes

Other Stations Penrith also has a station, but you then have to transfer by bus or other means to the Lakes. Carlisle is a main line station and connects with the amazing Cumbria coastal route - however did Beeching never kill it? - which hugs the west coast. Very handy for exploring the western Lakes and Furness, though it never actually touches any of the Lakes. (For transport *inside* the Lakes, see Chapter Three.)

By planning ahead, you can take advantage of *large* savings with a special saver ticket, or a Student Railcard, but it can take a large mount of time, working out all the conditions, most of which seem to have been dreamed up for your inconvenience.

Airport   There is no large Lakeland airport, though Carlisle does have a little one.   Contact the airport manager, 'phone 0228 73641.   If you own a private plane, this would be the handiest place to land.   (And if you own a private plane, would also like to buy a private publishing company?)   There is also an airfield on Walney Island, Barrow-in-Furness ('phone 0229 42442), with shuttles to Manchester and the Isle of Man.

Blackpool also has an airport, 'phone 0523 43061.   The nearest international airports are Newcastle, 'phone 0632 860966, or Manchester 061 437 5233.

Sea   Despite all that water which surrounds Cumbria on three sides, there are no regular passenger boats these days to any Cumbrian ports.   The nearest is Heysham in North Lancs, 'phone 0524 53802.

Coming from Abroad   Before arriving in Britain, it is possible to get information and advice about a holiday in the Lakes by contacting the nearest local office of the British Tourist Authority.   Most major cities in the US and most capital cities elsewhere have a BTA office.

Coming from London   English Tourist Board, Thames Tower, Black's Road, Hammersmith, London NW6 9EL. Phone: 01-730 3400.

Tourist Information in Cumbria

Cumbria Tourist Board, Ashleigh, Holly Road, Windermere, Cumbria.   Phone: Windermere (09662) 4444.

When you are planning your holiday, tell them in advance your special interest or problem.   This is their HQ address, where you can write or telephone, but don't call in person.

When you actually get to Cumbria, there are lots of local tourist information offices you can visit in the flesh. We'll come to them later in Chapter two.

Tourist Information   A 24 hour service of recorded events information is available on Windermere 6363.

Radio Cumbria broadcasts tourist information during the summer on 266 and 397m (MW) and 95.6 (VHF), or if you're in South Cumbria try Radio Furness on 358m (MW) and 96.1 (VHF).

Weather   Weather forecasts for the Lake District are available each day after 0800 on Windermere 5151.   These are usually reliable and essential if you are planning a day's walking.   An outlook for the following day is given after 1600.   During the winter the same number gives walking conditions on the fell tops.

Guide Books

Guide books to the Lakes first appeared around the 1770s. Since then, over 5,000 books have been published about the Lakes, more than on any similar sized region in the UK, so the choice is enormous and still growing.

Beware the over-glossy booklets with chocolate box covers with unbelievably blue skies and lakes. They have probably put their money and energy into colour reproduction at the expense of the words and new information. Also be wary of publications taking advertisements. How can they possibly give you real opinions?

Historic Books

☆ William Wordsworth, **Guide to the Lakes**. This was first published in 1835 but is now available from OUP in a facsimile edition. Fascinating reading, after you have had your holiday. Don't try to plan anything from it in advance. Notice how many subsequent Lakeland writers have pinched ideas and even phrases from Wordsworth, trying to capture the essence of Lakeland scenery.

☆☆ Dorothy Wordsworth, **Journals**. OUP. This is a facsimile of the Journals which Wordsworth's sister Dorothy kept of their life together at Dove Cottage in 1800-1802. It pays to know something of Wordsworth's life beforehand, to understand exactly what is going on, as it is very

*The Great Frost of 1895, Kendal, by A. Wainwright
(from the H. Davies collection)*

confused in parts but charming and illuminating descriptions of day to day life with her Beloved Brother, either helping him with his muse or baking his pies. Also now available in illustrated editions.

☆ **The Illustrated Wordsworth's Guide to the Lakes** edited by Peter Bicknell, Webb & Bower, 1984. Wealth of period illustrations to supplement the text (which, unlike OUP, is printed with a modern typeface and rather easier to read). A few modern photographs sit rather oddly among them. Spot the rogue picture of Grasmere masquerading as Rydal Water.

Educational Books

☆☆☆ **GCSE Resource Guides**. An ambitious series of books, aimed at GCSE students. Full of facts, information and ideas, presented in a lively manner. Three titles so far, with a fourth appearing towards the end of 1989. Additional backup available in the form of slide sets, an audio tape and computer material. Published by the National Park.

☆☆ **Field Studies in Cumbria**. Published by Cumbria Education Committee - invaluable guide for all teachers looking for sites in Cumbria which they can visit for environment-based educational purposes.

All Change! Published by the National Trust and Cumbria County Council. A teacher's pack on landscape conservation, for use in schools.

Walking Books

☆☆☆ A. Wainwright, **Pictorial Guide to the Lakeland Fells**, seven volumes published by The Westmorland Gazette, Kendal. Essential for all walkers. Wainwright divided the Lakes into seven areas, so buy the one you will be visiting most, or buy them all to take home and wonder at. In his own words and with his own pen (for there is not an ounce of printer's type in any of his books), he draws and describes exactly every walk up every fell you could possibly make. He spent thirteen years on his walks and though the first volume came out in 1955, they reprint endlessly and are still up to date. Each is a work of art, full of wit, wisdom and love of the Lakes. The first editions are collectors' pieces. Buy them **now** as they keep going up in price. They will be a joy for ever.

☆☆ John Parker, **Walk The Lakes**, Bartholomew. A peculiar-looking, spiral-bound book (it's easy to mistake for a calendar) describing forty, easy low-level walks. Excellent for the less ambitious walker. Each of the forty walks is graded, described in detail (including what you can expect to see around you) and is accompanied by a one inch to the mile colour map of the area described. Warning: because of the idiosyncratic binding and layout, it is worth spending some time at home getting to know your way round the book *before* you set off on the walks. (Follow up book in 1983 **Walk the Lakes Again** - reissued in 1988 as **More Walk the Lakes** - different title, different cover, same contents. Naughty..)

☆☆ Tony Hopkins, **Walks to Remember**, Polecat Press, 1984-5. 3 vols. Very well-produced, full of information on flora, fauna and general history of the area. Good family walks but some of the routes are very short - 2 or 3 miles on average.

☆ A. Wainwright, **Fellwalking with Wainwright**, Michael Joseph, 1984. Topped the British non-fiction lists but more a book to display on your coffee table so your friends all know you go walking in the Lake District.

☆☆ Colin Shelbourn, **Great Walks in the Lake District**, Ward Lock, 1987. Another coffee table book - when will publishers ever learn? - but superb colour photographs by David Ward and twenty-eight walks ranging from dead easy family strolls to day-long mountain hikes.

☆☆ Frank Duerden, **Best Walks in the Lake District**, Constable, 1986. The only serious rival to Wainwright which can still be stuffed in a rucksack.

General Books

☆☆ Norman Nicholson, **Portrait of the Lakes**, Hale. The late Norman Nicholson has been our most recent poet of the Lakes, born and bred in Millom. Good on history and geology. Perhaps the best-written present day book on Lakeland. Now out of print so look in second hand bookshops.

☆☆ AA - **Ordnance Survey Leisure Guide, Lake District**. First class production, excellent maps and very handy potted guides to the main places, arranged alphabetically. A very good seller when it first appeared in 1984. Short on comments but has almost all the facts that any beginner might want.

☆ Melvyn Bragg, **Land of the Lakes**, Secker & Warburg. Good photographs and lavish production, though in places a trifle thin on words. One of the most handsome of the present day books.

☆ John Wyatt, **The Shining Levels**, Penguin. Not a guide book, but the story of one man's return to nature, amongst the Lakeland fells. A nice book to take home and read once the holiday is over.

☆ Norman Nicholson, **The Lake District - an Anthology**, Penguin. Marvellous selection of stuff written about Lakeland, from the 7th century onwards. (But no Beatrix Potter - couldn't he get permission?) Ideal for literary buffs and browsers.

☆ W. Rollinson, **Life and Tradition in the Lake District**, Dalesman. A most original work of non-fiction. Describes and illustrates the vanishing or vanished folk culture of Lakeland, from stone walls, sports, dialects to diet and folk medicine.

☆☆ David McCracken. **Wordsworth and the Lake District**. Oxford Paperbacks, 1984. The best (by a wide margin) of the books connecting the poems and their places. Highly readable with maps, poems and some excellent guided walks around Wordsworth territory.

Hunter Davies, **A Walk Around the Lakes**, Arrow. Dreadfully out of date, why do they keep buying it in their millions? But a joy to read, the most loved general book on the Lakes ever written. Unquote.

Maps

The ordinary Ordnance Survey Landranger maps (1:50 000 series), are not much good for the Lake District. They're detailed enough for walking, yet you have to buy seven to cover Cumbria. You could go mad, trying to work out the overlaps. So find a good map or bookshop and go for the more specialised maps.

☆☆☆ **OS Outdoor Leisure Maps** (1:25 000 scale 2 1/2 inches to the mile). They divide the Lakes into four - SE, SW, NE, NW. Worth investing in all four. A pity the cover drawings have been dumped in favour of gaudy photographs.

☆☆ **OS Lake District Touring Map** (1 inch to the mile). This does at least give you the whole of the Lakes on one map. (Well almost. They have cut a nasty slice off the top of Caldbeck.) Good detail, but a bit cumbersome to use for those who are only exploring one area of the Lakes.
OS Six Inch Maps (1:10 000 and 1:10 560). For the absolute specialist, wanting to know a lot about a very little chunk, 5 x 5km square, down to individual fields, they usually have to be ordered. Only available as flat maps.

☆☆ **Cumbria - English Lake District**, Cumbria Tourist Board's Touring Map. Revised in 1988. Has tons of tourist info on the back (though if you've already bought this book you won't need any of it).

☆☆☆ **The A-Z Lake District**, published by the A-Z map people in London. 1 inch to the mile but a lot easier to read on the move than the OS 1 inch and with visitor attractions and places to visit marked out and *named* on the map (no confusing symbols as on the CTB). Excellent for road touring.

☆☆ **Lake District Lap Map**, published by Cardtoons Publications Ltd. A small, easy-to-use road map, designed for those who don't want the fuss and expense of larger-scale sheets. Loads of tourist info and suggested road tours on the back. Incredibly good value. (End of advt.)

Hint - A good source of local street maps are the estate agents - they usually have free ones available which are reasonably accurate.

Magazines

Magazines come and go. Since the last edition, we have lost *Preview of Lakeland*, that excellent source of day-to-day events listings. There remain four magazines you will see on book stalls in the Lakes. They tend to be short on opinions and true guidance, very cosy and old fashioned, but are normally reliable when it comes to listings. Being magazines, they are generally more up to date than any proper book with the latest details of Lakeland events. Even this wonderful book.

☆ **Cumbria**, monthly. Dalesman Publishing Co, Clapham, via Lancaster, Lancs. Rather old-fashioned, but more of a good read and less of an advertising sheet than the others.

Lakeland Life Magazine, monthly. PO Box 18, Carlisle.

Lakescene, monthly, 12 Lonsdale Street, Carlisle.

Cumbria Life, quarterly, Prestige Publications, 32 Lowther Street, Carlisle.

Newspapers

Best of all, for the *very* latest information, are the local papers. Here are the seven main ones, together with the areas they cover:

☆ **Whitehaven News** (Thursday) - Whitehaven and west coast of Cumbria. Queen Street, Whitehaven.

☆☆ **Cumberland News** (Friday) - Carlisle and N Lakes. Dalston Road, Carlisle.

☆☆ **Westmorland Gazette** (Friday) - Kendal and S Lakes. Stricklandgate, Kendal.

☆ **Barrow News** (Friday) - Barrow and Furness areas, round to Grange-over-Sands. Abbey Road, Barrow-in-Furness.

☆ **Cumberland & Westmorland Herald** (Saturday) - Penrith and E Lakeland. 14 King Street, Penrith.

☆ **West Cumberland Times & Star** (Friday) - Cockermouth and Workington. Oxford Street, Workington.

Keswick Reminder (every Friday) - Keswick and North Lakes. Station Street, Keswick.

The Lakeland Echo - S. Lakeland free sheet, published Thursdays. Not so hot on news (the editorial wears money-tinted spectacles) but has a weekly listing of local events.

The Lakes Leader - new competitor to the Echo, published Wednesdays. Far better on news, less good on events listings.

National Park Publications

☆☆☆ **The Lake District Guardian** - another freebie, published annually in vast quantities by the National Park Authority. Interesting articles plus a listing of visitor activities organised by the Park; guided walks, days with a ranger, farm open days. Available from TICs throughout the area. Residents get one delivered free with their local paper.

Events '89 - a new NP publication (we'll leave it to you to guess the title for coming years). NP events for the whole of the season, including useful listings of talks and slide shows. Free from TICs.

When to Come?

If you have school age children, then you are lumbered with coming in the school holidays. August is always a wicked month. For pretty scenery, May and June, then September and October are the best months, if you can make it. May and June are also the driest months, whilst September and October are the most colourful, with the bracken and trees finally turning from green to brown to gold.

The winter snows can be dramatic, and the views sensational, but apart from the fells, which never close, most man-made Lakeland things shut in winter. The Season' in the Lakes is shorter than the so called summer season elsewhere in England where most things open up at Easter for the visitors. In Lakeland, you'll find that many of the major attractions are not fully operational until Whit.

The Weather

Fascinating. Yes, that's what I think. There are few places in the world where you can get such variations from place to place, from day to day, in such a short distance. If you don't like it, move on a few miles, or come down a few thousand feet. Naturally, it could be *worse*, but at least it is unlikely to be the same.

Now for some hard facts about Lakeland weather. South Devon gets more rain that Carlisle. Honestly. It's the high bits at the head of the valleys which give the Lake District a bad name for rainfall. Elsewhere in Lakeland, the rainfall is normal-to-dry for Britain.

Seathwaite, at the head of Borrowdale, is admittedly the wettest place in England, with 130 inches a year, but if you go to Keswick, just eight miles away, it drops dramatically to 51 inches a year. Move on another 20 miles, into the Solway Plain at Carlisle, then it is only 30 inches a year. Positively arid.

Keswick has milder winters than London - and it's sweltering in the winter compared with really cold places like New York or Berlin. Though there is a great variation from day to day in Lakeland villages and valleys, there are not enormous seasonal *extremes*. You will notice that shepherds and farmers tend to wear the same clothes all the year round - usually a jacket and trousers that don't match and old shoes or boots, which sometimes don't match either. Inside their cottages, the fire is often lit all around the year.

The summer can be hot - remember the summer of 1984 and those weeks and weeks of eighty degrees, ahh - but don't bank on it. There has not been a summer in which I have not had a bathe in a Lakeland beck, if only for a few minutes, but it is best to come prepared, especially if you intend to do any climbing. It's always colder up top. And look out for mist. But note well, there is *never* any fog in the Lakes.

The nicest bonus of all for Lakeland lovers is that you get three quarters of an hour more daylight every summer's evening in the Lakes compared with London or the South. The weather often gets better as the day wears on and, with luck, you can have two days in one and organise two different expeditions. Climbers, even serious ones like Chris Bonington, often set out at six in the evening and get a day's climbing in before dark.

What to Wear Clothes, they're terribly useful. They don't like you going naked in the Lakes. It frightens the sheep. As for *what* clothes, then that's up to you. The experts and the officials and the organisation men would have you dressed for a simple fell walk as if you are going up Everest, with oxygen masks and ice picks and very bright colours.

The most important rule for walkers, and I stress walkers not climbers, is that Comfort is All. The second rule is that it won't last. So it is best to take a pullover, even setting off in the sun, and some sort of raincoat or waterproof anorak. Brightly coloured waterproofs are all the rage at the moment. At least they make you easier to spot if you get into difficulties on the fells. In the winter, or obvious bad weather, I take leggings as well. Third rule - always tell someone exactly where you are going and when you plan to return. Fourthly, take a whistle.

Climbing is a specialist sport, for which some participants dress like space explorers, but we'll discuss that later. Walking is natural. There's no secret. All you do is put one foot in front of the other. Easy peasy.

As for footwear, I walked happily for twenty years on the fells with plimsolls in summer and wellingtons in winter. Now, for winter and bad weather, I have to admit I've recently changed to lightweight boots. After two cartilage operations, caused by football not walking, I found that wellingtons hurt my calves. I now love my boots, but there is no need for you to buy them, if you don't want to. Nor any need to buy fancy climbing socks, pretty though they look, or those natty plus fours in that thick hairy tweed. I once got a pair as a present, and I looked terrific in them, but they itched like hell and I now never wear them. Have a second glance at the next shepherd you see working on the fells. How many are wearing climbing boots, plus fours and carrying ropes? Well then.

Accidents

What do you do if something awful happens? In the first edition of this book we gave no advice, but since then the accident rate has enormously increased. (Not our fault, I hope.) In the second edition, we reported that 1984 saw the highest number of deaths on Lake District Mountains since records began. Sadly, that record was broken again in 1987, with a total of 27 deaths. Five of the deaths were due to natural causes, such as heart attacks, but most of the rest occurred on the mountains, usually in snow and ice conditions and they mostly involved experienced mountain people, with adequate equipment.

The Mountain Rescue teams were called out for a total number of 275 incidents in 1987, including 33 where RAF helicopters had to be called out. Quite apart from the deaths, there were also 155 injuries, 64 serious. The Lake

District share of National call-outs stood at over 50% (not including Scotland).

Accidents to *ordinary* fellwalkers remain fairly steady over the years. Often the call outs are due to people being lost, or coming down in the wrong place and not notifying base. A large number of the injuries, however, can occur on wet grass, when it is very easy to slip. Plimsolls and wellingtons aren't much use here.

Rock climbers and specialist sportsmen and women have their own set of rules and guide lines. However, all users of the fells and mountains should take great care. In the events of a serious accident, do the following:

Summon help by six long whistle blasts, or torch flashes if you have one, then repeat after a minute. This is the recognised distress signal on mountains.

Go for help, if one of your party is able to, having made the injured person comfortable and administered any first aid. It is vital to memorise the exact spot, working out on the map the grid reference if possible.

Telephone for help, when you can find a box or the nearest farm. Dial Police 999. (You don't call out the Mountain Rescue Teams. The police will do this.)

You will be asked location of injured person, time of accident, nature of accident - they need to know this to decide if a helicopter is necessary. You will probably be asked to stand by the telephone, so the rescue team can reach you first.

The police will then contact the nearest Mountain Rescue team. There are sixteen in all, based at Keswick, Coniston, Cockermouth, Ambleside, Kendal, Furness, Penrith, Patterdale, Wasdale, Millom, Kirkby Stephen, Sedbergh, plus two Outward Bound Rescue Teams, a Dog Team and RAF Helicopter team based in North Yorks. When the leader is contacted he goes to his base HQ and puts out an emergency call to all his members. As soon as the first four arrive, usually including a doctor, they set off by Land Rover, taking first aid and radio equipment. They do a brilliant job. All voluntary. Please support them.

Winter Walking Increasingly, people are taking to the fells in winter and it is worth carrying and *knowing how to use* an ice axe if you plan to go on the high fells in snow conditions. The National Park runs a training scheme - details from Brockhole or one of the specialist outdoor shops.

Grid References Just in case you have forgotten, tut tut, this is how you work them out. They are always given in a group of six figures, such as 342 152, which in this case is the summit of Helvellyn, and they refer to a precise if 'imaginary' small square on an OS map.

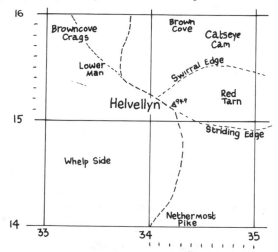

To find the exact site taking the example above, look firstly for 34 on the top or bottom margins of your Ordnance Survey map. Because the third figure is 2, you must look right two tenths of a square.

Now look for the 15 on either of the side margins and from this line count up two tenths of a square.

Mountain Accident Figures Each year, the Lake District Mountain Accidents Association issues an annual report. It makes fascinating, if morbid reading, detailing every incident. Usually costs about 80p. Enquire at the TIC's. The Secretary of the Association is - Mr Paul Horder, 36 Wordsworth Street, Keswick.

Hospitals

Assuming the accident is not too serious, and you can hobble or somehow get back on your own to your own transport, you might still want medical attention. Be careful. You might look up the nearest hospital in the telephone book and be unaware that it's only a titchy one, a cottage hospital perhaps, without any X-ray facilities or even doctors on the premises. This recently happened to a reader from Nottingham. She had been walking round Ullswater, as recommended by this very wonderful guide book, when a six year old in the party fell on a flat piece of grass, and appeared to have broken her leg. They looked up Hospitals in the *Good Guide* (first edition, alas, which didn't have them), so they worked out that the nearest town must be Penrith. They raced to Penrith, found the hospital, but were told the X-ray machine operator had gone off as it was after three o'clock. So back in the car and a mad dash up the M6 to Carlisle where they eventually found the Cumberland Infirmary. The leg was X-rayed, found to be broken, and treated. "They were very kind to us stupid trippers."

Here's a list of hospitals, just in case it happens to you. Hospitals starred have doctors available 24 hours a day and can cope with major accidents (though Kendal may refer people to Lancaster). The others all call on local GP's. Again, they will do this 24 hours a day, but for minor accidents, GP's are often available at the hospital where times have been indicated.

South Cumbria:

☆ **Furness General Hospital**
Barrow-in-Furness
Tel: Barrow 32020

☆ **Westmorland County Hospital**
East View
Kendal
Tel: Kendal 22641

West Cumbria:

☆ **West Cumberland Hospital**
Hensingham
Whitehaven
Tel: Whitehaven 3181

Cockermouth Cottage Hospital
Isel Road
Cockermouth
Tel: Cockermouth 822226

Victoria Cottage Hospital
Ewanrigg Road
Maryport
Tel: Maryport 812634

Workington Infirmary
Infirmary Road
Workington
Tel: Workington 2244
(GP available 9am-12 noon, Mon-Fri)

North & East Cumbria:

☆ **Cumberland Infirmary**
Newtown Road
Carlisle
Tel: Carlisle 23444

Keswick Cottage Hospital
Crosthwaite Road
Keswick
Tel: Keswick 72012
(GP and X-ray available mornings)

Penrith New Hospital
Bridge Lane
Penrith
Tel: Penrith 63647
(X-ray Dept. 10am-12 noon, 1pm-3pm, Mon-Fri).

Early Closing and Market Days

Unlike London and most Southern towns, Lakeland shopkeepers usually have one half day off every week when they close at lunch time. There is no geographical consistency. The favourite half day tends to be Thursdays, though several choose Wednesday and a handful opt for Tuesdays. It does not mean that *every* shop in that particular town or village will be closed. Many of the big ones and chain stores stay open. But you have been warned.

Market days are worth noting. They are often in covered market halls, selling mainly local vegetables and produce, clothes and domestic stuff. Often very colourful and full of country folk. Rarely something exotic to buy, but the faces are studies in themselves. Especially the egg ladies.

Early Closing (EC) and Market Days (M)

Alston: EC Tue; No Market. **Ambleside:** EC Thu (winter only); M Wed. **Appleby:** EC Thu; M Sat. **Arnside:** EC Thu; No Market. **Askam-in-Furness:** EC Weds; No Market. **Aspatria**: EC Wed; No Market. **Barrow-in-Furness:** EC Thu; M Wed, Fri and Sat. **Brampton:** EC Thu; M Wed. **Brough:** EC Thu; No Market. **Broughton-in-Furness** EC Thu; M Tue. **Carlisle:** EC Thu; M Mon to Sat (except Thu pm). **Cleator Moor:** EC Wed, M Fri. **Cockermouth:** EC Thu; M Mon. **Coniston:** EC Wed; No Market. **Dalton-in-Furness:** EC Wed; M Tue. **Egremont:** EC Wed; M Fri. **Grange-over-Sands:** EC Thu; No Market. **Grasmere:** EC Thu; No Market. **Hawkshead:** EC Thu (Winter only); No Market. **Kendal:** EC Thu; M Mon, Wed and Sat. **Keswick:** EC Wed; M Sat. **Kirkby Lonsdale:** EC Wed; M Thu. **Kirkby Stephen:** EC Thu; M Mon. **Longtown:** EC Wed; No Market. **Maryport:** EC Wed; M Fri. **Millom:** EC Wed; No Market. **Milnthorpe:** EC Thu; M Fri. **Penrith:** EC Wed; M Tue and Sat. **Sedbergh:** EC Thu; M Wed. **Shap:** EC Thu and Sat; M Mon. **Silloth:** EC Tue; M Sun. **Ulverston:** EC Wed; M Thu and Sat. **Whitehaven:** EC Wed; M Thu and Sat. **Wigton:** EC Thu; M Tue. **Windermere:** EC Thu; No Market. **Workington:** EC Thu; M Wed and Sat.

Recommended Markets

Keswick - Saturday
Carlisle - daily, except Thursday afternoon (in covered market)
☆ Whitehaven - Thursday and Saturday
☆☆ Kirkby Lonsdale - Thursday
☆☆☆ Ulverston - Thursday and Saturday (Thurs. best)

Calendar of Events

Check with the local newspapers, or with any of the tourist information centres (see page 00), for the precise dates each year, but these are the Big annual events which occur around the same time every year. Bear them in mind when planning your holiday.

Note Don't worry if you can't understand some of the words at this stage. No, Egremont Crab Fair has nothing to do with fish. We'll come to fuller descriptions of the major events and activities in Chapter Fourteen.

April

International Festival of Mime, Kendal - early April. Contact Brewery Arts Centre for details.

May

Cartmel Races - Bank Holiday weekend.

June

Appleby Horse Fair - second Wednesday.
Warcop Rushbearing - St Peter's Day (June 29) or preceding Saturday if the 29th is a Sunday.

July

Ambleside Rushbearing - first Saturday.
Great Musgrave Rushbearing - first Saturday.
Lakeland Rose Show, Grange-over-Sands - 2nd weekend.
Lake Windermere Festival - one week, early July.
Cumberland Show, Carlisle - next to last Thursday.
Penrith Show - Saturday (date flexible).

Keswick Convention - religious convention, two weeks, mid-July.
Wordsworth Summer Conference - late July or early August. Details from Dove Cottage.

August

Ambleside Sports - Thursday before the first Monday.
L.D. Summer Music Festival, Ambleside - late August.
Cockermouth Show - Saturday before the first Monday.
Grasmere Rushbearing - Saturday nearest St Oswald's day (5th).
Cartmel Show - Wednesday after first Monday.
Gosforth Show - third Wednesday.
Grasmere Sports - third Thursday after first Monday.
Lake District Sheep Dog Trials - Thursday after first Monday.
Rydal Sheep Dog Trials - second Thursday after first Monday.
Threlkeld Sheep Dog Trials - third Wednesday after first Monday.
Skelton Agricultural Show Penrith - third Saturday.
Carlisle Great Fair - third Saturday for about ten days.
Patterdale Sheep Dog Trials - Bank Holiday Saturday.
Keswick Show - Bank Holiday Monday.
Ennerdale Show - last Wednesday.
Lake Artists' Society Annual Exhibition, Grasmere - August and first week in September.
Lowther Horse Trials and Country Fair - weekend in early August.
Kendal Gathering - late August (date flexible).
Hawkshead Show - late August.
Kendal Folk Festival - August Bank Holiday. Contact Brewery Arts Centre.

September

Westmorland County Show, Kendal - second Thursday.
Egremont Crab Fair - third Saturday.
Loweswater Show - third Thursday.
Urswick Rushbearing, Ulverston - Sunday nearest St Michael's Day (29th)
Kentmere Sheep Dog Trials - last Thursday.
Eskdale Show - last Saturday.
Brough Hill Fair - 30th September.

October

Wasdale Show - second Saturday.
Wigton Horse Sales - last Wednesday.
Windermere Power Boat Record Week - late October. Contact Low Wood Hotel on Ambleside 33338.
Kendal Jazz Festival - late October. Contact Brewery Arts Centre for details.
Windermere Marathon - Sunday in late October. Contact Bowness Bay or Windermere TIC.

Chapter Two

Background
Briefing

The story so far - all you need to know about Lakeland geology and history, plus the National Park today and its wonderful services ...

Having arrived in the Lakes, the first thing is to try and get your bearings, not just how to get out of the bedroom or undo the tent flap, but to work out the shape of things to come, as well as the history and background and organisation of the area you will shortly be exploring.

It was Wordsworth who first likened the shape of the Lakes to a wheel, with the lakes and dales radiating from the centre like the spokes of the wheel. It's a good description. Things do radiate from a centre and it is very hard jumping from one spoke to another. To get to the outer spokes, especially on the West, you still have to make some very tortuous journeys.

But a handier image in your head is to think of the Lakes as *two* wheels, one in the North radiating from Keswick and the other in the South, radiating from Ambleside. Though the two towns are only fifteen miles apart, separated by the pass at Dunmail Raise, they often seem to be in different countries. They even talk differently, with the folks round Windermere and Coniston sounding almost Lancashire, while the rougher folks up North appear to have a Scottish influence in their dialect, at least to Southern ears.

The natives hardly move between the two divisions, but then Cumbrian natives have traditionally hardly moved anywhere. They often consider the folks in the next dale as foreigners. Most visitors who stay in the Northern Lakes, with Keswick as the nearest town, tend to stick there, exploring the lakes and mountains nearby. In the South, they look towards Ambleside and Windermere. Deciding to cross Dunmail Raise then becomes a major expedition.

Start by acquiring a general feeling of Lakeland as a whole, then concentrate on the names and places and character of the area where you are based. In a week's holiday, you probably will hardly venture into the other section. That will be for your next visit.

Geology

Yes, a tough subject to take in for absolute beginners, but come on, we can zip through it quickly. It's well worth it.

Roughly speaking, there are three major rock bands running across the Lake District and they have created three different types of scenery and buildings.

In the North, there are the Skiddaw Slates which give rounded, smooth hills and gentle horizons with not a great deal of colour. One result is that Skiddaw is relatively safe to climb with no dangerous crags. Skiddaw Slates were formed under the sea about 500 million years ago from shales and mudstones and are inherently weak. Skiddaw is considered to be the oldest mountain in Europe and the Lakeland hills as a whole are amongst the oldest in the world, more ancient even than the Alps or Himalayas.

The central zone is dominated by a band of Borrowdale Volcanic rocks which came just as the Skiddaw Slates had been laid down. Violent volcanic explosions threw up a much harder, more jagged rock and created dramatic,

Slate workers at Tilberthwaite quarry, 1889.

angular sky lines, such as Scafell and the Langdales. They're perfect for rock climbers. Something to get hold of, yet not fall off. They hope. The rocks and resultant vegetation are very colourful, rich in reds, pinks and greens, and provide technicolour autumn views for the photographers as well as the best rock climbs in England.

Next came the Silurian period, about 400 million years ago, and this resulted in a band across South Lakeland known as the Silurian Slates. These again have left more rounded hills. The distinctive green slate of the Coniston area, which you see in walls and roofs, are from this period. Around the edge of the Lake District, there are two other distinctive rock formations which should be mentioned - sandstone on the West Coast and in the Carlisle and Eden Valley area, which can clearly be seen in the local buildings, and limestone in the South and towards the Pennines.

Just to mess up these rather neat divisions, along came the Ice Age. It was quite recent really, under 2 million years ago. Everything was then put in the melting pot, or in this case the freezing pot, and the final shape of the Lakes eventually emerged. The effects of glaciation are easy to see, and much loved by school teachers on field courses. The valley floors were swept clean, tarns and lakes scooped out, valley heads built up, debris dumped, deltas formed, and all those cwms and corries created, the sort we all learned about at school. The variety, once again, is incredible for such a small area. Little wonder that for the last 200 years, the Lake District has become an adventure playground for geologists.

History

If there were inhabitants before the Ice Age, they left no clues, not even an ancient Kendal Mint wrapper. The earliest evidence possibly suggests some sort of primitive Stone Age settlements on the West coast, round about 4,000 BC.

There are quite a few definite Bronze and Iron Age remains scattered throughout the Lakes, such as stone circles and burial areas, but none as dramatic as elsewhere in England. Several are popular tourist attractions, notably Castlerigg near Keswick and Long Meg near Penrith.

The Romans They came, saw and conquered, led by Agricola who marched north to Carlisle, but stuck mainly to the plain. You will see on the OS maps of Lakeland numerous references to Roman remains but they are mostly small, though some are fairly interesting. To actually see first class Roman remains, you must go to Hadrian's Wall. Fortunately for all Lake District visitors, the Wall is quite near and has the best Roman military remains in the whole world.

The Celts After the Romans departed, around 400AD, the natives were left to their own devices, till the hordes of invaders from the coasts of Western Europe started arriving.

The ancient Celts clung on to their old ways for a long time in Central Lakeland, just as the Celtic people did in Wales, and there are strong connections between them. They each called themselves Cymry, or Cymri, hence Cumbria. There are many Celtic place names in Cumbria to this day which sound Welsh - such as those beginning with *pen*, meaning head or hill, as in Penrith or Penruddock; or *blaen* meaning summit, as in Blencathra or Blencow. Helvellyn *sounds* decidedly Welsh, though so far the experts have failed to explain its derivation.

The Invaders The Anglo Saxons invaded mainly the softer and easier Eastern coasts of England, though they did reach some of the fertile plains on the eastern slopes of the Lakes and their characteristic Anglian name endings of *ham* or *ton* can be seen in Brigham and Dearham, Dalton and Alston.

It was the Norse, rather than the Danes or Saxons, who colonised Cumbria, coming down the West Coast of Scotland to Ireland and the Isle of Man and establishing settlements in Cumbria. Some of the most typical Lakeland words have Norse origins - dales coming from *dalr*, fells from *fjall*, becks from *bekkr*, tarns from *tjorns*, and force (meaning waterfall) from *foss*. The ending 'thwaite', which you see everywhere, is Norse, meaning a clearing in the forest.

The Borders The northern half of present day Cumbria, the old Cumberland, has had its history, and its personality, fashioned by the very fact of being on the border between England and Scotland. For several centuries, there was constant conflict, looting and pillaging. Families and villages would swap loyalties, depending on who they thought would win. Much of Cumberland was in fact part of Scotland for many years. It has been romanticised by the novels of Walter Scott, but until as recently as the 18th century, it was a dangerous place in which to live. Many isolated North Cumbrians, even today, can be suspicious folk, preferring to winter you, then summer you, and winter you again. Then if you're lucky, they might say hello.

The legacy of all this Border conflict has been a large number of castles, fortified houses and pele towers, not beside the Lakes and Mountains themselves, but well away in the surrounding towns and plains such as Carlisle, Penrith, Cockermouth and Kendal. This was where the nobs lived and they were very keen on protecting themselves. Up on the fells, there was really not much worth stealing. Life, such as it was, went on, whether it was Agricola, William the Conqueror, Bonny Prince Charlie or Henry VIII who was out there causing all that nuisance, starting wars, leading rebellions or pinching land. The people who lived in the Lakes were 'statesmen', small time farmers with small estates and small farmhouses, much as they are today.

Trades and Industries

You'll see an awful lot of sheep in the Lakes, and not all of them are wearing orange anoraks. The four footed versions might well be Herdwicks, the native Cumbrian breed, which is supposed to have originally come from Spain, 400 years ago, when an Armada galleon was wrecked on the Cumbrian coast. Only a legend. Latest research indicates they were here in Roman times. They have white faces and only the males have horns. They have black wool when young which gets greyer with age. They never get fat and no wonder, living the life they lead out on the most barren of fells in the most barren of winters. They are reputed to be the hardiest breed of all sheep and when really hungry will eat their own wool to stay alive. (Well, they suck out the oils, just to keep themselves going.) There are fewer Herdwicks than there were and they are now in danger of becoming a rare breed. The more common breed are the Swaledales which are darker faced, with a light nose, and both sexes have horns.

Naturally, with all those sheep the woollen industry has always been strong in Cumbria. Kendal was the heart of it for six centuries and local cloths were known throughout the land. Shakespeare in Henry IV refers to a material as Kendal Green. It was a cottage industry in those days, with endless strings of pack horses carrying the raw and finished goods in and out of the town.

With the industrial revolution, Carlisle became a busy manufacturing centre for the cotton industry, till the main mass trade eventually moved to Lancashire and Yorkshire, though Carlisle today still has some high quality mills.

Mining in the Lake District is equally ancient and the Romans exploited the lead mines round Alston. All over the Northern fells you will find old mines, and round Coniston, one or two of which come back into temporary use as the price of the minerals goes up, or close when the prices fall. There is also extensive quarrying.

Heavy industry in Cumbria has always been restricted to the West, round Barrow and Millom, or up the coast around Maryport, Workington and Whitehaven, an important centre for many years for the coal and iron industries as well as shipping. At one time, around 1780, Whitehaven was the second port in the land after London - ahead of Liverpool and Bristol. It was one of the earliest planned towns in Europe.

The West Coast is now in decline, with heavy unemployment rather than heavy industry, though since the war some success has been made with new chemical and lighter industries, and the arrival of BNFL has been a huge financial boost to the area.

Today, the main industry of the Lake District is tourism, whatever the farmers will have you believe. Keswick, Ambleside and Windermere are largely tourist towns yet surprisingly, the towns just a few miles away are still *real* towns. Places like Penrith and Cockermouth, and to a lesser extent Kendal, are all market towns with old industries, hardly ruffled by slate lamps and signs boasting B and B in every second window.

Cumbria

The County today has a population of just under half a million (478,000 at the last count) and an area of 2,682 square miles. The County Council's main offices are in Carlisle (The Courts, Carlisle, telephone Carlisle 23456). There are six District Councils, four of which share the National Park between them - Copeland, Allerdale, Eden and South Lakeland.

District Councils

Barrow-in-Furness Borough Council, Town Hall, Barrow. Tel: Barrow 25500.
Carlisle City Council, Civic Centre, Carlisle. Tel: Carlisle 23411.
Copeland District Council, Catherine Street, Whitehaven. Tel: Whitehaven 3111.

Allerdale District Council, Holmewood, Cockermouth. Tel: Cockermouth 823741.
Eden District Council, Town Hall, Penrith. Tel: Penrith 64671.
South Lakeland District Council, Stricklandgate House, Kendal. Tel: Kendal 33333.

Lake District National Park

The National Park is that nice bit, right in the middle of Cumbria, but what *is* a National Park? Yes, visitors are always asking that. Read on.

There are ten National Parks in England and Wales and the Lake District National Park, set up in 1951, is the biggest, covering 880 square miles. It is looked after by the Lake District Special Planning Board (also likes to call itself the National Park Authority, or NPA) which protects the area for both farmers and holidaymakers. It doesn't own the land (the single biggest landowner is the National Trust with nearly a quarter of the land within the Park boundary) but has control over planning and development. They are very strict about all new buildings and are currently trying hard to restrict any more second homes (which currently account for nearly one fifth of all homes in the Lake District) and to limit the number of timeshares and leisure centres invading the area. People feel quite proud to be residents of the National Park, as if they were living in one of nature's listed buildings - until they want to add a new window or put a bed in the barn and they come up against the battle to get planning permission and they wish they were just a few feet outside the boundary. But they do a worthwhile job in protecting the Lake District for us all, keeping an eye on developments, protecting footpaths and open land. Once you get above the field line you can walk almost anywhere in the Lake District. The open fell is common land, still owned by someone but where the freedom to walk unhindered has been enjoyed for generations. There is no need to ask permission.

National Park Rangers The National Park also provides a bevy of nine full-time Rangers. They patrol the Park giving help and advice to visitors, working on Board properties, policing the bye-laws or leading parties doing a variety of jobs from litter-sweeps to repairing footpaths and dry stone walls. They wear green jumpers with a grey/green stripe across the front. In summer there are a number of Seasonal Rangers, who perform a broadly similar function. There are also around 350 Voluntary Wardens who help Rangers and can be identified by badges and oatmeal jumpers with a red stripe across.

Lake District National Park Statistics

	acres
Area of National Park	554 245
Area covered by lakes and reservoirs	16 062
Area under crops	9 227
Area under grass	188 446
Area of rough grazing	153 652
Area of common land	151 225
Area of broadleaved woodland	25 698
Total area of woodland	60 540

Who owns the National Park?

	acres
Areas of National Park Authority access land	20 554
Area owned and managed by NPA	18 723
Area leased to and managed by NPA	2 261
Area owned by National Trust	130 000
Area owned by Forestry Commission	31 466
Area owned by North West Water Authority	38 450
Area owned by Ministry of Defence	1 139
(MOD have firing rights over a further	1 196)

Population The population of the National Park is small, just 41,000, and is not growing. It doesn't include Carlisle, the county's biggest town, or Penrith, or the West Coast or - more surprisingly - either Cockermouth or Kendal, yet the Lake District Special Planning Board has its HQ offices in Kendal. (Lucky them, not having to apply to themselves for every planning permit.) They are still looking for premises inside the Park, so they say, but last time they considered it they came up against one of their own planning regulations which stopped them from changing a large country house from a dwelling place into offices.

Address The administration offices of the Lake District Special Planning Board are at Busher Walk, Kendal. Phone Kendal 24555. Enquiries to the National Park Officer.

☆☆ The National Park Visitor Centre

In addition to running nine tourist information centres throughout the area, the National Park also provides a Visitor Centre at Brockhole, Windermere. Telephone Windermere 6601.

The NPA's aim is to get you to start your holiday here, stock up on information and then sally forth among the lakes and fells, a better informed person. There are also things to amuse and entertain, especially aimed at family groups. A good place to wander around mid-week on a sunny day, when it can be less crowded (it gets very busy on wet days - Saturday is another quiet day, for some reason).

It's easy to miss, despite its size. From the name 'Visitor Centre' you might expect something modern, but it is in fact a stately home, a large detached building in its own grounds on the shores of Windermere, about two miles south of Ambleside on the A591. Keep an eye out carefully for the signs. Once inside the car park it is still confusing, as you can't tell the way to the house, or what's on offer before you part with your money, but they're hoping to change all that soon.

In the 19th century, Brockhole was the country home of a Lancashire cotton magnate, one of the many who built imposing residences along the shores of Windermere. It was converted in 1969 to its present use.

Once inside, there is a major exhibition, covering Lake District history, wildlife and present-day management. There are also audio-visual shows running throughout the day. Like any permanent exhibition, Brockhole suffers in that once you've seen it, there's little need to return. There are plans to update the exhibition during the winter of 1989/90, which should make the place more dynamic. The star attractions are often the special events and talks by local experts. Some of these can be excellent. It is worth finding out if there is anything special on during your stay. Ideas for 1989 include dog obedience courses (a one day affair to train owners and dogs to behave themselves in the country) and more family events, like the teddy bears' picnic (children with a teddy get in free - no, teddy boys don't count).

There's also a cafeteria, with reasonable home made fare. Huge car park. Excellent grounds of 30 acres, all of them open to the public, with picnic spots and play areas. Brockhole now has a landscape gardener and there are plans to make more of the gardens as a feature for the public to enjoy.

Launch trips to Brockhole - available from Bowness and Waterhead during the high season. Contact Bowness Bay Boating Company for details (Windermere 3360).

Admission: Adult £1.40, children 70p. Family tickets available. Buy an extra 20p ticket on first entry and you can get in for half price at any time in the following eight days. There are also season tickets. House and grounds are open daily from 10 o'clock, 16th March to mid-September in 1989, then closing early for work on the new exhibition. 1990 times should revert to normal - late March to early November.

Tourist Information Centres

Also referred to as TICs, these provide information on what to see and do; entertainments and events; places of interest; travel and transport and where to stay; even where to walk.

All the following tourist information centres should

have information on local accommodation. Most provide a free local booking service for personal callers. Centres offering the Book-A-Bed-Ahead scheme can make a provisional reservation for you at any other town which has a centre also operating the scheme (anywhere in the country).

All the centres operate a local bed booking service, with the exception of Brampton. Some centres only open during the summer months - these are indicated with a * .

Alston *
Railway Station
Tel: Alston 81696

Ambleside
The Old Courthouse,
Church Street
Tel: Ambleside 32582

Appleby
Moot Hall, Boroughgate
Tel: Appleby 51177

Barrow-in-Furness
Civic Hall, Duke Street
Tel: Barrow 25795

Bowness-on-Windermere *
Bowness Bay
Tel: Windermere 2895

Brampton *
Moot Hall,
Market Square
Tel: Brampton 3433

Brough
The 'One Stop Shop'
Tel: Brough 260

Carlisle
Old Town Hall,
Green Market
Tel: Carlisle 25517

Cockermouth
Riverside Car Park,
Market Street
Cockermouth 822634

Coniston *
16 Yewdale Road
Tel: Coniston 41533

Egremont
Lowes Court Gallery,
12 Main Street
Tel: Egremont 820693

Glenridding *
(The Ullswater Centre)
Car Park
Tel: Glenridding 414

Grange-over-Sands *
Victoria Hall,
Main Street
Tel: Grange 4026

Grasmere *
Red Bank Road
Tel: Grasmere 245

Hawkshead *
Main Street
Tel: Hawkshead 525

Kendal
Town Hall, Highgate
Tel: Kendal 25758

Keswick
Moot Hall, Market Sq.
Tel: Keswick 72645

Killington Lake *
M6 Servics (South),
Killington Lake
Tel: Sedbergh 20138

Kirkby Lonsdale
18 Main Street
Kirkby Lonsdale 71603

Kirkby Stephen *
Market Street
Kirkby Stephen 71199

Longtown
21 Swan Street
Tel: Longtown 791201

Maryport
Maritime Museum,
1 Senhouse Street
Tel: Maryport 813738

Millom *
Millom Folk Museum,
St George's Road
Tel: Millom 2555

Penrith
Robinson's School,
Middlegate
Tel: Penrith 67466

Pooley Bridge *
The Square
Tel: Pooley Bridge 530

Ravenglass *
Ravenglass & Eskdale
Railway Car Park
Tel: Ravenglass 278

Seatoller *
Seatoller Barn Dalehead
Base
Tel: Borrowdale 294

Sedbergh *
72 Main Street
Tel: Sedbergh 20125

Silloth-on-Solway *
The Green
Tel: Silloth 31944

Southwaite
M6 Service Area,
Southwaite, Nr Carlisle
Southwaite 73445/6

Ulverston
Coronation Hall
Tel: Ulverston 57120

Waterhead *
Car Park, Waterhead,
Nr Ambleside
Tel: Ambleside 32799

Whitehaven
St Nicholas Tower,
Lowther Street
Tel: Whitehaven 5678

Windermere
Victoria Street
Tel: Windermere 6499

Best Information Centres

So much for the official list, put out by the Tourist Board. They vary greatly in size, however, and in what they set out to do. The Cumbria Tourist Board publish these lists of information centres, implying that they run them all (which they don't, though they supply information to all of them). In the past, the best centres have been those run by the the National Park Authority. These not only supply tourist information, leaflets, news of events and so on, but also have displays and small exhibitions designed to enhance the visitor's knowledge and appreciation of the area. Some of these displays can be excellent and it is something the other centres don't really try to do. However, in recent years the NPA centres have concentrated more on selling than informing, and the service has suffered.

These are now our top five tourist information centres (either for service or for the excellence of the displays):

> **Appleby** - Moot Hall, Boroughgate
> **Glenridding** - Car Park
> **Grasmere** - Red Bank Road, Grasmere
> **Kendal** - Town Hall, Highgate
> **Windermere** - Victoria Street

Appleby, Kendal and Windermere are open all year round. Windermere is particularly useful as it is open from 9.00am to 9.00pm, seven days a week, between Easter and October (9.00-6.00 during the winter). Grasmere and Glenridding are NPA centres; the displays at Glenridding are particularly good. Outside, hidden in the car park under a tree, there's a relief model of the Helvellyn range, where walkers could trace their routes when they came off the fells.

Seatoller Barn is also worth an additional mention. Their craft days - when local craftsmen and women come in and give demonstrations - can be very interesting. Dates in the NP's *Lake District Guardian*.

National Trust Information Centres

These are basically recruitment centres cum gift shops and don't deal with general information. You can find them at:

Ambleside - The Bridge House, Rydal Road
Grasmere - opposite St Oswald's Church
Keswick - at the Boat Landings, Lakeside
Hawkshead - in the main square
(Also at **Sizergh Castle**, Kendal, **Wordsworth House**, Cockermouth and **Fell Foot Country Park**, Newby Bridge.)

The National Trust also has two shops, at 18 Finkle Street, Kendal (tel: Kendal 31605) and in The Square, Hawkshead (tel: Hawkshead 471).

The Friends of the Lake District

Finally, anyone interested in protecting the area could do no better than contact the Friends of the Lake District. They've been going for 50 years now and do a lot to protect the area by lobbying MPs, stirring up the press and generally keeping an eye on what is going on. Soon to have their own permanent HQ at Number 3, Yard 77, Highgate, Kendal. Or contact the Secretary at Gowan Knott, Kendal Road, Staveley. Tel: Staveley 821201.

You don't have to live in the area to be a member. Subscription details from the secretary.

Chapter Three

Transport

Travelling around inside the Lake District - by train, coach, car, taxi, bicycle.

Having got the background history of the Lakes in your mind, and picked up something of how it's organised today, the next thing is to leave the hotel or the caravan site and start exploring.

Train

There is not much scope for travelling by train inside the National Park, as the only BR line is the branch from Oxenholme to Windermere. But there are four main railway routes which skirt the Lake District:

☆☆☆ **The Lakes Line** This important route runs from Preston through Lancaster, Oxenholme and Penrith up to Carlisle. The Lakes branch starts at Oxenholme, running through Kendal, Burneside and Staveley to Windermere. The following are all manned stations and the telephone numbers are for passenger and timetable enquiries:
Preston (Preston 59439); Lancaster (Lancaster 32333); Oxenholme (Kendal 20397); (for Windermere times, ring Oxenholme); Penrith (Penrith 62466); Carlisle (Carlisle 44711).

Windermere Station The original site was sold and developed into a tasteful new supermarket (apparently the NPA has no jurisdiction over BR property in the Lake District). There is now a sweet little railway station round the back. It was developed after much local pressure, BR extracting £15,000 from the local community in the process. To combat any threat to the line, a Lakes Line Action Group was formed (their slogan is: "Helping BR to get there"). The Action Group's next target is Kendal station, which BR have allowed to become a dump.

☆ **The Furness Line** Runs from Preston and Lancaster through Carnforth up to Barrow-in-Furness. This is a list of the stations, with the telephone numbers given for the manned stations:

Carnforth (enquiries ring Lancaster 32333) (parcels Carnforth 732131); Silverdale; Arnside; Grange-over-Sands (Grange-over-Sands 2468); Kents Bank; Cark and Cartmel; Ulverston (Ulverston 53219); Dalton; Roose; Barrow-in-Furness (Barrow 20805).

☆☆ **The West Cumbrian Line** This almost forgotten service, which is second class only, meanders along the length of the Cumbrian coast from Barrow-in-Furness to Carlisle. Along the way it passes through Askam, Kirkby-in-Furness, Foxfield, Green Road, Millom, Silecroft, Bootle, Ravenglass, Drigg, Seascale, Sellafield, Braystones, Nethertown, St Bees, Corkickle, Whitehaven, Parton, Harrington, Workington, Flimby, Maryport, Aspatria, Wigton and Dalston. Of these, you'll not be too surprised to learn that only two are manned: Workington (phone Workington 2575) and Whitehaven (Whitehaven 2414). And at most of the others the train won't even stop, unless you ask the guard in advance.

To save time trying to ring Cumbrian stations (even the manned ones never seem to answer) pick up the latest timetables from the nearest Tourist Information Centre.

☆☆☆ **Settle to Carlisle Railway** This famous railway line runs the length of the Pennines to provide one of the most scenic rail routes in Britain. The line crosses the spectacular Ribblehead Viaduct (all 24 arches of it), and is the only way of reaching Appleby and the east Cumbria towns by train.

The route was run as a normal passenger service, but BR put it up for sale at the end of 1988. Even after they said it was not viable, they continued to promote it heavily as a tourist attraction. The problem lies with the expense of repairs to the famous viaduct. If no one buys the line, the service will be withdrawn and that will be that. By the time you read this, the line may be history, but let's hope not.

Special Tickets They're always changing the names of special tickets, but in 1988 a £25 NW Rail Rover ticket gave seven days' unlimited travel on BR throughout Cumbria, except the Settle-Carlisle line.

Apart from British Rail, there are three other short railway lines in Cumbria. All are popular tourist attractions, and all use steam locos.

☆☆☆ **The Ravenglass and Eskdale Railway** This runs from Ravenglass on the West Coast of Cumbria up to Dalegarth in Eskdale, on the edge of the Lake District. The trains run all the year round but with reduced service during the winter months. The miniature railway (known as La'al Ratty) takes forty-five minutes to make its journey. Timetables available from Tourist Information Centres or ring Ravenglass 226.

☆☆ The Lakeside & Haverthwaite Railway

Running on three and a half miles of track which was originally part of the Ulverston to Lakeside line, the railway connects with the southern steamer station on Windermere at Lakeside. Combined tickets are available for the railway and the boats, making it a useful way of getting up into the Lakes without taking the car north of Newby Bridge. Tel: Newby Bridge 31594.

☆ South Tynedale Railway.

Trains run between Alston and Gilderdale, following part of the old Haltwhistle to Alston branch line (just like something out of a Rowland Emett cartoon). Trains are usually hauled by steam engines at weekends and bank hols., otherwise by diesel. There is also a cafe and souvenir shop at Alston station. Tel: Alston 81696. (Alston, in case you were wondering, is in the extreme north-east of the county. In fact, British Telecom think it is in Northumberland.)

Cockermouth, Keswick and Penrith Railway - Parcel Stamps, 1894

Coaches

There are two major bus firms which cover the county, not as extensively or as regularly as they used to, but still fairly efficiently. Since deregulation, there are also a number of other companies hurtling round the area, trying to hijack passengers. In the main, though, these keep to the more popular routes.

Ribble

Strong on Central Lakes, North and South Cumbria. Bus services from Carlisle, Penrith, Kendal, Grange, Ulverston, Barrow, Ambleside, Bowness, Windermere. HQ - Preston 51177. Local bus stations - Lancaster 64228; Kendal 33221, Ambleside 33233, Ulverston 53196.

Ribble offer half day and full day excursions; express services between Lancaster and Keswick, and various special tickets (known as Ribble Ramblers).

Cumberland Motor Services (also known as CMS) Strongest on the West Coast, but covers Keswick as well. HQ - Tangier Street, Whitehaven 63222.

Local CMS bus stations - Keswick 72791; Wigton 42241; Workington 3080; Carlisle 48484; Penrith 63616. Also offers special tickets and excursions fares. One of their most useful services for the visitor is **The Borrowdale Bus**, which runs between Keswick and Seatoller. Information from tourist info centres, or ring CMS on their Workington number.

In addition to the national bus companies, **Wright Brothers** offer a handy service from Keswick and Penrith to Newcastle, during the summer. Telephone Alston 81200.

☆☆ Mountain Goat Minibuses

An enterprising minibus firm which sprang up in 1974 when Ribble started to cut down its rural services. It now offers 12-seater minibus schedules services, from Easter to October, on the following routes: Ambleside and Windermere to Patterdale and Glenridding, Keswick to Patterdale and Glenridding, Keswick to Buttermere, plus special expresses to Harrogate and York.

There are also special day tours to various Lake District beauty spots, often with picnic included. Trips stop frequently for photographs and some include guided walks. The Goat and Boat trip, combines the minibus service with a trip on the Ullswater steamers.

They're spreading their wings as they grow older. Latest developments include group travel for anywhere in Britain, and conference trips.

Hint: Theme days (trips to a number of visitor attractions linked by a common subject) are very popular but can get booked very quickly and don't operate every day. If you're only here for a week, check them out at the start of your holiday.

Mountain Goat, Victoria Street, Windermere (phone Windermere 5161) and Market Square, Keswick (phone Keswick 73962).

Timetables are usually available from Tourist Information Centres.

☆ Grass Routes

A newcomer to the scene, operating a similar service to Mountain Goat, but with the emphasis on countryside and scenic routes. Enquiries to Windermere 6760.

☆ Fellrunner

This is a small minibus company offering tours of the Eden Valley. A good way of seeing beautiful countryside without having to endure the traffic of the central Lakes. Bookings through any TIC in the Eden Valley, or ring Langwathby 648.

More traditional coach tours - of the sixteen lakes in an afternoon variety - exist in the Lakes. If this is what you're after, try **Brown's**, on Ambleside 32205, or **Silver Badge**, on Windermere 3215.

Post Buses This is a most ingenious scheme, hardly known elsewhere in England, whereby you can get a ride with the Postman. In various outlying districts, the GPO have made it possible for the mail vans to carry passengers as well as post. They use the familiar red coloured vehicles, though slightly bigger than normal, and with seats for a few passengers. They run scheduled services and are very handy. Martindale's celebrated its 21st birthday in 1988. Congrats.

Martindale Post Bus - enquiries Crown Square, Penrith 62700.
Duddon Valley Post Bus, Broughton-in-Furness Post Bus - enquiries Broughton-in-Furness 220.
Grizedale Post Bus - enquiries Head Post Office, Ulverston 52030.

The Duddon Post Bus, incidentally, gave John Cunliffe the idea for Postman Pat.

Coming down Dunmail Raise to Grasmere

Leaflets
A Guide to Public Transport in Cumbria - this used to be available, published jointly by Ribble and the Friends of the Lake District. An excellent idea which has since been discontinued. Why?

Timetables These all used to be available in a bumper collection, but Ribble have stopped doing that too. Individual timetables still available, free from bus stations and TICs. (NB: The main A591 route through the Lakes is covered in Ribble timetables number 14 and 16.)

Motoring

First a word of warning. In the middle of the season, it can take an age to get through Bowness and Ambleside on the A592 and A591. If you *have* to go through them, set off early. Keswick should be easier these days, with all those new roads and flyovers round the town, but if you have to go *through* Keswick to get to Borrowdale, then that too can be hell. So start early. Similarly, in July and August don't expect to get along the A592 from Bowness to Newby Bridge in a hurry. You *always* end up behind someone travelling at 19 miles an hour looking at the view. (This is a good road for spotting locals - they are the ones with steam coming from their ears.)

And if you have not already secreted a spare key on your car, do it now, before you hit the Lakes. Those little magnet boxes are best, hidden under the car somehow. All tourist info centres moan that one of the most common enquiries is from people who have locked themselves out of their own car.

Motoring organisations: AA 24-hour breakdown and information service - Carlisle 24274. Local services (operating from 0900-1730): Barrow-in-Furness 20665; Carnforth 732036 (24 hour); Kendal 27652; Keswick 73458. RAC Breakdown Service - Southwaite 73505 (if no reply, call Newcastle 281 4271). Breakdown service: Keswick 73071.

Garages

The following petrol stations remain open late during the summer season.

Ambleside - Hill's Garage (Ambleside 32144), 0700-2200.
Penrith - Town Head Garage, Penrith (Penrith 62175), 0700-2200.
Kendal - Lound Road Garage (Kendal 23914), 0730-2200. Ings Service Station, Ings, Nr Kendal (Staveley 821375), 0700-2100.
Crooklands - Central Garage, Preston Patrick (Crooklands 401), 24 hours.
Southwaite - Granada Service, M6 (Southwaite 73476), 24 hours.
Carlisle - Brunton Park Service Station (Carlisle 28715), 0700-2300
Harraby Green (Carlisle 20973), 0700-2300.
Traveller's Check Border (Carlisle 511213), 24 hours.

Bowness-on-Windermere - Rayrigg Motors, Rayrigg Road (Windermere 2716), 0800-2000.
Newby Bridge - Newby Bridge Motors, A590 road (Newby Bridge 31253), 0730-2130.
Grange-over-Sands - Grange Motors, Station Road (Grange-over-Sands 2612), 0730-2000.
Langdale - Chapel Stile Post Office (Langdale 301) 0830-2030 in tourist season.

Car Parks

In the season all the Lakeland towns are murder for parking - and even popular villages get quickly overrun.

Carlisle Has disc parking. You get a cardboard clock for free from a garage, Tourist Information Centre or traffic warden and use it to show your time of arrival in the car windscreen. Free, but two hours maximum. Look out for the signs.

To park, try near the Civic Centre. Otherwise use the major car parks. There are several large ones, all very cheap compared with metropolitan car parks. The Viaduct one is usually busy, so try West Walls, which has a short cut to the city centre, or try the one beside the Castle. If you're coming in from the east, try the two very large car parks off Botchergate.

Keswick Very poor. The central one, off Victoria Street, often has queues to get in during the summer, so try the one near the bus station. Always best to get into Keswick as early as possible. If all full, try going up to Keswick Spa and parking, then walk back down the hill into Keswick. Another possibility is the car park in Lake Road. Follow the signs for the Lake shore, park and then walk back into Keswick. Very cheeky visitors have been known to use the Pencil Museum's car park. Note well - Main Street is now pedestrians only on Saturdays.

Grasmere The police in Grasmere are very keen, so be warned. (A few summers ago one policeman even booked his own wife for parking on a yellow line.) There is a car park in Stock Lane just as you enter the village from the south - this is handy for Dove Cottage. If full, try the one behind the garden centre, opposite the church. Beware parking in the garden centre car park by mistake - their charges are huge, unless you go in and buy something. They're not very keen on giving change for the ticket machine in the other car park. Also try Broadgate - there's a nice riverside path from it which emerges by St Oswald's Church and misses the crowds.

Ambleside Parking in the street is limited to half-an-hour during the day. There are three main car parks in Ambleside. The one in the centre, by the library, is usually full, but there's often space in the other two and they are both quite good. If coming in the from north, use the car park opposite Charlotte Mason College. Handy for the town and it's a nice walk alongside the river and past the Bridge House. (Caution: do not be tempted at weekends by the College's large, empty, invitingly free car park - the caretaker is possessed of large, evil stickers which he is likely to place on your windscreen and which can take up to half-an-hour's scraping to get off.) From the south, use the car park just past Hayes Garden World. It's a five-minute walk into town, or about ten minutes in the opposite direction to Waterhead and the Lake. Waterhead has two good car parks - and the walk into town is pleasant.

Hawkshead Rapidly becoming one large car park with a small village adjacent. The village itself is nearly all pedestrians only, so use the main car park and saunter about the village without fear of being run over.

Windermere Limited street parking (if you're lucky). Use the car park behind the Library.

Bowness *The* place to avoid with a car in mid-season. There is limited street parking in Lake Road, coming down from Windermere, but you won't get in. (You will, however, get stuck behind someone else who is trying to get in and blocking the traffic.) There is also a small car park next to the cinema, usually full. The large car park in Rayrigg Road is good if you're early, but once past 11 o'clock there are often queues to get in. Far better are the two car parks down by the Bay. There's one behind the National Park information Centre and a large one along Glebe Road which often has spaces. Alternatively, if feeling like a nice stroll, use the car park at Ferry Nab (also useful for boat trailers - this is the SLDC launching site) and walk back into town along the lake shore and through Cockshott Point. Nearby Braithwaite Fold also opens as a car park in summer. Don't, whatever you do, just dump the car on the verge along Rayrigg Road. Bowness has a very efficient traffic warden these days, you know.

Coniston Use the main car park in the centre of the village. You have to pay, but it is by far the easiest.

Kendal Another horrid place to park. You always end up finding no spaces and having to go all round the one-way system to get back to the first car park you saw but decided to ignore in order to get closer to the shops. There is a good car park down by Abbot Hall, in Kirkland (the Council one-don't use the Museum car park, they will get cross, unless you're visiting the Museum). The best car parks are down on Blackhall Road, behind the new shopping centre. There's even a free car park by the river. It is always full. If you enter Kendal from the Kirkland end, you could turn up Gillingate and you might find a space by the road.

Car Rentals

Ambleside
Autohire Ltd., Knott Street (Ambleside 32322)

Bowness
Brantfell Garage, Kendal Road (Windermere 2000)
Eurocar, Belsfield Hotel (Windermere 5910)

Carlisle
County Motors, Montgomery Way (Carlisle 511760)
Grange-over-Sands
Autorent, Hadwin's Garage, Lindale (G-o-S 34242)

Kendal
Castle Garth Garage (Kendal 33582)
Lakes and Dales, 97 Valley Drive (Kendal 29311)

Crooklands (near Kendal)
Crooklands Self-Drive (Crooklands 414)

Keswick
Keswick Hotel, Station Road (Keswick 74422)

Penrith
Cumbrian Connection, Rudd's Yard (Penrith 67222)

Silloth
Coates Garage, Causeway Head (Silloth 31478)

Whitehaven
Autorent, 35 Central Road, Kells (Whitehaven 5078)

Taxis

Carlisle
Border Cabs, Carlisle 48153

Kendal
Blue Star Taxis (24 hour), Kendal 23670
Castle Taxis (24 hour), Kendal 26233

Windermere
Blezard Taxis, Windermere 2355/3439
Lakes Taxis, Windermere 6777

Whitehaven
Call-A-Cab, Whitehaven 63937

Keswick
Davies Radio Taxis, Keswick 72676

Cockermouth
Mike Collins, Cockermouth 822799

Penrith
Lakeland Taxis, Penrith 65722

Car Tours

Try **Knight Errant**, on Windermere 6501, or **Jeeves Tours**, on Workington 3016, who also offer a chauffeur-driven service.

Cycling

Cycle Hire is becoming more and more popular in the LD. Not just on the roads, either - they're increasing on the fells, thanks (if that's the word) to the advent of mountain bikes. Note that this is only permissible on bridle ways.

Cycle hire companies are springing up all over, with everyone from cycling shops to motoring accessories shops hiring them out. We have tried to sort out those which have been in it longest, know what they're doing and are involved with cycles as their main business, rather than jumping on a bandwagon. (Those marked MB also do mountain bikes.)

Arnside
South Cumbria Cycles, Silverdale Road.   Arnside 762065.

Elterwater
Lakeland Mountain Bikes, Yan Lane Ends. Langdale 370.

These are the original Lakes mountain bike specialists, having spotted their potential well before anyone else. They have a retail outlet in Staveley (Staveley 821748) and can arrange for hire bikes to be picked up there. They also offer repairs, tours and holidays.

Kendal
Brucie's Bike Shop, 187 Highgate. Kendal 27230
(Hire service summer only.)

Lowick Bridge
South Lakes Cycle Hire, Mill Farm, Lowick Bridge,
Nr. Ulverston. Lowick Bridge. 210. MB.

Penrith
Harper's Cycles. Penrith 64475. (Hire summer only.)
Eden Cyclo-Tours, Unit 8, Redhills. Penrith 64884. MB.
   Eden can also arrange routes, tours and repairs.

Wigton
Wigton Cycles & Sports, 23 West Street. Wigton 42824.
MB. (Hire summer only.)

Windermere
Lakeland Leisure, Station Buildings. Windermere 4786.
MB.
JDs , Spring Gardens, Station Precinct (Windermere 4786)

Typical Charges Charges vary - depending on whether you hire from a firm whose sole business is bike-hire, or from someone who is running it as a sideline to bike sales (usually the cheapest).

Charges for 1989: £5.00 per day; £20.00 per week (cycle hire business); £4.00 per day; £15.00 per week (cycle shop). Mountain bikes are usually more expensive - £10 a day, £50 a week.

Deposits in both cases are usually around £10.00 per booking (rather than per bike) and you usually find that the hire charge is per person, rather than per bike - so if you hire a tandem it will cost you double.

Cycle Tours

☆ **Cumbria Cycle Way** This is more a route, than a proper cycle way, despite its name, but it is an excellent ride. It directs you 280 miles (or 450k) along a circular route round coastal Cumbria from Furness up to the Solway plain, then through Carlisle (which is hell for cycling) and down the Eden Valley to Appleby and then to Kirkby Lonsdale. It is a carefully constructed route, through many miles of quiet minor roads, with an enormous amount of scenery - but none of it is in the Lake District.

There is also a **Forest Bicycle Route** in Grizedale Forest, using ten miles of signposted forest roads. No permission necessary and they can only be used by cyclists or pedestrians.

☆☆ **Cyclorama** A good idea for an unusual cycling holiday. Six nights spread between three hotels or bed and breakfasts, in three different places, starting and finishing at the Grange Hotel. You cycle between each hotel, but have alternate days off to explore each area when you arrive. Luggage transported between hotels, so nothing heavy to carry, and full maps and information pack provided. Distances about 16-20 miles between each hotel.

Price depends on the type of accommodation offered - from £155 based on B&B, to £248 for hotel with four night's dinner.

The same company also offers walking holidays, which are the same, but you walk between centres. Group bookings can also be arranged.

> Cyclorama Holidays
> Grange Hotel
> Grange-over-Sands.
> Tel: Grange-over-Sands 33666.

Cycling Guide

The best one is *Cycling in the Lake District*, by Richard Harries, Morland Publishing, 1984.

☆☆☆ Windermere Ferry

Four of the Lakes now have public transport of some sort on them - Windermere, Coniston, Ullswater and Derwentwater. (Details of the services are in Chapter 7.)

For road users it is worth pointing out at this stage that only Windermere has a car ferry. It runs all year round, except for Christmas and Boxing Day, from 0650 to 2150 (0950 to 2050 on Sundays and during the winter), crossing the Lake about once every twenty minutes.

1988 charges were: 10p for pedestrians, 90p for cars (including occupants). The ferry runs from Ferry Nab, just south of Bowness, across to Ferry House at Far Sawrey and the service is run by the Highways Department of Cumbria County Council.

Windermere Ferry, 1905

☆☆☆ A Recommended Excursion by Public Transport

A good method of spending the day without a car is to use the A591, especially between Ambleside and Keswick. It is a brilliant route for public transport, with buses about every hour, and is the only route in Central Lakeland where you will see a double decker. Set off early from Ambleside and get on the top deck (when you go over Dunmail Raise on the top deck of a bus on a good day the view is tremendous). Travel up to Keswick, stopping off at Dove Cottage, Grasmere, and Castlerigg Stone Circle (just before Keswick). Time each visit so you don't have to wait too long for the next bus along to the next stage. Spend some time in Keswick, then catch the bus back to Ambleside, this time stopping off at Rydal Mount on the way. Coleridge and Wordsworth did this route all the time when visiting each other. On foot of course. They were tough in those days.

But do set off as early as possible (Dove Cottage is open at 9.30, Rydal Mount closes at 5.30), or very quickly your precious hours will disappear.

Two Excursions by Car

Half-Day

Head south from Bowness and cross Lake Windermere via the ferry. Drive towards Hawkshead, passing Hill Top and taking the west road round Esthwaite Water (prettier). Look round Hawkshead (good for teas) and perhaps visit the Grammar School. Then continue towards Coniston, turning off for Tarn Hows. Carry on into Coniston, then return via Ambleside.

Full Day

Leave Bowness via the A592. Go over the Kirkstone Pass to Ullswater. Wonderful views over the Lake. Turn left onto the A5091 through Dockray to join the A66 at Threlkeld and blast along to Keswick. From Keswick go down the Borrowdale Valley. Don't forget the Bowder Stone. Over Honister Pass. Stop at Buttermere and walk round the lake. Then continue to Lorton, back over the Whinlatter Pass to Keswick. Leave Keswick via the A591 (stop off at Castlerigg Stone Circle), turn off and go round the west side of Thirlmere (quieter and prettier with places to park and explore the shore), then continue through Grasmere and Rydal (where you have the temptations of the two Wordsworth homes) and back via Ambleside.

Lonely as a coach at Wastwater, 1932

Chapter Four

Hotels

Where to stay - hotels, guest houses, farm-houses, caravans, camping, renting.

The choice is enormous, so all we intend to offer is a brief, personal selection, plus some broad general advice.

There are 750 hotels in the Lakes, 550 guest houses and bed and breakfast places offering 20,000 beds. Then there are all those farms and caravan sites. So what do you do? Well, it's relatively easy to get a list of the local beds available, and most of the tourist information centres will help. Just turn up and ask. But no official is going to tell you what they're really like.

If you are booking from afar, and want it reasonable and clean, then fine, go ahead and get a copy of their latest list.

Cumbria - English Lake District is the official Guide published by the CTB and available, free, from the CTB at Ashleigh, Holly Road, Windermere. TICs will also probably have copies. It is intended as a general guide but incorporates all the CTB accommodation information. (NB: worth pointing out - CTB only ever list their own members.)

Prices This time we are not giving exact hotel prices. We did so first time, and oh the moans and groans from proprietors when they put their charges up and expected us to reprint immediately. Just think of our extra printing costs, every time they muck around with their details. So we are lumping them all into three broad bands, A, B and C, ranging from cheap to expensive. Pricing varies enormously at the posh end of the market. Some don't offer a price for singles, others do but put on such a heavy penalty that the price approaches that of a double

Price Bands: For one person, for dinner, bed and breakfast.

> A £20 to £30
> B £30 to £50
> C £50 plus

De Luxe, De lightful Hotels

There are two hotels which stand head and shoulders above the rest for their high standards and attention to detail, for their food and service, for their furnishings and for their overall terribly good taste. Both are very expensive (expect to pay around £60-£100 for dinner, B & B) and both heavily over subscribed. Allow one week's notice in the summer to book dinner and around six weeks for a bedroom.

If you have the money, they are both well worth one night, if only for the experience. It will give you table talk for years wherever people of good taste are gathered together.

☆☆☆ Sharrow Bay Country House Hotel, Ullswater. Pooley Bridge 301. Price - C.

On Eastern shore of Ullswater, about two miles from Pooley Bridge.

Brian Sack and Francis Coulson still manage to keep it up, despite 40 years at the top. Still regularly awarded the top accolades by all the best hotel and food guides in the world.

Pluses - Food sensational, setting equally sensational, 29 bedrooms, each bedroom a work of art, drawing rooms very posh, always quiet and discreet, no bar (what a blessing - you have drinks served in the drawing rooms as if in a private home).

Minuses - Very few, though there are those sour pusses who find the food too much, in quantity and richness, and say the bedrooms are over fancy. Drawing rooms are a bit fussy and formal, and you can feel equally on display. Try to book into the hotel proper, not the annexes.

☆☆☆ **Miller Howe**, Rayrigg Road, Windermere 2536. Price - C. Overlooking Windermere, about 1 mile north of Bowness.

John Tovey is a much more extrovert character than the duo at Sharrow Bay. Look out for him in his white clogs, tripping round after dinner, unless he's off on tour, promoting his latest best seller, building his empire or off appearing on TV. He's also more theatrical and dinner is like a stage performance. Starting from scratch 18 years ago, he has also built up his hotel - and himself - so that it now has an international reputation - yet like Sharrow Bay it is totally English, using good Cumbrian materials and staff.

Pluses - Terrific food, very imaginative, sensational views, quiet but friendly atmosphere, handsome drawing rooms, 13 well equipped bedrooms.

Minuses - The lake views *are* brilliant, but the hotel is on a busy, boring road; some bedrooms are more flash than tasteful; despite Tovey's jovial personality, which makes his hotel not as intimidating as Sharrow Bay, some snotty people find it a trifle vulgar. Strict eating times, no choice. No lunch.

Classy Hotels

The success of the Big Two has had a great effect on the rest of the Lakes and standards of comfort and cuisine, taste and decor, have increased enormously in the last ten years. There are now several mini Sharrow Bays, less expensive, less publicised, but aiming for the same high standards and trying hard to avoid the mass produced, mass catering methods of the Trust House Forte type of hotels. They don't all succeed, but they are trying to stamp their individual personality and create hotels which they hope will appeal to the discerning.

☆☆ **Rothay Manor,** Rothay Bridge, Ambleside 33605.
Fine regency hotel, traditional fare and services. Price - B/C.

☆☆ **White Moss House,** Rydal Water, Grasmere 295.
Well established quality hotel. Great views of Rydal Water and ideally situated for any number of walks, but road can be very busy during daytime. Price - C.

☆ **Scale Hill Hotel,** Loweswater, Lorton 232.
Old coaching inn in a beautiful valley, off the main tourist routes. Friendly and relaxed. Good traditional food. Price - B.

☆☆ **Leeming on Ullswater**, Pooley Bridge 444.
Attempting in recent years to become very smart, but not quite yet in the Sharrow Bay class, though high quality

service and comfort. Can arrange deer stalking and fishing. Price - C.

☆☆ **The Old Vicarage,** Witherslack, Grange-over-Sands. Witherslack 381.

Small Georgian hotel, only seven bedrooms, in South Cumbria. Informal, quiet, but tasteful, good food. Price - B/C.

☆ **Greenriggs Hotel,** Underbarrow. Crosthwaite 387.

Old farmhouse, smallish and a delightful setting. Price - B.

☆ **Kirkstone Foot Country House Hotel,** Kirkstone Pass, Ambleside 32232. Price - B.

☆ **Lindeth Fell Country House Hotel,** Bowness-on-Windermere. Windermere 3286.

Run by Pat and Diana Kennedy. Small, friendly, high-class hotel set on the fells above town. Brilliant views and well away from the hordes. Strong emphasis on fresh food and local specialities (look out for the after dinner Kendal mintcake). Price - B.

☆ **Uplands,** Haggs Lane, Cartmel 248.

Spawned by Miller Howe (subtitled 'In the Miller Howe Manner') and run by two of John Tovey's former right hand persons, Diana and Tom Peter. All the quality and comfort you would expect from Tovey training, but at around half the price of Miller Howe. Only four bedrooms. Price - B.

Executive Hotels

First class hotels which have most of the accepted amenities, but often rather lacking in individual character or atmosphere. They are generally large, lots of bars, good for businessmen, large parties or, very important, good for children. Our top two De Luxe hotels actively discourage children under 13. Anyway, at those prices, who wants to take children. While the Classy Hotels are also rather wasted on children.

The following are not Executive in the Hilton, monster new building sense - and luckily nothing in the Lake District is like that - but in being large, functional and efficient. You might actually prefer them to some of the personal eccentricities and strange customs of the De Luxe and Classy hotels.

☆☆☆ **Lodore Swiss Hotel,** Keswick. Borrowdale 285.

Will still be saddened not to be classed as De Luxe, as they do try awfully hard, but somehow it's too big (72 rooms) and too functional to be hailed as an experience, but excellent at what it sets out to do. Very good for families.

Fine setting on Derwentwater, with the Lodore Falls behind, good restaurant, two swimming pools, tennis, dancing, sauna, film shows, children's playground, colour TV and phones in all bedrooms. Price - C.

☆ Wordsworth Hotel, Grasmere. Grasmere 592.

Will be cross not to be called Classy. A skilful conversion of an old building with lots of luxury amenities like indoor swimming pool and sauna and phones and TV in all rooms and conference rooms. Prelude Restaurant smart, but not yet a taste thrill. 38 bedrooms. Price - C.

Belsfield Hotel, Bowness. Windermere 2448.

Large Victorian house, 71 bedrooms, with lots of family amenities - swimming, clock golf, games, dancing. Price - C.

Old England Hotel, Bowness. Windermere 2444.

Old established mansion hotel with modern amenities - outdoor swimming pool, games room. 84 bedrooms. Price - C.

☆ The Crown, Wetheral, Nr Carlisle. Wetheral 61888.

Not in Lakeland proper, but one of the best of the county's executive hotels. Recently converted, at a vast expense, from old riverside hotel, with massive sports facilities, especially squash, very smart pine wood dining room and conference facilities. Handy for the Roman Wall and Borders as well as the Lakes. Price - B.

Keswick Hotel, Station Road. Keswick 72020.

Keswick is surprisingly poor in top quality or classy hotels, compared with Ullswater or Windermere. This one is quiet and comfortable with games room and putting. Price - B.

☆ Armathwaite Hall, Bassenthwaite Lake 551.

This should be a *Classy* hotel, because of its outstanding views over Bass Lake, its imposing mansion building and its good service, but somehow it *looks* more individual and special than it is, despite lots of recent promotional gimmicks. Food can be very good, other times not so good. Bedrooms 37. Price - B.

Low Wood Hotel, Windermere. Ambleside 33338.

Lakeland's biggest hotel with 148 bedrooms, but for many years its fine Lakeside setting, with 3/4 mile of lake frontage, was ruined by its passion for the charabanc trade. In the post war years it became little more than a transit camp for coach parties. Now aiming for family and executive trade. Continually adding new bits, like the waterski centre (much reviled by Friends of the Lakes), leisure and conference facilities. Price - B/C.

☆ **North Lakes Gateway Hotel**, Penrith 68111.

Penrith's answer for all busy businessmen. Opened in October 1985. 85 rooms and a leisure club. Price - C.

☆ **The Beech Hill**, Bowness-on-Windermere. Windermere 2137.

Modern hotel, right on lake shore, 3 miles south of Bowness. Conference rooms, plus own sauna, solarium and swimming pool. Links with Westmorland Watersports enable water skiing and windsurfing courses to be offered. Price - B.

Underscar Hotel, Keswick 72469.

With its wonderful conservatory dining room, terrific setting under Skiddaw and fifty lush acres, this should also be one of nature's classy hotels, but recent changes of ownership have led to varied reports. Worth checking on though as it has lots of facilities for jolly family hols, also very good self-catering apartments. Price - B.

Hotels with Swimming Pools

Just in case that's really what you're after, here's a selection:

1 Beech Hill Hotel, Bowness-on-Windermere. W'mere 2137.
   Pool (open to non-residents), sauna & solarium.
2 Hillthwaite House Hotel, Thornbarrow Road, Windermere.
   W'mere 3636. Pool (res. only), sauna & solarium.
3 Old England Hotel, Bowness. W'mere 2488.
   Outdoor pool (res. only), sauna.
4 Belsfield Hotel, Bowness. W'mere 2448.
   Pool (res. only), sauna.
5 Burnside Hotel, Bowness. W'mere 2211.
   Pool and sports facilities (eg squash, badminton, gym, etc.) for residents, with a club for non-residents.
6 Regent Hotel, Waterhead, Ambleside. Ambleside 32254.
   Pool (res. only).
7 Pillar Hotel & Country Club, Elterwater. Langdale 302.
   Pool (club membership available), sauna & solarium.
8 Whitewater Hotel, The Lakeland Village, Backbarrow, Newby Bridge. Newby Bridge 31133. Pool (club memb.), sauna & solarium.
9 Wordsworth Hotel, Grasmere. Grasmere 592.
   Pool (club membership), sauna, solarium, jacuzzi and gymnasium.
10 Eccle Riggs Hotel, Foxfield Road, Broughton-in-Furness.
   B-in-F 398. Pool (open to non-res.), sauna & solarium.
11 Damson Dene Hotel, Lyth Valley. Crosthwaite 676.
   Pool (res. only), squash court, sauna & solarium.
12 Lodore Swiss Hotel, Keswick. Borrowdale 285.
   Pool (res. only), sauna & solarium.
13 Crown & Mitre Hotel, English Street, Carlisle. Carlisle 25491.
   Pool only (club for non-residents).
14 Swallow Hilltop Hotel, London Road, Carlisle. Carlisle 29255.
   Pool (club for non-res.), sauna & solarium.
15 The Appleby Manor Hotel, Roman Road, Appleby. Appleby 51571.
   Pool (club for non-res.), sauna & solarium.
16 North Lakes Gateway Hotel, Ullswater Road, Penrith.
   Penrith 68111. Pool, sauna, solarium (club for non-res.).

Small Hotels and Inns

A handful which have got individual character and one day might well jump up to be classed as Classy.

Sun Hotel, Coniston 41248.

Regulars rave about the comfort and food. Beautiful setting. Price - B.

Pheasant Inn, Bassenthwaite Lake 234.

Old style inn, can be a bit like a road house in high summer with passing tourists, but very attractive. Price - C.

Three Shires Inn, Little Langdale. Langdale 215.

Despite several changes of ownership, still comfortable, simple, small hotel with friendly atmosphere. Price - A.

☆ Dale Head Hall, Thirlspot, Nr Keswick. Tel: Keswick 72478.

Nice, quiet location with lovely views; the only privately-owned building on the side of Thirlmere. It was opened in 1986 by Mr and Mrs Hosey and only has nine rooms - some with four poster beds. Price - B.

☆ Temple Sowerby House, Kirkby Thore 61578.

Not in the LD proper, being six miles the other side of Penrith, on a main road, but a handsome Georgian house with a growing reputation for good imaginative food. Could eventually be in the Classy category. Price - B.

☆ Lupton Tower, Lupton, Nr. Kirkby Lonsdale. Crooklands 400.

Another of Derek Hook's enterprising ventures (see chapter 5 for more about Mr Hook), this time in partnership with the Smith family. A nice, quiet, vegetarian hotel which opened in July 1987. Nine rooms. Price - A.

☆ Lancrigg Vegetarian Country House Hotel, Grasmere 317.

Pleasant hotel, hidden away from the crowds in Easedale. Ten rooms, some with whirlpool bath (hardly seems in keeping with the veggie image ...). Price - A/B.

Bower House Inn, Eskdale. Eskdale 244.

Pretty Inn in a pretty valley. Bedrooms have TV and bathroom. Price - B.

Blue Bell Hotel, Heversham. Milnthorpe 3159.

Not really a small hotel - it has 26 rooms and a dining room which can take eighty people. It prefers to call itself a hostelry. The dining room is popular with locals. Just as we went to press, we heard that it had been sold. Let's hope the stardards keep up. Price - B/C.

Bargain Places

A random selection - all around £25 for dinner, B & B.

☆☆ High Greenrigg House, Caldbeck 430.

Absolutely isolated, traditional Cumbrian farm house, out on the Caldbeck fells, away from all those nasty tourists, but handy for all the Northern Lakes. Very friendly, simple bedrooms, comfortable sitting room, bar, snooker, table tennis, first class home cooking, good packed lunches. Perfect for *real* open air lovers, especially families or parties. Personally run by Robin and Fran Jacobs. She's American. He's English. Price - A.

☆ Howtown Hotel, Howtown, Ullswater.
Pooley Bridge 514.

Complete opposite of High Greenrigg, being chintzy and rather old fashioned and not really very suitable for boisterous families (though they have separate cottage accommodation), but delightful, cosy and olde worlde, with brilliant views, right beside Howtown Pier. The Sharrow Bay bosses often drop in here to relax. Price - A.

☆ Low Hall, Brandlingill, Nr Cockermouth. Cockermouth 826654.

Recently converted 17th century farmhouse near Lorton. Perfect for exploring Loweswater and Crummock. Only six bedrooms. Hard to find, so get exact directions, which means it's beautifully quiet. David and Dani Edwards, she ex-teacher, he ex-social worker, have done it all by themselves, their little dream come true. And it is. Terrific food, comfy bedrooms, nothing too much trouble. Price - A.

Guest Houses

There are hundreds of guest houses in the Lake District - here is a selection of good ones, recommended by our spies. Prices vary between £10.00 to £25.00 per person for B&B (1989 prices). The difference between a Guest House and a Hotel is that hotels have to offer lunch or dinner to non-residents.

Ambleside

Meadowbank Guest House, Rydal Road, Ambleside. Tel: Ambleside 32710.

Holme Lea Guest House Church Street, Ambleside. Tel: Ambleside 32114.

Cartmel Fell

Lightwood Farm Guest House, nr. Bowland Bridge, Cartmel Fell. Tel: Newby Bridge 31454.
(NB this is not a working farm.)

Grange-over-Sands
Thornbank Guest House, 6 Thornfield Road,
Grange-over-Sands. Tel: Grange 2664.

Grasmere
Banerigg Guest House, Lake Road, Grasmere.
Tel: Grasmere 204.

Hawkshead
Bracken Fell Guest House, Outgate, Ambleside.
Tel: Hawkshead 289.

Kendal
The Hillside Guest House, 4 Beast Banks, Kendal.
Tel: Kendal 22836.

Keswick
Charnwood Guest House, 6 Eskin Street, Keswick.
Tel: Keswick 74111.

Linnett Hill Hotel, Penrith Road, Keswick.
Tel: Keswick 73109.

Milnethorpe
Milton House Barn, Crooklands, Milnethorpe.
Tel: Crooklands 628.

Penrith
Howscales Guest House, Kirkoswald, Penrith.
Tel: Lazonby 666.

Rydal
Foxghyll Guest House, Under Loughrigg, Rydal.
Tel: Ambleside 33292.

Rydal Holme Guest House, Rydal. Tel: Ambleside 33110.

Windermere
Brendan Chase Guest House, College Road, Windermere.
Tel: Windermere 5638.

Glenburn Hotel, New Road, W'mere. Tel: W'mere 2649.

Hawksmoor Hotel, Lake Road, Windermere
Tel: W'mere 2110.

Meadfoot Guest House, New Road, Windermere.
Tel: W'mere 2610.

Bargain Farmhouse
☆ **Foldgate Farm**, Corney, Bootle. Tel: Bootle 660.
　　Run by Mary Hogg, this is a real Cumbrian farmhouse,
with plenty of sheep and cattle around. Has a delightful
cobbled courtyard and old stone barn. Inside it has old
furniture and rag rugs, homely and friendly; thoroughly
nice. Dinner, B & B - £13.50.

☆ **Picket How,** Brackenthwaite, Loweswater, Cockermouth. Tel: Lorton 209.

A real farm, though the farmer, Philip Walling, is now a barrister, but his wife, Julia, turns out a pretty farmhouse bed and breakfast, £10, plus dinner if required.

Other farmhouses They're everywhere, just look for the signs, and usually very cheap - around £12-£15 for B and B and evening meal.

Self-Catering

There are a number of private agencies operating in the Lake District, all of which have a selection of properties on their books:

Cottage Life (mainly Central Lakes, 17 properties)
1 Elterwater, Ambleside. Tel: Langdale 292.

Grey Abbey Properties (mainly North, 72 properties from caravans to cottages)
PO Box 23, Coach Road, Whitehaven. Tel: W'haven 3346.

Holidays in Lakeland (All Lakes - 200 properties)
Stock Park Estate, Newby Bridge, Nr Ulverston.
Tel: Newby Bridge 31549.

Lakeland Cottage Holidays (Keswick area - 40 properties)
Keswick. Tel: Keswick 71071.

Lakelovers (mainly South - 90 properties)
The Toffee Loft, Ash Street, Bowness-on-Windermere.
Tel: Windermere 6561.

Prices vary enormously, especially between central Lakes and the fringes. A cottage sleeping six in Cockermouth could cost you £190 a week in the high season; something similar in Ambleside would cost £290. Big differences too between high and low season; a typical cottage in Borrowdale costing £105 in the winter will be £285 at the height of the summer. The rate often depends on the owner's reasons for needing the money (i.e. it might not be his full-time business), so you can get some good deals through the independent lists.

The Cumbria and Lakeland Self-Caterers' Association seeks to provide 'realistic minimum standards' for properties. They have a free leaflet which lists members, prices and details, available from the Secretary, CLSCA, Jonathan Somerville. Tel: Kendal 821325. CLSCA also has a vacancy advisory service, open all year - tel: Ulverston 57668.

Camping and Caravanning

There are sites all over the Lake District - some spectacular, some good, some awful.

The English Tourist Board run a Rose Award scheme to distinguish the best of the caravan parks, describing them as "first class caravan holiday homes (sic) set in delightful, well-managed settings ...". There are five of these so far listed in Cumbria:

Greenhowe Caravan Park, Great Langdale, Ambleside. Tel: Langdale 231. (Static caravans only.)

Lakeland Caravan Park, Moor Lane, Flookburgh. Tel: Flookburgh 556.

Stanwix Park Holiday Centre, West Silloth. Tel: Silloth 31671.

Fallbarrow Park, Rayrigg Road, Bowness-on-Windermere. Tel: Windermere 4427.

Bassenthwaite Lakeside Lodges, Bassenthwaite Lake 641.

Sites for Caravans and Tents is a booklet available from most of the Tourist Information Centres. It lists all the sites but does not give charges. You have to be careful; some sites double their charges at the height of the summer (claiming that actually they discount the rest of the year, which is rubbish). Some say 'family groups only', usually to avoid problems with groups of young lads.

National Trust Camping Sites

The NT have three excellent places, open from Easter to October:

Great Langdale, Ambleside (at the head of the Langdale Valley). A 9-acre site with room for 300 tents. Shop, toilets and showers on site.

Wasdale Head, Seascale (at the head of the Wasdale Valley, on the west side of Wastwater). An 8-acre site, room for 100 tents and all the facilities mentioned above.

Low Wray Farm, Low Wray, Nr Ambleside (3 miles south of Ambleside on the west side of the lake). 150 pitches, plus lakeshore access.

At one time, anyone using a National Trust site who had a green (ie, unobtrusive) tent would get a reduction. This practice stopped, however, once the NT realised that people were using car spray paints and tents were returning a bright orange after a downpour ...

Five Recommended Caravan Sites

☆☆☆ **Wild Rose Caravan & Camping Park,**
Ormside, Appleby. Tel: Appleby 51077

☆☆ **Ashes Lane Caravan & Camping Park,**
Staveley, Nr. Kendal. Tel: Staveley 821119.

☆ **Thirlspot Farm,** Thirlspot (Thirlmere).
Tel: Keswick 72224.

☆☆☆ **The Cove Caravan & Camping Site,**
Watermillock, Penrith. Tel: Pooley Bridge 549.

☆☆ **The Quiet Site,** Watermillock, Penrith.
Tel: Pooley Bridge 337.

All are recommended on the basis of being quiet and in a good setting - not for the fun park activities which some sites boast. Ashes Lane has sites for 200 tents and 100 vans, Wild Rose can take 50 tents and 175 vans. The rest are comparatively tiny, so don't expect to be able to turn up at the height of the season and get on without booking.

National Trust Caravan Site

Fell Foot Country Park, Newby Bridge, Ulverston.
Tel: Newby Bridge 31273.
Sites available (along with chalets) at the Trust's property at the southern end of Lake Windermere, with lake shore access.

National Park Site

Not to be outdone, the National Park people have a caravan and camping site, though slightly out of the tourist mainstream:

Silecroft Caravan & Camping Site, Silecroft, Millom. Tel: Millom 2649.

Hints Most sites get very busy at bank holidays - those around the major towns in particular. The nearest campsite to Bowness or Windermere is 3 miles away - very handy if you've just slogged in from the Dales Way and are looking for a late night campsite.

Accommodation for the Disabled

There is a Trust operating in Cumbria specifically to encourage the disabled to try a range of outdoor activities, making the most of the National Park:

The Calvert Trust Adventure Centre
Little Crosthwaite, Under Skiddaw, Keswick.
Tel: Keswick 72254.

The Calvert Trust has accommodation for 36 people (plus self-catering for 12) and run a number of activities, including archery, angling, bird watching, hill walking, nature trails, rock climbing, canoeing, pony trekking and sailing. They will take able-bodies people, but all their facilities are aimed at the disabled. For further details contact the warden.

Bendrigg Lodge
Old Hutton, Kendal.
Tel: Kendal 23766.

This is another centre catering specifically for the disabled. It has accommodation for 35, plus self-catering for 20 (minimum booking of 10 for self-catering). They also provide a range of outdoor activities.

General Hints on Accommodation

In the summer and school holidays, anything in a town like Bowness, Windermere, Ambleside and Keswick is bound to be busy, noisy and hectic. Unless you love that sort of thing, try a rural spot or a small village or head for the fringes, such as Furness, Cockermouth, Eden Valley. In those places, you will at least be able to park your car outside your digs.

At most of the hotels and larger guest houses, it is worth asking about winter prices and bargain breaks. There are all sorts of price incentives to get people into the area out of season.

Accommodation Registers

There are four of these available for the LD. Each covers a specific area and gives around 80% of the accommodation available. They give loads of addresses, prices and facilities, but no pretty pics. Available from local TICs or from the following:

South Lakeland
SLDC Where To Stay Guide. Price 35p.
Available from Kendal Tourist Information Centre. Tel: Kendal 25758.

Keswick
Keswick Publicity Association Guidebook and Accommodation List (covering a 10 mile radius of Keswick).
Price 75p including postage.
Available from The Moot Hall TIC. Tel: Keswick 72803.

Eden Valley
Eden District Council Accommodation List. Free but enclose a SAE. Available from: Penrith TIC, Robinson's School, Middlegate, Penrith. Tel: Penrith 67466.

Copeland (W Coast, Eskdale, Ennerdale & Wasdale)
Where To Stay In Western Lakeland. Free.
Whitehaven TIC, St Nicholas Tower, Lowther Street, Whitehaven. Tel: Whitehaven 5678.

Complaints?

It's no use letting off steam at the first tourist information assistant you see, as TICs cannot handle your complaints for you, so if you want to air a legitimate gripe about accommodation, write to:

Senior Accommodation Officer,
Cumbria Tourist Board,
Ashleigh,
Holly Road,
Windermere. Tel: Windermere 4444.

Personal Choice Even with money to burn, I would not spend the whole of a week's holiday at either of the Big Two post hotels, Sharrow Bay and Miller Howe. Despite a picnic lunch and trying to be sensible at dinner, it is hard not to feel bloated and soporific after just three days. You can have too much of a good thing. So even if you have the money, save them to the end of the hols as a treat, perhaps booking in for one or two nights, with dinner of course, as that's the highlight. Before that, book into a cheap Inn or Guest House in a completely different part of the Lakes for the first part of the week, such as our Bargain Places, and have some active days and hearty simple meals, then finish off with a guzzle. If of course you are on a very tight budget, or you have teenagers you want rid off, then the cheapest accommodation by far is . . .

Youth Hostels

There are 30 youth hostels in Cumbria, 22 of them inside the National Park:

Alston, Ambleside, Arnside, Black Sail, Buttermere, Carlisle, Carrock Fell, Cockermouth, Coniston - Coppermines, Coniston - Holly How, Derwentwater, Dufton, Elterwater, Ennerdale, Eskdale, Grasmere - Butharlyp How, Grasmere - Thorney How, Hawkshead, Helvellyn, High Close, Honister, Kendal, Keswick, Kirkby Stephen, Longthwaite, Patterdale, Slaidburn, Thirlmere, Wasdale and Windermere.

They all vary in standard and scale. Some, like Ambleside, have all mod cons, look right over the lake, with 240 beds, while Black Sail is little more than a remote mountain hut with only 18 beds. In general, though, the standard of them is getting better all the time.

Here are the three nicest Youth Hostels, in our opinion:

☆☆ **Black Sail Hut,** Ennerdale (OS Ref: 194124). No telephone.

☆☆☆ **Patterdale Youth Hostel,** Goldrill House, Patterdale, Nr Penrith. Tel: Glenridding 394. (OS Ref: 399156).

☆☆ **Carrock Fell Youth Hostel,** High Row Cottages, Haltcliffe, Hesket Newmarket, Wigton. Tel: Caldbeck 325. (OS Ref: 358355).

Which are best often depends largely upon the warden, but these three were considered excellent in recent years. Black Sail is rightly renowned for people wanting to get away from it all; tucked away at the head of Ennerdale it is very simple and completely inaccessible by motor vehicle.

Membership Apply to YHA, Trevelyan House, St Albans, Herts, or any hostel. Adult Membership in 1989 is £7.00 per year. Don't forget you don't have to be a Youth - any age is welcome - and these days Hostels have car parks, many cater for families and they are still incredibly cheap, from £2.60-£5.00 per night. A neat way of using them, if the adults prefer more comfort in their old or middle age, is to book into a good hotel - but put the children in the nearest YHA.

Regional Office YHA, Barclay's Bank Chambers, Crescent Road, Windermere. Tel: Windermere 2301.

Regional Handbook *Youth Hostels in Lakeland*, lists full details. Every year, around 1/4 million people stay in Cumbrian Hostels. Excellent value for money.

Chapter Five

Eating

The Palm Lounge, Royal Oak Hotel

A selection of the top Lakeland restaurants, plus some good lunch and tea places in the various towns, followed by a few reasonable pubs, and some recipes for doing it yourself, Cumbrian style.

Restaurants

In London and Manchester and the big towns, it's a general rule that hotel meals are poor and that it's best to look for a proper restaurant. In the Lakes, the opposite often applies. A good hotel in the Lakes usually offers the best food in that area, while most of the street restaurants are little more than caffs, producing fry-ups for the tourists. But there are exceptions, and they are increasing all the time. There is not the huge selection of good and cheap ethnic restaurants, which London and most large British towns now offer these days, but if you go slightly up market for the more ambitious restaurants, some with definite pretensions and others boasting top class home fare, then there is quite a choice.

We have whittled down our own tastings, and taken expert soundings, and offer what we think are the top Lakeland restaurants. This time, however, there are so many good ones that we have split it up into two lists - the Top Four, plus The Others. Recommended Vegetarian and Ethnic Eating are listed separately.

Prices The range is A, B and C, from cheapish to expensive, according to the average price for one person having dinner, without wine or service.

> A under £15
> B £15-£25
> C over £25

Top Four Lakeland Restaurants

☆☆☆ Sharrow Bay Country House Hotel,
Howtown Road, Ullswater. Tel: Pooley Bridge 301.
  See Hotel listing for details. Price - C.

☆☆☆ Miller Howe, Rayrigg Road, Windermere.
Tel: Windermere 2536.
  See Hotel listing for details. Price - B.

☆☆ Porthole Eating House, 3 Ash Street, Bowness-on-Windermere. Tel: Windermere 2793.
  Italian-French, run by an Italian-Cumbrian, Gianni Berton, and his Manchester-Cumbrian wife, Judy, since 1972. The mixture works, brilliantly. Always very popular, efficient yet informal, with great care taken over everything, from the yummy treacle bread to start with, to the Windermere char, if it's on. Don't forget to take coffee or pre-drinks upstairs. Easy not to realise they have a large lounge bar, hidden away. Price - B.

☆☆ Quince and Medlar, 13 Castlegate, Cockermouth. Tel: Cockermouth 823579.
  It's a veggie restaurant, shock horror, at least that was my reaction on first going, being a dedicated meat eater. But you'd never realise, as it's all so tasty, filling, ingenious, using vegetarian and ethnic dishes from all over the world. Don't miss the Dominican twice cooked souffle. Delish. Small Georgian building, few tables, rather bijou, always best to book. Run by Jonathan Whitehead-Whiting, who waits, and wife Susan who cooks. No smoking, which is another plus. In 1988, it was number two in a nationwide best veggie restaurant of the year. Good wine list. Excellent value. Price - A.

Other Top Restaurants

☆☆ Jackson's Bistro, St Martin's Square, Bowness.
Tel: Windermere 6264.
  Frank and Christine Jackson ran Greenriggs at Underbarrow for ten years and have now gone urban with this smart, cheerful bistro. Two floors, attractive decor, excellent value for money. Price - A.

☆☆ Merewood Country House Hotel,
Ambleside Road, Windermere. Tel: Windermere 5284.
  Windermere's newest restaurant and hotel. Aiming for the same market as Sharrow Bay and Miller Howe but trying to do something a little different from the other two. Lovely old house in a superb setting, good atmosphere and excellent food. Price - C.

☆☆ **The Old Vicarage**, Witherslack, Grange-over-Sands. Tel: Witherslack 381.

A Lakeland dream come true - how two couples, absolute amateurs, gave up London commuter living after 25 years, fled to the Lakes, started a little guest house, doing B&B at first, now blossomed into one of the best small, select hotels in South Lakes. Five course dinners, all works of art. Price - B.

☆☆ **Roger's Restaurant**, 4 High Street, Windermere. Tel: Windermere 4954.

Owned and run by Roger Pergl-Wilson. A smart, modern French restaurant offering some of the best quality cooking in the district. Menus change daily and home-grown herbs play an important part. Price - A/B.

☆☆ **Rothay Manor Hotel and Restaurant**, Rothay Bridge, Ambleside. Tel: Ambleside 33605.

A Regency hotel, built up by the late and greatly missed Bronwen Nixon and her two sons, famed for its soups and starters. Five-course dinners are good value, usually traditional French or English. Lamb a speciality, along with game when in season. Sweets are excellent . Price - B.

☆☆ **Kirkstone Foot Country House Hotel**, Kirkstone Pass. Tel: Ambleside 32232.

A 17th century manor which has been converted into a luxury hotel with self-catering apartments. Begun by the Batemans thirteen years ago and they continue to provide a personal service. All fresh food with a traditional English main course and imaginative sweets and starters. One sitting at 8 o'clock prompt - set menu but specialities can be catered for if you give plenty of warning. Elegant and very good value for money. Price - B.

☆☆ **Leeming-on-Ullswater Country House Hotel**, Watermillock, Ullswater. Tel: Pooley Bridge 444.

Classically-designed restaurant. In the evening there is a fixed price menu based on excellent local supplies, ranging from roast beef to guinea fowl with celery and walnut stuffing. Delicious, beautifully presented sweets. Price - B.

☆☆ **Uplands Country House Hotel**, Cartmel. Tel: Cartmel 248.

A Miller Howe offshoot, but less pretentious. Excellent evening meals at reasonable prices. Price - B.

☆ **Passepartout**, 51 Castlegate, Penrith. Tel: Penrith 65852.

Now under new management, and lacking some of the flair and finesse of the old order, but still a pleasant eating place in an arid eating area. (Strange that with all those aristocratic families around Penrith there should be so few high class places for them to eat. Perhaps it's always visitors who are prepared to spend their dosh, not locals.) But let's welcome the Robinsons, she an ex-French teacher and he a former senior lecturer in catering. (Hmm.) Efficient French-English cuisine. Hurrah, it's now non-smoking, but boo to a salad that comes with beetroot in it. They also offer an attractive flat, £26 per night, sleeps two to five, handy for those who can't stagger back to their tent. Price - A.

☆ Rampsbeck Hotel, Ullswater.
Tel: Pooley Bridge 442.

A sensational situation right on the shore, with a reputation for first class cuisine nouvelle which is well worth trying, though on our test lunch we were the only ones in the dining room. A delightful surprise, though, when you consider how boring the bar meals are. Price - A.

☆ Michael's Nook Country House Hotel, Grasmere. Grasmere 496.

Run by Reg Gifford with imaginative five-course dinners, but some find the antiques and decor a bit fussy. Price - C.

☆ The Bay Horse, Canal Foot, Ulverston.
Ulverston 53972.

It's actually a pub, overlooking Morcambe Bay, but there is a bistro attached which is building up a fine reputation for good food. Yet another part of the Miller Howe empire. Price - A.

☆ Tullythwaite House, Crosthwaite, Nr Bowland Bridge. Crosthwaite 397.

A small farmhouse at the back of Cartmel Fell, between Kendal and Lake Windermere. Originally run by Mary Johnson and raved about in the first edition of this guide. New owners Mr and Mrs Greenwood no longer serve high teas, but produce excellent evening meals (Wednesday to Saturday only and lunches on Sundays). Small, personal service, using local produce. Price (evening meals) - B.

☆ Aynsome Manor, Cartmel, Nr Grange-over-Sands.
Cartmel 36653.

Another new entry. Good reports coming in about this pleasant manor house set in parklands just outside Cartmel village. Price - A.

☆ Field Head House, Outgate, Hawkshead.
Tel: Hawkshead 240.

Another newcomer to the book, this is a small hotel between Hawkshead and Ambleside which provides a set evening meal for non residents (but only if the hotel is not full). Price - B.

Smaller Restaurants, Good Teas and Light Lunches

A speciality of Lakeland is the small tea or coffee shop, where you can get home-baked cakes and light lunches. Often these are combined with some other attraction, such as a historic house (eg, Brantwood, Dalemain and Hutton-in-the-Forest). They tend to be popular with locals as well as tourists. The cafe at the Kirkstone Slate Gallery was so popular that there was a public campaign which got it reopened after a year. Here are some recommendations for good teas and lunches throughout the Lakes, town by town.

This list also includes some of the smaller, less pretentious eating places which haven't quite made it into our Top Restaurants. Some of these also do teas and lunches, but not all the cafes do evening meals. We have indicated which of them do. Closing times can vary enormously, compared to the cities, often as early as 7.30pm.

This time we've also indicated those places where food has priority over the dreaded weed. These are either completely 'no smoking' or have banished smokers to a separate room (merely putting them on separate tables never works.)

Ambleside

☆☆ **Sheila's Cottage**, The Slack.
Tel: Ambleside 33079. No smoking.
One of the best tea shops around Ambleside. Evening meals (early evening only).

☆ **Zeffirelli's Wholefood Pizzeria**, Compston Road. Tel: Ambleside 33845. No smoking.
An event in itself, as it's part of a cinema, shops, coffee lounge, all very arty and stylish. (Chelsea comes to Ambleside.) But great fun and good food. There's no Mr Zeffirelli by the way, so don't ask for him. The owner is Derek Hook from Blackpool. It's a cinematic joke, gerrit. **Pizzeria** does evening meals; during the day go to the **Garden Room Cafe** downstairs.

Cervetti's, Kelsick Road. Tel: Ambleside 33676.
Small coffee house. Proprietor is Italian - authentic dishes, snack meals and a la carte.

Stock Ghyll Snacks and Grills, Central Buildings. Tel: Ambleside 33334.
Best sausage, egg and chips in the Lake District?

Kirkstone Slate Galleries, Skelwith Bridge. Tel: Ambleside 33296. No smoking.

Appleby
The Copper Kettle, 17 Boroughgate. Tel: Appleby 51605.

Bowness-on-Windermere

The Alpine, Crag Brow. Tel: 2884.
   Looks unprepossessing but good value coffee and home cooking. A good budget cafe.

Broughton-in-Furness

Beswick's Eating House, The Square.
Tel: Broughton-in-Furness 285. No smoking.
   Open during the day in summer, evenings all year.

Caldbeck

Priests Mill, Caldbeck. Tel: Caldbeck 369.
   Recently converted watermill, very tastefully done. Modest but healthy lunches and teas. Also craft shops, with persons crafting away, and very good little second-hand bookshop.

Carlisle

Hudson's, Treasury Court, Fisher Street.
Tel: Carlisle 47733. No smoking.

☆ **Lordy's**, 10 Lonsdale Street. Tel: Carlisle 42014.
   More of a restaurant but very reasonable.

Mr Pickwick's, 13 Globe Lane. Tel: Carlisle 49346.
   Pleasant but busy tea room in The Lanes precinct.

Cartmel

St Mary's Lodge. Tel: Cartmel 379.
   A pleasant and homely tea room near the Priory.

Cockermouth

Old Court House Restaurant, 2 Main Street.
Tel: Cockermouth 823871.
   Relaxed atmosphere and generous food in the past - let's hope the new owners keep it up.

Courtyard Coffee House, Headford Crescent, Main Street.
Tel: Cockermouth 823971. No smoking.

Over The Top, Kirkgate . Tel: Cockermouth 827016.
   Healthy, home cooking. Best cappuccino in Cockermouth. It's 'over the top' of The Fig Tree Craft Centre.

(And don't forget **Wordsworth House** does very good teas; worth the entrance fee.)

Coniston

Bridge House. Tel: Coniston 41278.
   Home-made fare served all day. Licensed.

Blue Bird Cafe, Coniston Boating Centre.
Tel: Coniston 41649.
   A neat little cafe just by the lake.

Jumping Jenny, Brantwood. Tel: Coniston 41396.

Yes, Ruskin's House - now does good teas and lunches. Open to non-visitors to the house. Welcoming wood-burning stove in winter.

Dent

Stone Close, Main Street, Dent. Tel: Dent 231.

Excellent lunches, teas and evening meals (latter by booking only), all in a 17th century cottage, complete with flagged floors and cast iron range. (They also do bed and breakfast at very reasonable rates.)

Grasmere

Baldry's, Red Lion Square . Tel: Grasmere 301.

A nice cafe in an area which is otherwise starting to slip a bit. Good home-made fare, especially the apple pie.

Hawkshead

Minstrel's Gallery, The Square.
Tel: Hawkshead 423. No smoking.

Grandy Nook Coffee Shop, Vicarage Lane.
Tel: Hawkshead 404. No smoking.

Excellent coffee shop, which also does evening meals in summer.

Kendal

Brewery Arts Centre, 122 Highgate. Tel: Kendal 25133.

Pizza Plus serves from 5.30-7.00pm so a good to eat before going into their new cinema.

☆ **Farrers Coffee Shop**, Stricklandgate.
Tel: Kendal 31707. No smoking.

A real, old fashioned, excellent value coffee shop. The coffee comes in one of those plunger thingies. You can also buy packets of coffee and tea in the shop, along with various arcane implements for brewing same.

☆ **The Moon Restaurant**, 129 Highgate. Tel: Kendal 29254. No smoking.

With that name it would be tempting to say it lacks atmosphere, but it wouldn't be true. However, this is one which serves evening meals only.

☆☆ **Nutter's Eating House**, Yard 11, Stramongate.
Tel: Kendal 25135. No smoking.

Very friendly cafe and eating house, probably the most entertaining in Kendal. Look out for Simon's poems at the entrance to the Yard.

Union Jack Cafe, Kirkland. Kendal 22458.

Since the sad demise of Crumpets a few years back (although a glossy photo of it continues to appear in the CTB guide to the area), Kirkland has lacked a nice, family cafe to encourage shoppers down to this part of town. Welcome the Union Jack, now less of a transport cafe than formerly. They even do vegetarian snacks (though usually with chips).

Keswick

☆☆ **Maysons**, 33 Lake Road. Tel: Keswick 74104.

My favourite Lakeland place for a light meal - something tasty and unusual available almost any time of day. Keswick has desperately needed somewhere nice for yonkers.

Bryson's Cake Shop, 42 Main Street.
Tel: Keswick 72257. No smoking.

Doubled in size since the last edition. Still good value and very pretty, but getting a bit noisy. Do they really need muzak?

☆ **Wythop Mill**, Embleton. Tel: Bassenthwaite Lake 394.
Small but terrific home cooking.

Old Sawmill, Dodd Wood, Underskiddaw.
Tel: Keswick 74317.

Part of the Mirehouse estate, but there is no charge to get in. The cafe makes the best fruit cake in Cumbria.

Lorton

White Ash Barn, High Lorton. Tel: Lorton 236.

One of the few places for teas in a very pretty vale. Friendly couple (she's from Brazil) in a neatly converted barn.

Maryport

☆ **The Retreat Restaurant**, Birkby. Tel: Maryport 814056.
No smoking.

A rare find. Open for lunches and evening meals only.

Melmerby

☆☆ **The Village Bakery**. Tel: Langwathby 515.

A tiny village, 10 miles north east of Penrith, so not exactly on the usual tourist round but a wonderful stopping off point if you're making the trek to Newcastle. Excellent cafe in a converted eighteenth-century barn. Home produce using locally ground flours, much it available to take away.

Newby Bridge

Fell Foot Cafe, Fell Foot Park. Tel: Newby Bridge 31274.

Penrith

☆ **Bluebell Bookshop**, Angel Square.
Tel: Penrith 66660. No smoking.

Good teas and light lunches amongst the bookshelves.

In Clover, Wholefood Restaurant, Poet's Walk.
Tel: Penrith 67474. No smoking.

Ravenstonedale
☆ **The Fat Lamb Inn**, Fell End, Ravenstonedale.
Tel: Newbiggin-on-Lune 242.

An old coaching inn set high on remote moorland. You can't miss it. In the field there is the only remaining member of a rare breed of Long Necked Sheep (it's actually a Llama).

Seatoller
☆ **Yew Tree Restaurant**, Seatoller. Tel: Borrowdale 634.

Sedbergh
Ye Old Copper Kettle, 43 Main Street.
Tel: Sedbergh 20995.

Don't be put off by the name. A little known gem.

Staveley
Wedge Hall Gallery & Tea Room, Windermere Road.
Tel: Staveley 821130.

Just what Staveley needs to divert people from thundering past on the new bypass. Locally made goodies - both food and crafts.

Watendlath
Caffle House. Tel: Borrowdale 219. No smoking.

Very modest, but what a joy to have their farmhouse teas after a long walk.

Whitehaven
The Good Food Store, 153 Queen Street.
Tel: Whitehaven 66628. No smoking.

Bit variable since change of ownership (some while ago now) but still worth checking out.

☆ **Bruno's Restaurant**, 9 Church Street. Tel: Whitehaven 65270.

Very good Italian, though rather cramped. Nice 'tree' in the centre of the restaurant.

Windermere
Lakeland Plastics, Alexandra Buildings (right behind the Railway Station). Tel: Windermere 2255. No smoking.

Don't laugh - go right to the end and there's a very good cafe, now run by Miller Howe.

Victoria Cottage, Victoria Street. Tel: 5234. No smoking.

Good 'foody' ideas, cosy L. Ashley decor but oh, the painfully slow service.

Vegetarian Eating

There has always been a tradition of veggie eating in the Lakes, but usually of the faintly eccentric kind, popular with Wizened Wonders with hairy knees clutching Fabian pamphlets. The point was to make it politically veggie, not artistically tasty, so non-veggies scoffed or laughed at the very idea of nut cutlets, and never ventured in.

Now the world and his wife, or at least their children, have gone veggie mad. (My three children are all veggie, but I am allowed meat on Wednesdays.) It's part of the healthy living, healthy eating kick, and let's not be horrible to the poor animals. Interesting that it should have taken off so much in Lakeland, where the main sport for centuries has been doing horrible things to animals, such as foxes.

This new breed of veggie restaurants and hotels are ever so homely and artistic, and welcome the unconverted. They've had a good effect on ordinary, meaty places, who more and more publicly offer the choice of a veggie dish or menu. (In the old days, you had to force it out of them.) You also now get many places which offer the meat dish as the eccentric alternative, such as Sheila's Cottage in Ambleside or Over The Top in Cockermouth, both of which are keenest to see you guzzling their healthy stuff or the fruity cordials.

Here's a selection of specialist veggie places, some of which are also mentioned above.

Veggie Restaurants

☆☆ **Quince and Medlar**, Cockermouth.
The best in Cumbria, if not all Britain. (See **Top Five Restaurants** for details.)

☆ **Hedgerow Vegetarian Restaurant**, Lake Road.
Tel: Windermere 5002. No smoking.
Various changes of ownership over the last few years, but it seems to have settled down now. Very attractive and welcoming. Does evening meals and light lunches.

Harvest Vegetarian Restaurant, Compston Road, Ambleside. Tel: Ambleside 33151. No smoking.
Again, a recent of ownership. Variable reports so far.

☆ **Zeffirelli's Wholefood Pizzeria**, Ambleside.
See above for details.

☆ **Lupton Tower**, Lupton, Nr. Kirkby Lonsdale. Crooklands 400.
Nice, quiet vegetarian hotel and restaurant. See Chapter Four for details.

Finally, **The Moon**, in Kendal, is "50% vegetarian".

Vegetarian Cafes

Waterside Wholefoods, Waterside. Tel: Kendal 29743. No smoking.

Good veggie stuff, but slightly pricey.

Eat Fit, Stramongate, Kendal. Tel: Kendal 20341.

The Good Food Store, Whitehaven.
In Clover, Penrith.
Zeffirelli's Garden Room Cafe, Ambleside.

(See Restaurants and Teas for details of the last three.)

Veggie Guest Houses and Hotels

Lancrigg House, Easedale, Grasmere. Tel: Grasmere 317.

Set in 27 acres, in an area loved by the Wordsworths. The Whittingtons used to run the Rowan Tree, so they can be trusted to provide high class veggie cuisine, but now in their small hotel they are also offering such wicked things as a sauna and whirlpool baths. Price - B.

Orchard House, Borrowdale Road, Keswick.
Tel: Keswick 72830.

Long established veggie guest house, going back 30 years. They still talk about the veggie lasagna. Price - A.

Fair Place, Watermillock on Ullswater.
Tel: Pooley Bridge 235.

Small guest house with classic overtones. (The owners were in a string quartet, so the music is always high class.) Price - A.

Ethnic Eating

Do you come all the way to the Lakes to eat foreign? They seem to think so in Bowness where you can't move for all the Greek, Italian, Swiss, Chinese and Indian restaurants. The hard bit is finding good English nosh.

Here's our recommended selection of Chinese and Indian restaurants:

The China Boat, Church Street, Bowness.
Tel: Windermere 6326.

Good value - also take-aways.

☆ **Jade Fountain Chinese Restaurant,** Ulverston.
Tel: Ulverston 55047.

Universal rave reports from our spies.

Rajah Tandoori and Curry Restaurant, Ash Street, Bowness. Tel: Windermere 5852.

Lakeland's only Tandoori? We shall see.

Pub Meals

Pubs are becoming increasingly popular eating places for tourists in the Lake District and some of them are very good indeed. Here are twenty of the best, ordered roughly north to south:

The Sun Inn, Ireby. Tel: Low Ireby 346.

The Old Crown, Hesket Newmarket. Tel: Caldbeck 288. Real beer, brewed on the premises.

The Sun Inn, Bassenthwaite Village. Tel: Bass Lake 439.

Kirkstile Inn, Loweswater. Tel: Lorton 219.

Pheasant Inn, Wythop Village, Bassenthwaite Lake. Tel: Bass Lake 234 (also see Hotels).

Borrowdale Hotel, Borrowdale, nr Keswick. Tel: Borrowdale 224.

Bridge Hotel, Buttermere Village. Tel: Buttermere 252.

The Outgate Inn, Outgate, Hawkshead. Tel: Hawkshead 413.

Britannia Inn, Elterwater. Tel: Langdale 210.

Queen's Head Hotel, Hawkshead. Tel: Hawkshead 271.

Tower Bank Arms, Near Sawrey. Tel: Hawkshead 334.

The Mortal Man, Troutbeck, Windermere. Tel: Ambleside 33195.

Hare and Hounds, Bowland Bridge. Tel: Crosthwaite 333.

Angler's Arms, Haverthwaite. Tel: Newby Bridge 31216.

Farmer's Arms, Lowick Bridge. Tel: Greenodd 376.

The Crown, High Newton. Tel: Grange-Over-Sands 3073.

Hare and Hounds, Levens Bridge. Tel: Sedgwick 60408.

Royal Oak Inn, Bongate, Appleby. Tel: Appleby 51463.

Mason's Arms, Strawberry Bank, Cartmel Fell Tel: Crosthwaite 486.
Famed for its selection of exotic beers, now including its own, brewed on the premises. Food also very good.

Lindale Inn, Lindale, Grange-o'-Sands. Tel: G-O-S 2416.

In addition, **The Blue Bell Hotel**, Heversham (tel: Milnthorpe 3159) gets a mention for its excellent afternoon teas. Hope it continues under the new owners.

Best Pub Meals

Best in the North: Still the Sun Inn, Bassenthwaite Village.
Best in South: Queen's Head, Hawkshead - heading upmarket at a rate of knots but still good value for money.

Good Beer

So much for the food, now for the liquid stuff, the real stuff of course, which real ale drinkers drool over while making skitty comments about that fizzy beer which the Big Breweries pump out everywhere. John Ogden, a terribly keen amateur drinker of northern brews, recommends four which can be found in most parts of Lakeland, plus two he is not so keen on. (The comments are all his.)

Best Brews

Jennings Very popular with enthusiasts. The brewery sits majestically on the banks of the Cocker in Cockermouth and from it come beers of distinction. A local trad brewery, as much a part of the Lakes as Herdwick sheep. Jennings Mild is superb, rich and creamy. Their Marathon Bitter also excellent.

Matthew Brown Well done Blackburn, for giving us Wainwright and Matthew Brown. Much of it is sold in the Lakes and perhaps in recognition of this they have a nice John Peel bitter. The beer was named after him, not the other way round.

Not Best Brews

Hartley's Brewed in Ulverston. Seems weak and characterless. Could explain Stan Laurel's early departure to the USA. They drink Hartley's in Barrow. Enough said.

Younger's Not to my liking either. Seems fizzy and gaseous. Wouldn't give it to my dog, except to put it out of its misery.

Cumbrian Recipes

Tatie Pot

The traditional 'hot-pot' supper of the shepherds' meet.

1lb (450gms) potatoes
1 1/2lbs (680gms) middle neck of lamb
1 black pudding
2 onions
salt and pepper
1/2 pint stock or water
dripping or butter
pickled red cabbage

Peel and slice vegetables, trim fat from meat, slice black pudding.

Layer potatoes, onions, meat and pudding, seasoning each layer and finishing with potatoes, in a good sized casserole dish.

Pour over hot stock, sprinkle with salt, cover and cook 1 1/2 hours in a moderate oven (350°F, 177°C, gas mark 4).

Remove lid, brush potatoes with melted dripping or butter, return to the oven for a further 1/2 hour, to brown them, raising heat of oven slightly if necessary.

Decorate with parsley and serve straight from the cooking dish, accompanied by pickled cabbage. Serves four.

Grasmere Gingerbread

There is only one, genuine Grasmere Gingerbread, invented by Sarah Nelson in 1855 and still sold today from her original tiny shop by St Oswald's Church, Grasmere Village. The recipe is a strictly-guarded secret and is kept in the National Westminster Bank. This is a reasonable facsimile:

1oz (28gms) crystallised ginger
8ozs (227gms) plain flour
1/2 teaspoon bicarbonate of soda
1/2 teaspoon ground ginger
1/2 teaspoon cream of tartar
4oz (115gms) butter
4oz brown sugar
1oz (28gms) sultanas
1 tablespoon golden syrup
1 teaspoon granulated sugar

Sift flour, bicarbonate of soda, cream of tartar and ground ginger. Rub in butter until mixture resembles fine breadcrumbs.

Mix in brown sugar, crystallised ginger, sultanas and golden syrup. Press into a greased sandwich tin and sprinkle with granulated sugar.

Bake in a warm oven (325°F, 163°C, gas mark 3) for 45-50 minutes, until golden brown. Cool in the tin for 15 minutes, cut into wedges and turn out.

Cumberland Rum Butter

1/2lb (227gms) unsalted butter
1lb (450gms) Barbados sugar
1 glass rum (5-7 fl. oz. [150-200mls] according to taste)
1/2 grated nutmeg

Sieve sugar and nutmeg into basin and add the rum slowly, beating all the time. Meanwhile, *gently* melt the butter and when liquid beat it bit by bit into the sugar. Continue beating thoroughly until combined - about 20 mins (!). Then pour into a bowl or small tubs and allow to set. (NB Always add the butter to the sugar, not the other way round.)

Best eaten on scones, with mince pies and Christmas Pudding.

Cumberland Sausage

Traditional Lakeland sausage made from fresh pork and herbs, with little or no 'filling'. It is sold in a continuous strip. Just cut off what you think you can eat. Best cooked in a buttered roasting tin, kept in a fairly tight coil, pricked carefully every three inches or so. Cook in a moderate oven (350°F, 180°C, gas mark 4) for 30-40 minutes and turn once whilst cooking.

Good ones available from butchers in Ambleside, Kendal, Penrith and Cockermouth. They all seem to have their particular recipe. Best eaten with apple sauce.

Cumberland Apple Sauce

a little brown sugar
pinch of powdered mace
several Bramley apples
knob of butter

Peel, core and slice apples and boil in a very little water until cooked and fluffy.

Add sugar to taste, mace and butter and mix well. Serve hot.

Kendal Mint Cake

A local form of teeth rotter, but terribly tasty and not half as sickly as all those mass produced chocolate and candy bars you see elsewhere in the world. The ideal present to bring home, something very special to the Lakes, and they come in small bars for only 10p. You can get them either with brown sugar or white sugar, or even chocolate coated, which is sacrilege. They are genuinely made in Kendal and the four main firms are Romneys, Quiggin, Wilson and Wiper. Most of them boast on their wrappers, "As supplied to expeditions world-wide". All true. Chris Bonington took some with him on Everest trips, and so have many others. Very energy giving. Better than a Mars Bar on the mountains.

1lb white sugar
3oz glucose syrup
teaspoon mint essence
3 fl oz water

Boil the sugar with the water in a pan until sugar dissolves. Add glucose syrup and bring up to 250°F.

Remove from the heat. Allow to settle for 10 minutes, then add mint and stir vigorously (very important) until cloudy white. Pour into moulds. (It is the stirring which gives it its colour and texture.)

For brown mint cake remove 20% of the white sugar and substitute brown (not all brown or it will come out black).

Cumbrian Treacle Bread

I pinched this recipe from the Porthole Restaurant in Bowness, for which many thanks. It really is brilliant. And so easy to make. Must be - I now make it myself every Sunday morning, just to hear the rest of the family going yum yum.

2lbs wholemeal flour
1oz. dried yeast or 2oz. fresh yeast
11/4 pints of warm water
2 tablespoons treacle
1/2 oz. salt
3oz. cracked wheat or bran

Stir the treacle into the 1/4 pint of warm water, sprinkle the yeast on top, put in a warm place until a nice froth has formed - 7 to 10 minutes - then add the rest of the water. Put the dry ingredients into a large mixing bowl, add the yeast mixture and mix well. Divide between 4 1lb loaf tins, greased, press down with the hand - the mixture will be sticky so dampen the hand - leave to rise in a warm place for about 40 minutes, then bake at Gas 6 or 400°F for 30 minutes. Take out of tins, bake for a further 5 minutes for a nice crisp loaf.

Recipe Book
Lakeland - A Taste to Remember, by Mavis Downing. Cicerone Press, 1985, £3.95. Good collection of Lakeland tea recipes.

Specialist Food Shops
Yes, Cumbria does have them. Some export all over the country. Here are three of the most famous:

Alston Cheeses, The Butts, Alston. Tel: Alston 81913.
Specialise in local and North Country cheeses (including Smoked Tynedale and North Pennine).

Ashdown Smokers, Skelleragh Farm, Corney, Nr. Bootle. Tel: Bootle 324.
Dry curing and smoking, wild game and Herdwick Macon (macon is mutton bacon).

Bar Woodall Cumberland Hams, Lane End, Waberthwaite, Nr. Millom. Tel: Ravenglass 237.
Makers of the famous Waberthwaite Cumberland sausage (probably the county's best). They use traditional ingredients - ale, molasses - and no artificial preservatives. Has a postal service (and currently supplies the London Hilton Hotel) and various outlets throughout the county.

Chapter Six

Towns and Villages

Details and descriptions of the main towns and larger villages in the Lake District, plus their history and main amenities.

☆☆ Bowness and Windermere   Population 8,500

The largest town in the National Park.   And it can certainly seem it on a bank holiday when it becomes the number one tourist attraction of the Lake District - especially for day trippers as it is the only central LD town to have a railway station. Has the feeling of a seaside resort, rather than an inland town, with most of the usual seaside amenities, but manages, if only just at times, to avoid the worst of seaside squalor and things like amusement arcades and tries hard to remain dignified, despite the hordes.

History   Technically, it is two towns, but they are virtually joined together and always considered as one. Bowness is an ancient village, right on the lakeside, centred round the 15th century St Martin's Church. (Martin was a Roman Officer who divided his cloak in half to help a beggar. Jolly kind of him.)   The name Bowness comes from Bulness, meaning a promontory which looks like a bull's head, and it does, if you study the map, jutting out into the lake beside Bowness Bay.

Windermere was originally a little village called Birthwaite, about a mile away inland.   It only became known as Windermere after the arrival of the Railway in 1848. Wordsworth, fearing that the horrid Lancashire hordes would soon be rushing round the lake to gape at him at Rydal and so ruin his tranquillity, tried to stop the railway. He predicted that the little village would be inundated by 'The Advance of the Ten Thousand'.   He was right.   A veritable explosion took place and Bowness and Windermere changed almost overnight.   It wasn't just the hordes but the New Wealthy from Lancashire who built splendid mansions, many of them Italianate or Gothic

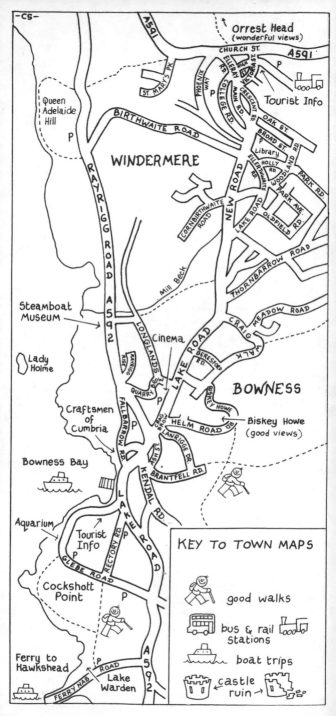

fantasies, grand holiday homes to show off their own grandness. There still is a lot of money around Windermere, and quite a few palatial homes and private yacht harbours, but many of the bigger Victorian mansions are no longer private homes. Brockhole, the National Park Centre, used to be one, and so was Belsfield, now a hotel. Belsfield was built by H W Schneider, who used to commute each day to his industrial empire in Barrow, going on his own launch down Windermere to Lakeside, then by a special carriage on the Furness Railway to Barrow. Ah, those were the days.

Amenities Railway station; cruisers on the lake; regular ferry across the lake from Bowness; bus station; masses of hotels and boarding houses; shops; boats; TIC in Victoria Road and at Bowness Bay; Mountain Goat Minibus HQ; Windermere Steamboat Museum; aquarium; cinema; snooker hall; de luxe hotel, Miller Howe, on Rayrigg Road; good food at Porthole Restaurant and Jackson's Bistro; brilliant view of Lake from Orrest Head, just outside Windermere, where on a very clear day you might glimpse Morecambe Bay.

Handy for Beatrix Potter countryside across the ferry; National Park Centre at Brockhole. But oh, those summer crowds.

☆☆ Keswick Population 4,762

'The full perfection of Keswick consists of three circumstances, beauty, horror and immensity united' - that was said by an earlier guide book, some two hundred years ago. Also sometimes regally referred to as 'The Queen of Lakeland'. Keswick has a fantastic setting, sandwiched between Derwentwater and Blencathra and Skiddaw. In fact, it is most impressive when seen from a distance as bits of it nowadays scarcely live up to its promise. It is now a major tourist centre and has more bed and breakfast and guest houses per head of population than anywhere else in the country. It is the favourite centre for Lakeland climbers and serious fell walkers. Always busy in the summer and only really attractive to walk round in the winter.

The lakeshore walk, along Lake Road, is becoming spoilt too with a rather unpleasant tea garden and the collection of portacabins housing the Century Theatre. The theatre itself is first class and a commendable venture, but its setting is tatty. It is soon to have a permanent building, in the same place, when they get all the money. Meanwhile, the latest attraction in Keswick is Keswick Spa, near the site of the old railway station, a leisure pool, open to the public, for those who can't afford the Med. Behind, hidden away is the new Timeshare, Keswick Bridge.

History The oldest building is Crosthwaite Church at the north west corner of town. The foundations date from 1181, but most of the fabric of the building dates from the 14th century and later. Inside is a memorial to Robert Southey, with an inscription written by his friend William Wordsworth. Canon Rawnsley, co-founder of the National Trust, is buried in the churchyard. Brandlehow, on Derwentwater, was the first property acquired by the Trust in 1902.

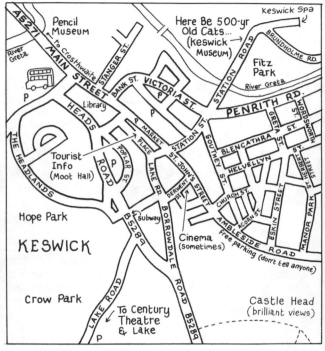

Originally a small market town, Keswick became prosperous with the arrival of the mining industry in the 16th century. Mining engineers were imported from Germany to look for copper, lead, silver and iron. They were treated with suspicion by the locals and forced to make their homes on Derwent Island, but they must have overcome the hostility as German surnames can still be found amongst the local population. The town also became famous for the black-lead mined in Borrowdale and so the Cumberland Pencil Company was born. Southey and Coleridge lived in Keswick at Greta Hall (now part of Keswick school) and overlooking the town is Windebrowe, where William and Dorothy Wordsworth lived for a short time before moving to Dove Cottage.

In 1865 the Cockermouth-Penrith railway line opened and put Keswick on the tourist map. Most of the town's central buildings are Victorian. The Moot Hall, in the market square, was built in 1813. Look out for an unusual one-handed clock. One visitor described it as a cross between an art gallery and a public lavatory, but it actually contains a very good tourist information centre and a small gallery.

The railway line no longer exists, unfortunately, and it has been replaced by the horrid and unloved A66. One of the Special Planning Board's notable failures - they fought hard to stop it but were overruled by central government.

Amenities Cumberland Bus Station; Derwent Launch Company; Mountain Goat Station. Loads of small hotels - the Station Hotel is the oldest in Keswick; Fitz Park Museum; Pencil Museum; Railway Museum; Keswick Spa. Very good information centre in the Moot Hall; cinema; Century Theatre in Lake Road.

Handy for Derwentwater and Bassenthwaite, Thirlmere, Skiddaw, Blencathra, Borrowdale (and the famous Bowder Stone), Castlerigg Stone Circle. Access to the western lakes - Loweswater, Crummock, Buttermere and Ennerdale.

☆☆ Ambleside Population 2,671

Beautifully situated in the Rothay valley, one mile north of the head of Lake Windermere. Ambleside is more centrally situated than Bowness and is one of the major centres for the climbing and walking fraternity. It is good, too, for the general visitor and has more escape routes to the surrounding fells and lakes than anywhere else in the Lake District. It gets very, very busy in the summer but, unlike some (eg, Grasmere), it doesn't die in winter and can still be quite lively and interesting when the winter fell walking enthusiasts start arriving.

History The name itself comes from the old Norse for riverside pastures and the town has a long history due to its position at the crossing of many old pack-horse routes. The Romans had a fort at Waterhead, one mile south of the town. Probably built around AD79, Galava fort protected the road which ran from Brougham over Hardknott to Ravenglass. Few stones remain, but the layout is still visible from the surrounding fells - especially Todd Crag on Loughrigg.

The town's most famous building is the Bridge House, which stands in Rydal Road *over* Stock Beck. Local legend says that it was built by a Scotsman to avoid Land Tax, but it was actually the apple-storing house belonging to Ambleside Hall, when this part of the town was all orchard. It is now a National Trust Information Centre but has also been a weaver's shop, family home, cobbler's and a tea shop.

The oldest part of the town dates from the 15th century and is on the Kirkstone side of the river. This was once a centre for corn and bobbin mills and a restored waterwheel can be seen just below the bridge on North Road.

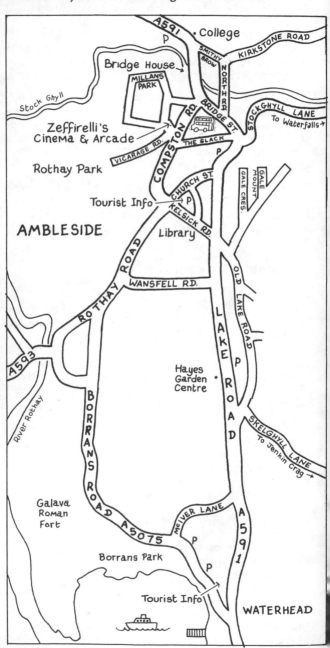

Originally, the railway was to have come right through to Ambleside (there were plans to carry it on up to Keswick and put a tunnel through Dunmail Raise) but it was shelved and 19th century tourists had to come up from Windermere by steam launch and charabanc. Recently an enterprising gentleman by the name of Mr Parsons reinstated the horse and carriage and now offers trips from the steamer pier at Waterhead into the centre of Ambleside.

The teacher-training college in the centre of town is named after Charlotte Mason, one of Ambleside's famous residents. Others included the diarist and close friend of Wordsworth, Harriet Martineau, Dr Arnold of Rugby and W E Forster.

Amenities Bus station; Tourist Information Centre in Church Street; cinema; Armitt Collection; good waterfall and walk (much loved by the Victorians) beside Stock Ghyll, behind the Salutation Hotel. At Waterhead there is another Tourist Information Centre, plus the Windermere cruisers, launches and rowing boat hire; putting green.

Handy for Rydal Mount, Windermere steamers, Tarn Hows, Elterwater, Townend at Troutbeck, Loughrigg Fell, the Langdales, Skelwith Force ... virtually anywhere in the South Lakes.

☆☆ Grasmere Population 841

Grasmere is everyone's idea of a picturesque Lakeland village and now forever associated with William and Dorothy Wordsworth. Grasmere looks very pretty, especially if seen from Loughrigg Terrace, looking down over the lake with the village against the background of Helm Crag and Dunmail Raise, but the surrounding fells can give it a damp, claustrophobic air, especially in winter. The village is almost wholly orientated towards tourists with cafes and tourist shops. In winter it used to die completely - even the two banks still close down for most of the week - though the presence of sheepskin shops now encourages the village to stay open out of season. In the summer, it is overrun - the sports field becomes an unsightly mass of caravans and the roads into the village become blocked with coaches disgorging hordes of Americans in search of Dove Cottage. For all this, Grasmere thinks rather a lot of itself - disdaining what it sees as the commercialism of Dove Cottage and the Museum whilst continuing to feed off the visitors they bring to the area.

In 1979 a member of Grasmere WI compiled a short history of the village which contained the following notable sentence on the subject of 'off-comers':

"Grasmere is the poorer for the losses it has sustained during the last 25 years, losses of people who are not matched by the newer people who have come into the village, many of whom may be good and nice people but are not of the same calibre as their predecessors". So, please don't spit or swear, especially near a resident.

History An ancient road ran through the valley. The village itself is really a string of hamlets along the old pack-horse route to Whitehaven. The road used to come over White Moss and past Dove Cottage, which was originally an inn. The present main road was built in the 1830's. Coming from Ambleside you encounter a rather nasty bend, just before coming into view of the lake; this is known locally as Penny Rock because blasting the rocks to put the road through added a penny to the rates. There is a corpse track over White Moss from Rydal. Coffins were once carried along here to Grasmere church. Up the hill, past Dove Cottage, there is a large, flat stone known as a coffin stone, where the bearers used to rest.

Most of the village buildings are 19th or early 20th century, though the surrounding farms are far older. Grasmere Church, dedicated to St Oswald, dates from the 13th century and is the scene of one of Lakeland's rush-bearing ceremonies. The Wordsworth family graves are in the churchyard and the poet's great-great-great grandson now lives in the valley.

Grasmere Sports Day is one of the oldest and most popular traditional events in the Lake District (probably dating back to Viking times) and involves people from all over the North. At one time even Dove Cottage would close down on Sports Day, so that the staff could go along. Now they have to keep at it, catering for the hordes.

Amenities Tourist Information Centre; boat hire in the village; Dove Cottage and the Wordsworth Museum; used to have a good garden centre, though now more of a clothes shop masquerading as one. During the summer months the Grasmere Players put on amateur theatrical productions for visitors.

Handy for Helvellyn, Fairfield, Thirlmere, Rydal, Loughrigg and Easedale Tarn. Grasmere is at the traditional dividing line between North and South Lakeland - Dunmail Raise - now the main transport artery, the A591. If going south, a nicer route is over Red Bank to Elterwater and back into Ambleside through Clappersgate. This route is also handy for Coniston and Hawkshead and the Langdales.

☆ **Coniston** Population 868

Probably the most disappointing of the major Lakeland villages. It has a magnificent setting but the grey, stone-built village has little character of its own and almost wholly given over to the tourist industry. Its best feature is the way the Old Man rises dramatically behind the houses when seen from the village centre. The road from the south can be rather dreary, apart from Blawith Common. Still, a good centre for walkers, though climbers now seem to prefer the Langdales and Borrowdale.

History Coniston grew up in the 18th century as a mining village, though copper was mined locally as far back as the Norman times. In the 16th century, Keswick's resident German miners were brought in and the ore extracted was sent up to Keswick for smelting. The area around Church Beck is still referred to as Coppermines Valley.

Coniston was once served by a railway line which came up from Furness. The closure of the line rendered the village rather inaccessible compared to the central Lakeland villages. Its most famous resident was John Ruskin and the 16th century St Andrew's church in the centre of the village contains his tomb. On the village green, just opposite the car park, a large, green-slate seat acts as a memorial to Donald Campbell, who died attempting the world water speed record on the lake in 1967. The name Coniston means 'the king's farm'.

Coniston's oldest building is Coniston Old Hall, a 15th century building once associated with the area's largest landowners, the Flemings. It is now owned by the National Trust and is being restored to its 17th century condition.

Amenities A good Tourist Information Centre and bookshop in Yewdale Road; Ruskin Museum; launches and boat hire on the lake, plus Gondola.

Handy for Coniston Old Man, the Furness Fells, Hawkshead, Brantwood.

☆☆ **Broughton-in-Furness** Population 478

An old market town, built largely in the 18th century. Broughton has a quiet character and the market square has hardly changed in the last two centuries. You can still see the old stone fish slabs. The market itself no longer exists. Because it has been largely missed by the tourist hordes, Broughton is a nice little village, unspoilt and a friendly place to shop. The obelisk in the square was erected to commemorate the jubilee of George III.

Nearby is Broughton Tower (now a school and not open to the public) which was once an old pele tower. The Broughton family are associated with this area back to before the Norman conquest. the name 'Broughton' means 'the hamlet by the stream' - the '-in-Furness' bit was added later to distinguish it from the innumerable other Broughtons dotted about the north-west.

Amenities Broughton is a good base from which to explore the Duddon Valley, Furness Fells and Swinside Stone Circle.

☆☆☆ **Hawkshead** Population 530

In lowland countryside near the head of Esthwaite Water, Hawkshead is generally reckoned to be the quaintest and prettiest village in the Lake District. Consequently it gets very crowded in mid-summer. Cars are banned from the village itself, which is a good idea, but gives the village something of the air of an open-air museum. It has an attractive muddle of squares and cobbled streets, overhung by timber-framed 17th century buildings. It isn't *too* difficult to imagine what it must have been like when Wordsworth went to school here.

History An important wool town in the Middle Ages. It once contained seven inns. St Michael's Church, up on the hill overlooking the village, is one of the most interesting Lakeland churches. There has been a chapel or church on this site since the 12th century but the present building dates from about the 15th. Inside are decorations and painted texts dating from around 1680.

Ann Tyson's Cottage is in the centre of the village, in Vicarage Lane. It is identified by a plaque, but when William Wordsworth lodged with her, Ann Tyson lived at Colthouse, just outside the village.

In 1548, William Sawrey, the Vicar of Urswick, stayed at what is now the Old Courthouse. Local records say that he was besieged for two days by a 'tumult of insurrection', man armed to the teeth with swords, clubs and daggers. They demanded that he should come out "for they would have one of his arms or legs before going away". Eventually, they were dispersed by neighbours. Why, or what it was all about, no one knows. The name of the village is Old Norse and means' Hauk's summer pasture'.

Amenities Best reached via Windermere Ferry if you are in a hurry. Tourist Information Centre in the main car park. Hawkshead Old Courthouse; Grammar School; Beatrix Potter Gallery. Good pubs, reasonable tea shops.

Handy for Rusland Valley, Grizedale, Beatrix Potter country, Esthwaite Water, Tarn Hows.

☆ **Patterdale and Glenridding** Population 444

Two rather shapeless villages at the southern end of Ullswater, separated by less than a mile. Patterdale is the prettier and more of a real village. But the setting is spectacular, surrounded on almost all sides by mountains with the only open view over towards the lake. It is a superb centre for walking. The name is a corruption of 'Patrick's Dale'. The patron saint of Ireland is supposed to have preached and baptised here once and along the road towards the boat landing at Glenridding there is St Patrick's Well, which was once thought to have healing properties. Glenridding was a mining village until the mines closed in 1962. Lead was discovered in the area in the 17th century and mining was at its height in the early 19th century with Greenside being one of the best lead mines in the country. Glenridding is best used as a walking centre and as an access to the lake.

Amenities Tourist Information Centre. The two hotels opposite sell reasonable bar lunches. Lake steamers; boat hire and a yachting and windsurfing school available at Glenridding.

Handy for Ullswater, Aira Force, Seldom Seen (a small row of mining cottages hidden up the valley from Glenridding), Brotherswater, Fairfield, Striding Edge - Patterdale is the best place from which to approach Helvellyn - Place Fell. As a centre for walking, Patterdale is excellent.

☆ Caldbeck Population 600

As Grasmere is to Wordsworth, so Caldbeck, in its own little way, is to John Peel, the famous huntsman and hero of the song. Set near open fells to the 'back o' Skidda', on the Northern boundary of the National Park, it has a traditional village green, duck pond, a 12th century church and an amazing river gorge called the Howk. Look out for the signs. Behind the church is St Mungo's Well. The churchyard has the bodies of two famous Lakeland characters - John Peel and Mary Robinson, the Beauty of Buttermere. Caldbeck is a real, working village, not yet overrun by tourists, despite a gift shop in a barn. Home of Chris Bonington the mountaineer.

Amenities No hotels, but one pub, Odd Fellows Arms; good village shop; Priests Mill - tourist information, craft shops, books and light meals. On a busy bank holiday, the Caldbeck Fells will still be quiet and uncrowded. Promise.

Handy for Caldbeck Fells, Skiddaw, Mungrisdale, Bassenthwaite, the Solway Coast.

Cumbrian Towns

The above towns and villages are all in the National Park, but there are many towns and villages on the fringes of the Park which you are likely to visit. Places like Kendal and Cockermouth are assumed to be in the National Park because they are so Lake Districty. These are the main ones you might visit.

☆☆ Carlisle Population 70,000

A bustling market and industrial town. Carlisle is Cumbria's capital city, the home of the County Council, Radio Cumbria, Border Television, Cumbria's only Football League team and a host of industries. Not a huge place by southern standards, but it makes up for it with an exciting and confusing one-way system. The city has a long history, much of it reflected in the architecture of the buildings. It also has a castle and Cumbria's only cathedral.

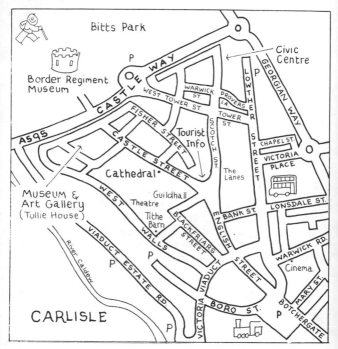

History It became an administrative centre during the Roman invasion, much of its subsequent history revolving around its proximity to the border (which was not always north of the city - there were times when Carlisle itself was part of Scotland). The Romans called it Luguvalium and placed a fort at Stanwix, on Hadrian's Wall which ran along the northern outskirts of the city.

There has been a castle at Carlisle since 1092 (the first was probably built of wood), occupying a good strategic position which was easily defended. Throughout the Middle Ages it was continually plundered, attacked and generally demolished by marauding Scots. The castle became more and more important and walls were built around the city. In 1568, Mary Queen of Scots fled her own country and was imprisoned at the Castle.

Amenities The castle still stands and today houses the Border Regiment Museum. Carlisle has an excellent museum at Tullie House, a fascinating town trail and a good cathedral. It has a good main-line railway link with Newcastle, Scotland and the south. Carlisle has its own airfield (with a rather limited range of services) and an array of tourist attractions and amenities. Leisure centre at the Sands. Very good new shopping precinct in The Lanes, flashy yet tasteful. Excellent Victorian covered market. Guildhall Museum. Tithe Barn.

☆☆ Penrith Population 12,000

A friendly, sandstone-built market town on the eastern fringes of the Lake District. Its character is rather muted, spoilt by traffic during the week. A little overlooked and forgotten, compared with Carlisle, but a nice, friendly place for shopping - especially during the week. One of its best attractions is the view from Penrith Beacon, which stands on a hill overlooking the town. It gives a superb view west across the plain to the Lakeland Fells.

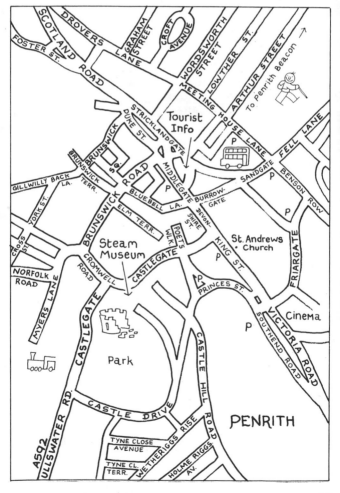

History Dates back to Roman times and was beloved by the marauding Scots once the Romans had gone. An unusual castle, originally merely a defensive tower, was built around 1400 and enlarged in subsequent years, falling into disuse during the 16th century and providing a stock of building material the local houses. The oldest and most interesting buildings are to be found around the church, most of which date from the 1700's. William and Dorothy Wordsworth went to school in Penrith, for a time, and in later life William wrote of the town's famous Beacon. This structure was once a link in a communication chain which ran the length of the country and was a useful early warning system when the Scots were on the rampage again.

Amenities Penrith makes a reasonable base for a Lakeland or Eden Valley holiday and is improving all the time. Railway station (though trains from Carlisle to Oxenholme don't always bother to stop). The castle - now in ruins - is open to the public and lies in the public park. St Andrew's Church area is very attractive. There is a cinema (which is nothing special and lags behind those in Bowness and Ambleside) but no theatre. Interesting Steam Museum. Very nice bookshop, The Bluebell, in Angel Square, an attractive new shopping area.

☆☆ Kendal Population 23,000

Kendal has suffered in the last three years. Whereas we rated it highly in the first edition, nowadays Penrith seems the friendlier, more attractive place to shop in. Kendal is being spoilt by the traffic and the usual plague of estate agents and building societies springing up all over the place. The one-way system is diabolical.Take a navigator to make notes of likely parking places as you are swept past them, then aim for them on the second time around.

It is a shame, because Kendal is a busy market town and is quite lively culturally, largely thanks to the Brewery Arts Centre. The best part of Kendal, right at the southern end of the main shopping street, is Kirkland (often referred to as Kirkland Village). If you're coming in from the south, park at the parish church, then walk along the riverside and go up into the town centre via Kent Street and Market Place. In the town centre is a brand new shopping development, the Westmorland Shopping Centre. Very clean and attractive, with much use made of local stone and natural lighting. Pity they had to spoil it with 'Arndale Centre' background muzak.

History It used to be the largest town in the old county of Westmorland, now the administrative centre for the Lake District Special Planning Board (despite being outside the National Park). There was once a Roman fort just south of

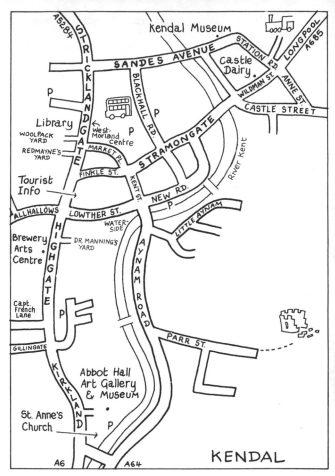

KENDAL

the town, called Alauna. Suffered from the Scots (like everywhere else) but settled down a little during the 14th century and became famous for Kendal Green, a heavy cloth advertised by Shakespeare in 'Henry IV'.

The castle, which stands on the hill to the east of the River Kent, was built by William Rufus and once belonged to Thomas Parr. His daughter, Katherine, later achieved fame as one of the wives of Henry VIII. Today it is a ruin, but commands a fine view over the town.

Amenities It has one of the best art galleries and museums in the region, Abbot Hall, along with a fascinating Arts Centre at the old Brewery in Highgate. Also has a cinema, now at Brewery Arts, and a good leisure centre. Not too brilliant an area for restaurants, however, but good tea places. Kendal itself has a railway station in the town, cunningly disguised as derelict building, plus the mainline station at Oxenholme, hidden miles from anywhere to the east of the town. The town is still reasonable for shopping of all kinds - including some unusual little shops tucked away from the shopping centre. The town also has a thriving insurance industry.

☆☆ Cockermouth Population 7,000

For some reason, the National Park boundary line does a rather vicious loop around Cockermouth, excluding it from the Park. A pity, as it well deserves to be inside. Cockermouth is a fine little town, far easier for everyday shopping than Keswick and distinctly on the way up. Main Street, Market Place and Kirkgate are very attractive and the area around All Saints Church, beside the River Cocker, is pretty. The church too is good, although the wall-to-wall carpet looks a bit odd. Cockermouth has a nice community air about it, the worst aspect of the tourist industry being notably restrained. Perhaps there are advantages in being outside the National Park, after all.

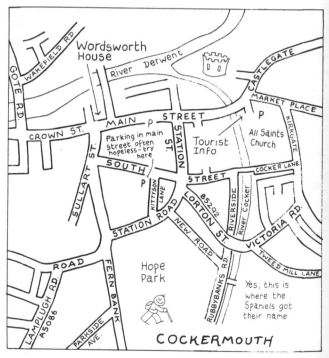

History Cockermouth's most famous building today is undoubtedly Wordsworth House, a fine, Georgian building which dominates the main street. Cockermouth's other notable building is the castle, built originally in the 13th century, though most of what remains dates from 100 years later. Much of it is in ruins, though part is still lived in, by Lady Egremont. It is rarely open to the public, but if you ask nicely, you might be let in. The best time to try is during Cockermouth Festival. The town was subject to the usual Scottish raids and the castle was besieged by Royalists during the Civil War.

Amenities Cockermouth probably has more attractions for the resident than visitor, though of all the towns lying just outside the Lake District, it is probably the quietest and most interesting to escape to when the crowds of the central Lakes begin to annoy. No cinema or theatre (although Rosehill is within striking distance) and no rail links. Wordsworth House remains the town's main tourist attraction, but don't miss Market Place and Kirkgate. Cockermouth is good for provision shopping, especially since the new Walter Wilson opened - not so hot for gifts and Lake District souvenirs. Good teas, antiques, excellent veggie dinners at Quince and Medlar.

Villages
In alphabetical order, ten villages we think worth a detour.

☆☆☆ Askham
An ancient and pretty village a few miles south of Penrith. Many houses dated between 1650 and 1750. Askham Hall is 14th century in parts and was developed on the site of a pele tower. It is now the home of the Earl of Lonsdale. Lowther Castle is only a facade, now mostly ruins. It was not a genuine castle but a Gothic mansion built in the 19th century. Nearby is Lowther Park. The village is handy for Haweswater, Penrith, Ullswater and the Eden Valley. Good pubs.

☆ Elterwater
The village of Elterwater lies at the foot of the Langdales and is quite small and picturesque, especially if you first see it from the road from Ambleside or Grasmere directions. Once a thriving mining area, the old gunpowder works is now an exclusive timeshare holiday estate, though well screened from the road. The Britannia Inn, at the centre of the village, is a popular place in the summer, especially on a fine evening.

✩✩ Grange-in-Borrowdale

Once a grange of Furness Abbey. Only a small hamlet but beautifully situated alongside the River Derwent. One of Lakeland's prettiest villages.

✩✩ Hesket Newmarket

A northern hamlet, well out of the tourist beat. Once an important market, now it is just a pleasant village built around a long green. Dickens stayed in the village in 1857 whilst on a Lake District tour. Hesket Hall is a dull but odd building with a peculiar roof and twelve, angular projections forming the walls. The corners of these projections are supposed to make an effective sundial. Good pub, with their own real ale.

✩ Ireby

On the northern edge of the Lakes. It gained a market charter in the 13th century but in time Wigton and Cockermouth proved too much competition for it. Look out for the original church, a simple Norman affair, stuck in a field 11/2 miles outside the village on the Torpenhow road. Ireby is good as a base for the Solway Coast, Bassenthwaite and Skiddaw.

✩✩✩ Maulds Meaburn

Not in the LD proper, as it's across the M6, towards Appleby, but many discriminating Cumbrians consider it the county's prettiest village. Fascinating stone houses, each one different, on either bank of the River Lyvennet. No pub.

✩ Rosthwaite

A little hamlet in the Borrowdale Valley, useful as a base for setting off for Watendlath, Seatoller, Langstrath and Sty Head. The footpath up to Watendlath used to be quite attractive but now appears on the landscape as a mini-motorway.

✩✩✩ Troutbeck

One of the Lakes' most famous villages. Strung along a hillside just north of Windermere, it is really a series of hamlets grouped about a series of wells. The cottages and barns date from the 17th to 19th century - the finest of all being Townend, built in 1626 and now looked after by the National Trust and open to the public. There are two old, restored inns, the sign to the Mortal Man being quite famous for its rhyme:

O mortal man that lives by bread,
What is it makes thy nose so red?
Thou silly fool that looks so pale,
'Tis drinking Sally Birkett's ale.

Note that there is another Lakeland Troutbeck, just off the A66 near Threlkeld. Even Pevsner got the two muddled.

☆☆ Warcop

Near Brough, on Pennine slopes (so not true Lakeland), but a nice, unspoilt little place, complete with village green and a beautiful 16th century bridge over the River Eden. The village holds a very pretty rushbearing ceremony in summer.

☆☆☆ Watendlath

A moorland hamlet of farms, set artistically beside a large tarn. It is situated to the east of Rosthwaite and was the remote, isolated setting for Hugh Walpole's 'Judith Paris'. Now it is a magnet for tourists and is to be avoided on summer bank holidays. It can be reached by leaving the main Borrowdale road and crossing Ashness Bridge. This road is a menace in the high season and it is better to leave the car and walk. Good teas.

Best Kept Cumbrian Villages

For those who like their villages terribly clean. The Best Kept Village Competition has been run by Voluntary Action Cumbria for the past twenty-five years, awarding large and small villages that have been kept neat and tidy. It covers the whole county, not just the NP. For the past ten years, these have been the award-winners:

Best Kept Large Village		Best Kept Small Village	
1979	Natland	1979	Wreay (Carlisle)
1980	Morland	1980	Ravenstonedale
1981	Dalston	1981	Underbarrow
1982	Braithwaite	1982	Ireby
1983	Braithwaite	1983	Warcop
1984	Lazonby	1984	Bassenthwaite
1985	Grasmere	1985	Bouth
1986	Dalston (Carlisle)	1986	Great Salkeld
1987	Natland	1987	Wreay (Carlisle)
1988	Thursby	1988	Bassenthwaite

Chapter Seven

Lakes

Facts and facilities of the Major Lakes, including steamers, sailing, fishing and other amenities. Plus a look at some rather interesting Tarns.

There are sixteen lakes in the Lake District, so most experts agree. The other bits of water are tarns. A few tarns, despite their second division status, are in fact bigger than one of the so-called lakes, but most tarns are small, in fact very small, and some have not even the dignity of being named. It's the Sixteen Lakes which are the glamorous attractions, the crowd pullers.

Only one of the Sixteen Lakes should technically ever have the word 'Lake' attached to its name. All the Lakes, you see, either the word 'mere' or 'water' already in their name, so there is no need for the word 'Lake'. Except one. Which is it? Read on ...

Lakes	Length (miles)	Width (miles)	Height above sea level (feet)	Depth (max. feet)
Windermere	10 1/2	1	130	219
Ullswater	7 1/2	3/4	476	205
Coniston Water	5 1/4	1/2	143	184
Bassenthwaite	4	3/4	223	70
Haweswater	4	1/2	790	198
Thirlmere	3 5/8	1/2	583	158
Derwent Water	3	1 1/4	244	72
Wastwater	3	1/2	200	258
Crummock Water	2 1/2	5/8	321	144
Ennerdale Water	2 1/2	3/4	368	148
Esthwaite Water	1 1/2	3/8	217	80
Buttermere	1 1/4	3/8	329	94
Loweswater	1 1/4	3/8	429	60
Grasmere	1	1/2	208	75
Rydal Water	3/4	1/4	181	55
Elterwater	1/2	1/4	187	50

☆☆☆ **Windermere**

Windermere is not just Cumbria's, but England's largest lake - 10 1/2 miles long and one mile wide with a maximum depth of 219 feet. It is named after a Norse hero, Winand or Vinandr, and until this century it was a busy highway, probably used by the Romans for ferrying troops and then later used for transporting iron ore and charcoal and passengers. Now, for the last 80 years, the boats are purely pleasure bound - but there are still hundreds and hundreds of them. In the season, they glisten from afar like tadpoles with hardly enough water to go round, or so it often appears.

Windermere in summer is not a place for peace and quiet. It is still a beautiful lake, with well wooded shores and some dramatic mountain views looking east and north across and up the lake, but it is essentially a playground, with more aquatic diversions than any other English lake.

To escape the crowds, yet still savour the lake, get across quickly from Bowness on the ferry and walk the western side. There is no road nor any towns or villages along the western shore. You can walk a lakeside public path, most of the way, then gaze across at the mansions, and the masses, on the other side and try to pretend you can't hear the motor boats.

Amenities

Windermere Cruisers The cruiser operations on Windermere has now reverted to its original, 1848, name of the Windermere Iron Steamboat Company. (After the trading standards people looked long and hard at the word 'steamboat', but they've let it go.) They run three boats, Swan, Teal and Tern. There is a regular service up and down the lake, from Lakeside in the south up to Bowness and then to Ambleside, a one way trip of approximately 1 1/4 hours. First boat from Lakeside is usually about nine o'clock in the morning.

Services run from Good Friday to early November, seven days a week, with evening cruises on Wednesdays and Saturdays during the summer season. All boats are fully licensed.

Special Fares Lots of permutations, such as all day sails between any of the piers, family tickets, seven day tickets, special pensioner rates.

Best Bargain Rail-Sail tickets; you can start on the little private steam railway line at Haverthwaite, go by train to Lakeside, then into a cruiser and up the lake and back. The Rail-Sail ticket is a good way to get a feeling of the lake and surrounding area - and it is also good for parking as there's ample car parking near Lakeside and at Haverthwaite. Parking in Bowness or Ambleside can be hell in the season.

Further details Timetables from any TIC, hotel foyers, or the Manager, Windermere Iron Steamboat Co, Lakeside, Ulverston. Tel: Newby Bridge (05395) 31188.

Bowness Bay Boating Company
Regular launch services from Bowness and Waterhead all year round, except Christmas Day. They call in at the Windermere Steamboat Museum and Brockhole on selected trips. Special winter services, including Winter Wonderland cruises. Evening cruises with wine and trips round the islands. Guided commentary on all trips. Also motor and rowing boats for hire.

Bowness - telephone Windermere 3360
Waterhead - telephone Ambleside 33187.

Windermere Ferry
Regular, all round the year, all day long, public service from Bowness Nab across the lake, for cars and pedestrians. Queues form in the height of the summer, so heed the notices about any delays. Takes only seven minutes.

The ferry is a vital link for holiday makers and for those who live on the western shores of the lake as by road, round the lake, can put up to an hour and at least ten miles on the journey.

There has been some sort of ferry using this exact crossing for about 500 years. Wordsworth went across it as a school boy, on his way to Hawkshead. Today, it's a motorised service, but if you look carefully you'll see the boat pulls itself across the lake on two chains. Very ingenious.

Windermere Boat Registration Scheme
All power-driven boats must be registered for use on Windermere - this means power-driven vessels of any kind, even sea-planes. (There are already microlights, equipped with floats, on the registration list.) Once registered, the vessel has to display a registration number of a certain size and type. Full details from the Lake District Special Planning Board, Busher Walk, Kendal. Leaflets available from Bowness Bay Information Centre. There is a yearly charge to register (the old five year rate has now gone) of £7, plus £4 for a set of numbers (you only need these once as your registration number will stay the same each time you renew). There is now a registration disc which boats must display, which changes each year, like the car tax disc.

Navigation Rules
(Windermere is a navigable highway) available from the Board, or South Lakeland District Council, Town Hall, Highgate, Kendal.

Since the scheme was started in 1978, over 32,000 boats have registered (including those two microlights) and over 13,000 are currently registered. When you register, one of the details you have to give is the length of boat. If all the boats currently registered were placed bow to stern and strung along the length of the lake, they would more than cover the distance from Fell Foot to Waterhead, back and up to Waterhead a second time.

Lake Rules The only lake with no maximum speed limit, but there are 10mph and 6mph speed zones. Look out for speed cops. Yes, they do exist.

Lake Windermere Collision Rules Copies available from South Lakeland District Council, Town Hall, Highgate, Kendal - telephone Kendal 33333.

Sailing on Windermere Sailing tuition, water skiing, sailing holidays - Westmorland Watersports, Beech Hill Hotel, Bowness - telephone Windermere 5756.

Sailing Clubs Royal Windermere Yacht Club - tel. W'mere 3106; Lake District Boat Club - tel. W'mere 3595.

Sailing Holidays Windermere Lake Holidays Afloat, Shepherds Boatyard, Bowness Bay - telephone Windermere 3415. Hire sailing cruisers and motor cruisers by the weekend or week.

Water Skiing The 6mph restriction applies to all boats in the speed limit areas - anyone exceeding the limit is liable to prosecution. Water skiing can become dangerous on summer weekends, the lake gets so crowded. A good club exists - Low Wood Water Ski Centre, Low Wood Hotel. Telephone Ambleside 34004.

Lake Warden Public slipway, Ferry Nab, Bowness-on-Windermere - telephone Windermere 2753. Summer - open daily between 0800-2200 hrs, winter - 0900 - 1700. Closed Christmas Day.

Moorings Contact South Lakeland District Council for residential moorings. Holiday moorings, contact the Lake Warden.

Launch Sites
1. Public slipway, Ferry Nab (1/4 mile south of Bowness). Two launch facilities with car parking and room for trailers. Lake Warden's office. Fee payable (but usually the cheapest).
2. Windermere Aquatic, Glebe Road, Bowness - telephone Windermere 2121. Fee payable.
3. Waterhead Marine, Waterhead, Ambleside - telephone Ambleside 32424. Fee payable.
4. Low Wood Ski School, Low Wood Hotel, Ambleside - telephone Ambleside 33338. Fee payable - higher than the others but includes use of all facilities and is for a day, not per launch.
5. Unofficial launching across the shingle at Bellman Landing, 2 miles south of Bowness. Right beside the road, so access is hell with a trailer and parking very poor. Free.

These sites are all for powered craft. Launching for small (under 5hp) craft available at Waterhead and Fell Foot (latter owned by the NT and only open from March to October). Charge made at Waterhead by Bowness Bay Boating Co, who lease the beach.

Launching for non-powered craft available from NT land at Millerground (north of Bowness on Rayrigg Road) - contact Mr J W Cockman, Low Millerground, Windermere - and along the eastern shore between Ferry House and Wray Castle - contact A Langstaff, Harrowslack Cottage, Far Sawrey. Fee payable in both cases.

Other Attractions

Belle Isle 38 acre island with beautiful round house, said to be the only truly round house in England. Visits by appointment. (See chapter 12.)

Windermere Steamboat Museum (see chapter 10). Rayrigg Road, Windermere - telephone W'mere 5565.

Brockhole National Park Visitor Centre (see chapter 2).

Wray Castle On the western shore, just north of the Ferry landing stage. Owned by the National Trust. Grounds open to the public.

Lake Windermere Festival runs for 10 days in early July. Lots of events and attractions, mostly centring on Bowness and Waterhead. Also helicopter flights, water ski displays, power boat races. Contact Bowness Bay TIC for dates.

Windermere Power Boat Week based at the Low Wood Ski Centre. A week of attempts on various world records. Usually held the beginning of October. Contact the Ski School on Ambleside 33338 for further details.

Swimming You can swim almost anywhere, if you can escape the private gardens and private launching sites. And if you can stand the cold. But it is very cold, even at the height of the season, and can be dangerous, with all the power boats zooming about. Best place is Fell Foot Park, the National Trust place at the southern end of the lake. There is some talk of renewing the public swimming area at Miller Ground (just north of Bowness) - there used to be a roped off area with diving platforms. Watch this space.

First man to swim the entire length of Windermere was Joseph Foster of Oldham in September 1911. An annual Windermere swim is held every spring.

Motor Boat Racing takes place regularly at Windermere Motor Boat Club, Broad Leys (tel: Windermere 3284). First races were held in 1918. In 1930, Sir Henry Seagrave was drowned while speeding on Windermere.

☆☆☆ Ullswater

Windermere is bigger and has more going on, Derwentwater is more compact, but Ullswater has variety and grandeur and is bordered by some of the best walks in the Lake District. If we had to choose just one lake, for amenities and for beauty, it would be Ullswater.

At the Pooley Bridge end it is gentle, flat, almost boring, but as you work your way along its length, the landscape around becomes more picturesque and then, finally, you get the grandeur and magnificence of the southern end at Glenridding. A good view is also to be had from Kirkstone Pass, looking down with Brothers Water in the foreground.

Ullswater is a serpentine lake, snaking its way through the landscape for seven and a half miles. It is three-quarters of a mile wide and 205 feet deep. It is best explored from the southern end, where the lake is dominated by St Sunday Crag, Place Fell, Fairfield and Helvellyn. Walk along the path on the eastern shore from Howtown to Patterdale and you'll appreciate the lake at its best. The opposite side, where the main road is, is usually crowded in summer and best avoided by walkers.

During the 1960's, Ullswater was the scene of a battle between the National Park Authority and Manchester Corporation, who wanted to extract water to feed the reservoir at Haweswater. As a compromise, the pumping station was hidden completely underground at the northern end and now the average visitor is not even aware of its existence.

Ullswater is probably the best lake for sailing. The peace used to be spoilt somewhat by large numbers of water-skiers, until the effective ban in 1983 when the speed limit over the whole lake was dropped to 10mph. Someone has actually managed it at that speed, so water-skiers haven't been outlawed (which would have been unfair). It just isn't very exciting any more.

The name comes from the first Lord of Ullswater, a Norse settler named L'Ulf. Ullswater is a public highway and was once used for transporting miners and ore from Glenridding. At the lake foot is a hill called Dunmallet which was once the site of an Iron Age fortification.

Amenities

Anyone can launch a boat on Ullswater, either sail or motorised, and there is no registration scheme like Windermere. There is, however, a speed restriction which covers the whole lake.

Steamers Two 'steamers' run up and down the lake. They resemble the cruisers on Windermere (and like them, 'steamer' is a courtesy title since they all run on diesel). These are run by the delightfully named Ullswater Navigation and Transit Company Limited and both are around a hundred years old. 'Lady of the Lake' was first launched in 1877 and 'Raven' twelve years later. They run from the pier at Glenridding to Pooley Bridge, stopping off at Howtown. The main service runs from the Sunday before Easter until the 30th September. During October, a reduced service runs from Glenridding to Howtown, which takes 35 minutes. Going the whole length of the lake takes about an hour.

Ullswater Navigation and Transit Company Ltd
13 Maude Street
Kendal
(telephone Kendal 21626 or Glenridding 229).

Boat Hire Rowing and motor boats from Glenridding and Pooley Bridge. Also from Ullswater Caravan and Camping Site Marina, Watermillock. Tel: Pooley Bridge 666. Canoes from Lake Leisure, Pooley Bridge. Tel: Pooley Bridge 401. Sailing craft from Glenridding Sailing School (see below).

Sailing Ullswater is excellent for sailing (especially now the water-skiers have gone). Launching can take place at Willow Trees, just north of the Glenridding steamer pier, or at Glencoyne Bay or Howtown.

The Glenridding Sailing School is based at The Spit, Glenridding; contact Celleron Cottage, Tirril, Penrith, telephone Pooley Bridge 601 or Glenridding 541. Sailing craft can be launched for a small charge and a rescue service operates, rescuing "everything in sight".

Warning - there is a 10mph speed restriction over the whole lake and as at Windermere, the National Park people have a patrol boat. (Incidentally, one of our researchers, putting in time, analysed the Ullswater steamers' timetable - and found they must be averaging 12mph . . .)

Launch Sites
    1. Howtown - access from the B5320, 3 miles south of Pooley Bridge, at a public launch site. All craft, max. length 20'.
    2. Glencoyne Bay - 1 mile north of Glenridding on the A592. Light powered craft only.
    3. National Trust land - north of steamer pier by the Willow Trees, or on the adjoining beach at Glenridding. No powered craft.
    4. Ullswater Yacht Club. Pooley Bridge 333.
    5. Park Foot Caravan Site. Pooley Bridge 636.
    Also from Ullswater Caravan and Camping Site Marina and Glenridding Sailing School.

Other Attractions Gowbarrow Park, now a National Trust property, open to the public and the site of Wordsworth's daffodils. Aira Force; Askham; Dacre.

☆☆ Coniston Water

If you travel along the busy road near the western shore, Coniston can be a little disappointing. You can see the lake, but it is against a background of low fells and forest plantations. This is also the most 'touristy' route, with ice cream vans in every layby. It is quieter and more satisfying along the narrow road on the east and from here you can see Coniston Water at its best, with the Old Man and its neighbours rearing up magnificently in the background. (This can often happen with the lakes - you get there, wonder what all the fuss is about, trundle about a bit - then suddenly it hits you.)

The lake is 5 1/4 miles long, half-a-mile wide and 184 feet deep. It has three small islands, all owned by the National Trust. Peel Island featured in Arthur Ransome's *Swallows and Amazons* as Wild Cat Island. On some very old maps, Coniston appears as Thurston's Mere. It has been a public highway for centuries. Ore mined at the head of the lake used to be carried down to the foot and then transported to the quay at Greenodd (yes, that jumble of roads and bypasses - which cunningly conceals one or two nice houses - was once a busy port).

The lake is famous as the scene of Donald Campbell's attempts at the world water speed record. In 1959 he established a record of 260.35mph in Bluebird. He was killed trying to break the record in 1967 and his body has never been recovered. There is a memorial in the village. Photographs of his attempts can be seen in the Ruskin Museum.

Amenities

Coniston has a lake transport service, but it seems a shame to classify it mundanely as an 'amenity' as it is really one of the lake's star attractions . . .

☆☆☆ Gondola

In 1859, a steam yacht, Gondola, was launched from Coniston Hall and ran a regular service up and down the lake for nearly 80 years. Eventually it was taken out of service, its engine sold to power a saw mill and the hull became a house boat. It was washed ashore in 1963 and lay derelict until the National Trust started taking an interest in the mid-70's. With some daring, they decided to try and restore her. Now owned and operated by the Trust, this unique and beautiful craft has been back in service since 1980. It takes over 80 passengers, is decked out with luxurious upholstery and fittings and is the only silent method of powered transport anywhere in the Lake District. It is uncanny. Highly recommended, just for the experience. Best to sit at the front - there can be specs of soot at the back.

Gondola runs from April to the beginning of October,

daily except for Saturdays. It travels the 25 minute route between Coniston pier and Park-A-Moor, on the south-east shore, and stops off at Brantwood on the eastern shore.

Note: If the weather is bad, Gondola sometimes cannot run. To check, ring High Waterhead, Coniston, on Coniston 41288, or the Tourist Information Centre, Coniston 41533.

Boats Coniston is still a public highway, but launching is restricted due to land access. The best place - also for boat hire - Coniston Boating Centre at the north of the lake (telephone Coniston 41366). It is run by the National Park people. They hire rowing and motor boats, sailing dinghies and Canadian canoes and can offer assistance with launching and recovery, for a small charge.

Rowing boats can be launched from the two car parks at either end of the lake - Monk Coniston and Brown Howe. At Coniston Hall there is a sailing club and RYA members are welcome - apply to Coniston Old Hall, Coniston, Cumbria.

There is a speed restriction of 10mph over the whole lake.

Launching Sites

1. Coniston Boating Centre, telephone Coniston 41366. All craft. Fee payable.

2. Access from car park at north end of the lake (not power).

3. Access from Brown Howe car park at south-west end of the lake. No power craft.

Other attractions The star of Coniston's shoreline is Brantwood, Ruskin's home, which stands on the eastern bank. (See chapter 11.) There are nature trails available for this part of the shore. The road down the east side has several nice little car parks tucked amongst the trees.

☆ Bassenthwaite Lake

This is it - the only true 'lake' in the Lake District; the others are all 'meres' or 'waters'. However, just to confuse matters, Wordsworth called it Broadwater. It is one of the largest lakes but also one of the shallowest - 4 miles long, 3/4 mile wide, but just 70 feet deep. It is the most northerly of the lakes and has no real settlement on its shores. Apart from the hideous A66, which blasts its way up the west side, the shores are relatively unspoilt and as the lake is now owned by the Lake District Special Planning Board, it should be kept that way. It is a good lake for bird life, although there are no recognised hides.

Towering over the lake at the Thornthwaite corner is a craggy white rock which looks down over the A66. This is known as 'The Bishop'. Legend has it that a bishop once tried to ride up the screes at this point to demonstrate his faith in God. His horse, however, must have been less pious because it fell and they were both killed. By tradition, the rock is kept whitewashed by the landlord of the nearby hotel. (Volunteers welcome.) On the day of the Silver Jubilee in 1977, the stone appeared red, white and blue - painted by hands unknown.

An excellent view of the lake and the surrounding countryside is available from Dodd, on the east side.

Bassenthwaite can look very mysterious - which is how Tennyson saw it when he stayed by its shores and wrote *Idylls of the King*.

Amenities

Very few. Because of attempts to conserve wildlife in the area, shore access is limited and all powered craft are banned. There are no public launch sites. The only way to get onto the lake is to be a member of the RYA in order to make use of the private Bassenthwaite Sailing Club. (Contact the secretary at 8 Rose Lane, Cockermouth.)

Canoeing is permitted but rather restricted. The situation is improving, however, and the Planning Board, at Busher Walk, Kendal, will supply the latest details.

There is a Bassenthwaite Sailing Club. Contact the secretary: D.P.Nuttall, 4 Sycamore Close, Whitehaven. Tel: Whitehaven 2965.

There is a shore path which runs the length of the west shore, though this isn't the best point from which to view the lake. The only access to the east shore is at Mirehouse, which has a wooded walk in the grounds. The house is now open to the public. (See chapter 11.)

☆ Haweswater

One long reservoir - 4 miles long, half-a-mile wide and 198 feet deep. It *used* to be only 2 1/2 miles long a 3/8 of a mile wide and the water level was 96 feet lower. At its head stood the attractive village of Mardale, whose farms in the middle of the last century used to send 3000lb of butter a week to Manchester. There was also the Dun Bull, a renowned inn. Then, in 1940, the Manchester Water Corporation stepped in, spent £5,000,000 on building a 120 foot high dam and Haweswater became a reservoir. Mardale is now under the water.

Haweswater is one of the most isolated and difficult lakes to reach. From the central lakes you have to make a long detour by road and travel out towards Penrith. It is only accessible from the north-east and south-east sides and is in wild and unspoilt countryside. Rather lonely and if you're only in the area for a short time you might not think it is worth it, but loved by Lakeland experts. The best way to discover Haweswater is to park at the head of the

Kentmere Valley (turn up from Staveley) and walk over the Nan Bield Pass. Haweswater remains the largest reservoir in the north-west. The National Park people and the North West Water Authority are plotting better access for the future, but its very wildness has attracted nature conservation proposals, so the public may end up no better off. In very dry weather, when the water is low, the shore line goes bleached and looks very strange and moon-like. In very, very dry weather, look out for signs of the sunken village.

Amenities None, except for the scenery.

☆☆ Thirlmere

Another reservoir. Thirlmere was once two much-smaller lakes, called Leatheswater and Brackmere, with a footbridge across their narrow middle. In 1879, the area was purchased by Manchester Corporation Water Works, a dam was built at the north end and the water level raised by 54 feet. It is now called Thirlmere, which means the lake with the hollow (the hollow presumably being where the two earlier lakes joined). It is now just over 5 1/2 miles long and half-a-mile wide. At its deepest it is 160 feet.

Thirlmere is in fact quite a pretty lake, very clear and pure and the woods along the west shore have a wild look about them, despite being conifers. It is best appreciated from the lovely little road which threads its way along the west shore line, through the trees. From the A591, it can look rather barren, especially in mid summer when the water level drops, leaving a ragged, white scar round the 'rim' of the lake. One of the best and most peculiar viewpoints as at Hause Point, about half-way along the west road. You have to climb some metals steps and find yourself on top of a rock along with a garden seat. The view to Dunmail Raise is good although Helvellyn is uninspiring from this angle.

The lake is now being opened up to the public by the NWWA. There is access at most of the laybys along the west road and from the Station Coppice car park, half-way along the east side. There is a forest trail on each side of the lake, although the Launchy Gill and Swirls nature trails have suffered from tree felling recently and are very difficult to negotiate. On the west side is a new footpath, constructed by the British Trust for Conservation Volunteers, which leads to Raven Crag, an excellent viewpoint.

Unspoilt lakeshore footpath and access for boating at Armboth, on the west shore. Strictly no powered craft, but sailing dinghy, canoes and sailboards permitted. No permission necessary and no fee payable. The lake is open to fishing to holders of NWWA rod licences. No permit necessary.

Finally, no swimming is allowed.

☆☆☆ Derwentwater

Now we enter an area of raging controversy; which is best, Ullswater or Derwentwater? We think Ullswater just makes it, thanks to its magnificent scenery and variety, but Derwentwater has been called 'the Queen of the Lakes' and it is nicely compact and very pretty. Friars Crag, which is along Lake Road, less than a mile from the centre of Keswick, has one of the finest views in the country, looking across the lake and down into Borrowdale. Derwentwater is great for walking, but don't bother with the road. For a really spectacular excursion use the launch service - there are piers all round the lake and good walks are available from any of them.

The name means the 'lake of the river which abounds in oak trees'. The shores are still heavily-wooded and largely in the care of the National Trust. It is 1 1/4 miles wide and therefore the widest of the lakes. (Most of them have a superlative of one sort, if you search hard enough.) It's three miles long but its maximum depth is only 72 feet. The average depth is 18 feet, which means that this is one of the first lakes to *freeze* over. Famous for skating.

It has five islands - Derwent, Lord's, Rampsholme and St Herbert's. Lord's Island used to be the site of the house of the Early of Derwentwater, hence the name. St Herbert's is reputed to have once been the home of St Herbert or Hubert, a disciple of St Cuthbert. It became a place of pilgrimage and the spot where the monks and friars used to wait for the boat to take them across is now called Friars Crag.

The fifth island is a real oddity. Marked on the maps as Floating Island, it is down in the south-west corner and only appears once every three years or so. No, it isn't a ghost - it's a mass of weeds and rotting vegetation which pops to the surface now and then, buoyed up by marsh gases. More of an event than an island.

Derwentwater is a public highway and was used for transporting charcoal, graphite and ore. Keswick's miners used to live on Derwent Island.

Amenities

The Derwentwater Launch Company operates a launch service which runs from Lake Side, just outside Keswick. The launches are unlike those on Ullswater and Windermere, being a lot smaller and with no pretensions to being called steamers. The launches leave every half-hour (every 15 minutes during July and August); the first goes round the lake clockwise, then anti-clockwise. The clockwise route takes you to the piers at Ashness Bridge, Lodore Falls, High Brandlehow, Low Brandlehow, Hawse End, Nichol End and back to Keswick. The round trip takes 50 minutes and the time between piers is about 10 minutes each. The service runs from a week before Easter to the last

Sunday in November. It is a good way of getting to a number of walks, but the launches themselves can be noisy and uncomfortable.

Derwentwater Launch Co
29 Manor Park
Keswick
(telephone Keswick 73013, or for the Lake Side, Keswick 72263).

Launching Sites

1. Derwentwater Boat Club, Portinscale, Keswick, telephone Keswick 72912. Daily charge.

2. Derwentwater Launch Co, telephone Keswick 72263. Facilities for launching between March and November. Any size but no power about 6hp. Small charge.

3. Nichol End Marine, Portinscale, telephone Keswick 73082. Charge according to length of craft.

4. NT land near the B5289, opposite Barrow House Lodge. Not power craft, and only if can be manhandled - no trailers.

5. LDSPB car park at Kettlewell, half-a-mile north of Lodore. No power craft.

Walks Roads runs along either side of Derwentwater, but the one on the western side is narrow and can become quickly congested, especially during Bank Holiday week-ends. Typically, it has the best views. You can walk around most of the lake and the surrounding fells give some fantastic views. Travelling on the lake is the best way of getting to Lodore Falls and Ashness Bridge, if you can stand those noisy launches.

☆☆☆ Wastwater

Wasdale was the original name, meaning the valley with the lake, so the 'water' part is redundant, strictly-speaking. It doesn't matter - this is the deepest, most dramatic and most haunting of all the lakes. It is well over towards the coast and the only way to it by car is over Wrynose and Hardknott, or from the West Coast. Approach through Greendale and you suddenly come within sight of a view which is in almost every book on the Lake District - the famous Wastwater screes. Nearly two thousand feet high, thy plunge into the lake, presenting a sheer wall which goes down to the maximum depth of the lake, 258 feet. Although it looks vertical, it's not, as you can see if you manage the walk along the shore. There is a path along the foot of the screes, but it is exceptionally tough going. Best seen on a still, sunny day when the screes are reflected in the lake and can look frightening. Look up the lake and you see a view which is also familiar - Great Gable flanked by Kirkfell and Lingmell. Recognise it? It is the emblem on the National Park badge.

Wastwater is three miles long, a quiet, unspoilt lake, a favourite starting point for walkers and mountaineers. No boating. There is a good walk along the entire length of the west shore - the road is usually pretty quiet. At the head of the lake there is a very small village and the Wasdale Head Inn, which has good bar meals and a smart climbing shop. The hotel is famed among the mountaineering fraternity.

Don't miss St Olaf's Church, hidden in a field behind a clump of fir trees, said to be the smallest church in England. In the little graveyard are memorials to dead climbers, killed on Scafell, Gable and the Himalayas.

After Ullswater, this is our second choice lake. If you have only time for two lakes, Wastwater gives you the perfect antidote to those bigger, over-populated busy lakes. Although there are no amenities on the lake itself, the valley offers you England's deepest lake, highest mountain and smallest church. And the attractive Wasdale Head Inn (telephone Wasdale 229) was once run by Will Ritson, the biggest liar in England . . .

Shush . . . Wastwater is now becoming a sailboarder's paradise, despite the fact that it is strictly illegal. Hands up all those who saw the Countryside Commission's National Parks campaign poster a few years back? This featured a picture of Wastwater - complete with sailboard! (Thereby completing a hat-trick of errors - not only is the lake a reservoir and therefore administered by the NWWA, but the fell in the background - the screes - is owned by the NT. Nothing to do with the NP appeared in the picture.)

☆☆ Crummock Water

The name is Celtic, hence its Scottish sound, meaning a crooked or bent lake. It is curved, 2 1/2 miles long by 5/8 mile wide and 144 feet deep. It is separated from Buttermere by a narrow, half-mile strip of land and they were probably both one lake, back in the ancient, geological past. It is bigger than Buttermere, very attractive, but nowhere as busy. The approach from Loweswater, going along the east shore is a very pretty road with the lake in the foreground against Mellbreak and Ling Crags. There is a footpath along the west shore, going from Buttermere village to Loweswater and this gives some excellent views up the valley. The lake is now owned by the National Trust. There is no public launch site, but small dinghies can be launched from access land at various points by the road. Permission has to be obtained from Mrs Beard at Rannerdale Farm, Buttermere.

The inns at Loweswater and Buttermere offer the only amenities in the area, with reasonable accommodation and good bar meals.

☆☆ Ennerdale Water

Like Wastwater, it is on the western flanks of the Lake District and is one of the wildest and remotest lakes. It has a good name for solitude and quiet, with the result that you might meet lots of other people who've also gone there to be alone. The Forestry Commission have recently rather drawn people's attention to it by making noises about their valley forest trails. The valley is dominated by their plantations, but at least they have kept out the cars and allow free access. You can walk all around the lake, although things get a little scree-y on the southern shoreline. Park at Bowness Point, where the road ends and there's a good car park with toilets. Walk along the shore to the lake foot - good place for picnics - then back by the other side.

The lake is owned by the North West Water Authority and no private boating is allowed. It is actually a reservoir, but the dam is hardly noticeable.

Amenities are few, apart from car park and picnic points. No hotels, pubs or village. Access from the central lakes is difficult and means either coming down via Cockermouth or heading towards the coast from Buttermere, leaving the fells and then turning back in again.

The big thing about Ennerdale is that it is the only completely road-free lake in the whole of the Lake District. Every other lake, even Wastwater, has a road along at least part of its shore. So it makes a perfect, peaceful circular walk. Easy going most of the way, even with children. Allow about four hours.

☆ Esthwaite Water

Wordsworth knew this lake well as a boy, but nowadays it can be easily missed if you're rushing up to Hawkshead. Not a very spectacular location, but conventionally pretty, surrounded by low fells and minor roads. In some ways similar to Rydal or Grasmere, but without the crowds and cars. A public footpath runs from near the village to the shore at the north-west and down in the south-west is a good car park and access point. This gives a good view across the lake and is the only public launch point for rowing boats (the only form of craft allowed on the lake.) Rowing boats can be hired from Hawkshead Trout Farm, telephone Hawkshead 541.

☆☆☆ Buttermere

The name is a dead giveaway and means 'the lake by the dairy pastures'. It is a perfect little lake. You can walk right round it, with only a few yards on the road, and the views are superb. The early tourists used to rave about it being "the quintessence of natural beauty" and if you're based in the north and have time for only one low-level, easy, family walk, do this one. Park in the village, follow the footpath across farmland to the lakeshore. Go round anti-clockwise and along the north shore you'll enter a short tunnel, cut through the rock. The story goes that the local landowner had it blasted through because he was annoyed at not being able to walk all round the lake. The lake is only 1 1/4 miles long and 3/8 wide, so the entire walk won't take you much more than two hours.

If you're feeling too lazy, you can park at the southern end and look across the water to High Stile. You can also launch rowing boats from here, but you have to get permission, either from Gatesgarth Farm in the village, or the Kirkstile Inn, Loweswater. The lake is now owned by the National Trust. Buttermere village has two reasonable inns, with good beers, but they can get very busy.

☆☆ Loweswater

Probably the most forgotten of the sixteen lakes, which is a great shame as it is very pretty. Its uniqueness lies in the fact that it is the only one whose waters flow in towards the centre of the Lake District. There, that's one for the record books.

Loweswater is a nice, gentle lake, though looking east over it there are some rather grand views. There is a small car park at the southern end and from here you can follow a footpath right round the lake. If you prefer something more gentle, go into the woods along the west side, owned by the National Trust and provided with variously-placed seats. It is popular with locals as a Sunday afternoon sort of a place. The car park at the foot has room for only about 20 cars, which gives you an idea of how remote it is. Loweswater means 'the leafy lake', referring to the woods which flank one side. It is about 1 1/4 miles long, 3/8 wide and about 60 feet deep, which makes it another early lake to freeze over in winter. Very good pub meals at Kirkstile Inn, Loweswater.

When doing Loweswater, make sure to take in the Lorton Valley, which has some of the most attractive, lushest scenery in the Northern Lakes, and don't forget that Crummock Water and Buttermere are round the corner. The three lakes go together, making a perfect string of pearls. With clever car parking arrangements, you could walk them all in a day, sticking each time to the road-less shores, taking in refreshments at the Loweswater and Buttermere pubs. What bliss.

☆☆☆ Grasmere

Everyone likes Grasmere. And with all that fame and literary name, how could we begrudge it three stars. It is a 'delightful' little lake, completely surrounded by fells, nice to took at from every angle. It has one island, centrally-placed, no piers or steamers, and on the west side the fields come right down to the water's edge. The only thing which spoils it is the 'beach' at the foot of the lake, under Loughrigg Terrace, which can get quite busy in summer. The other drawbacks are the crowds in Grasmere Village and the A591, which runs along the lake's east side. Lots of people stop along this road to take photographs. Don't. If you want to be different, go back and park at White Moss, then walk over the old road towards Dove Cottage. About halfway you'll see a seat in some woods on your right. A little farther along there is a gate. From this seat you get a good, if less panoramic, view of the lake with Silver How as its backdrop. When the lake is still and the sun is shining in the early morning, the island seems to be sitting on a mirror and the view is absolutely magic. Another classic view is from the top of Loughrigg Terrace, with Dunmail Raise in the background.

You can walk right round the lake, although you are on that horrid road a lot of the way. There is a nice little wood at the southern end. The island belongs to the National Trust. William and Dorothy Wordsworth used to picnic there and the stone barn was used to shelter sheep, which were taken across in flat-bottomed boats. Arguably the best place from which to see Grasmere vale is from a rowing boat in the middle of the lake and the island is great for picnics (but no camping).

No powered craft allowed, although sailing is permitted and you'll see the occasional windsurfer. The only public launch site is Allonby's, in the village at Pavement End. They also hire rowing boats and provide teas (telephone Grasmere 409).

The name, by the way, simply means 'the lake with the grassy shore'.

☆☆☆ Rydal Water

A reedy little lake, usually mentioned in the same breath as Grasmere - the advantage of both for the passing rubber necks is that you can get a good view of them from the road as you whizz past in your car.

The river which flows out of Grasmere enters Rydal, then flows out at the foot down to Waterhead. If you are keen, you could canoe all the way from Grasmere to Lakeside, although the walk back wouldn't be much fun. It used to be called Routhermere or Rothaymere (after the river which flows 'through' it). It gets its name from Rydal village, though it isn't actually in Rydal 'dale' at all.

There's a lovely old bridge just to the south, called Pelter Bridge, where you can turn off the A591 onto the Under Loughrigg road. Park here and walk up the lane back to the lake. The view from the bench as you come into sight of the lake is a classic and especially lovely in winter.

Carry on and walk right round the lake up to White Moss, then follow the road back. The 'beach' on the south shore is good for swimming. No public launching or boats allowed, although you may see the odd canoeist. Rydal isn't very large - just 3/4 mile long by 1/4 mile wide, but it can be absolutely superb first thing in the morning or in the winter when there is no one else about. In summer it gets very busy and for all its charm it is best avoided on busy days for the more remote lakes - unless you get up very early in the morning.

Elterwater

This is a peculiar little lake, with a funny shape, the smallest of the sixteen - in fact, it sometimes gets omitted altogether and Brothers Water often gets included instead. Tucked away at the foot of the Langdales, you get glimpses of it as you travel along the B5343. It is only half-a-mile long and has not got much to offer in the way of walks or boating. It is best reached by parking in the car park at the eastern end, crossing the road and entering the wood. A footpath runs along the side of the lake and up to the little village. Its chief distinction is the good view this path gives you, looking over the lake to the Langdales. Nice for a quiet stroll - that one view apart - but not really typical Lake District. The name is rather nice, though - Elter is the old Norse for 'swan', so this is - 'swan lake' - presumably because of the Whooper swans which call in when migrating from their Siberian winter.

Tarns

So much for the lakes. Now for their less famous, less popular little brothers, the tarns. It's impossible to tell how many there are as the smallest have no names and are therefore rather difficult to count, but the Lakeland artist, W. Heaton Cooper names and paints or draws 103 of them in his classic study, *The Tarns of Lakeland* (reprinted by Frank Peters, Kendal, 1983, price £15.95).

One of them (Tarn Hows) is in fact more visited than any of the lakes and two of them (Brothers Water and Devoke Water) are as large as the smaller so called lakes. One of the 'un-named' tarns has been given a name to show it hasn't got one - Innominate Tarn. That's on the top of Haystacks, one of the most beautifully situated tarns in the entire Lake District. Its claim to fame is that this is the spot where the Blessed Wainwright has said he wants his ashes scattered.

Meanwhile, here is a brief selection of the bigger, better known tarns which are worth considering for a visit, if you want to see a tarn.

☆☆ Tarn Hows

One of the most popular places in the entire Lake District. You see it on postcards all over the area. Very heavily visited during the summer. It's free and open and so impossible to count but in 1974 it was estimated that 3/4 million people came to Tarn Hows.

It lies between Hawkshead and Coniston and is sign-posted simply as 'The Tarns'. There are two car parks, some public toilets and one of the most delightful views in Lakeland. It is a beautiful tarn, lush and very chocolate box, only 1/2 mile long, surrounded by woods and with a path all the way round. To the west, the immense bulk of Wetherlam looms. Walk a little way and you get a good view down over Coniston Water.

It is usually referred to as a man-made tarn, but there used to be several much smaller tarns here, originally called Monk Coniston Tarns. Then, about 70 years ago, the local landowner built a dam and converted the marshy ground into one tarn, with two little islands. The present name really refers to the farm to the south west. It has been in the hands of the National Trust since 1930 who do much to control the level of erosion, but with the number of footbridges, paths and fences springing up, it is becoming more artificial every year. Avoid it on bank holiday weekends and during the school holidays. Or go very, very early. It is really only at its best during the winter, when it can be very beautiful - and good for skating.

Brothers Water

Sometimes classed as the sixteenth lake - an idea which seems to come in and out of fashion - which means down-grading Elterwater into a tarn. It lies just to the south of Ullswater, forming a well-known view from Kirkstone Pass. it may once have been part of Ullswater. A footpath skirts its shores on the west and the road on the east. Not really worth stopping for, not with Ullswater beckoning.

It used to be called Broadwater and is said to have got its present name when two brothers drowned in it, whilst skating, in 1785.

☆ Devoke Water

As large as Rydal, but still reckoned to be a tarn. It is rather out of the way and in a rather austere moorland setting, due east of Ravenglass. Only approachable by foot. From the central lakes it involves a long drag over Wrynose. Hardly worth going specially all that way, unless you're into Bronze Age settlements - there are about 400 ancient cairns and 'hutments' in evidence around the tarn, dating from around the time when the area was first cleared of forest. Much-loved by Norman Nicholson for its desolate feeling. The name says it all, really - 'the dark one'.

Overwater Tarn

Just north of Bassenthwaite, on the very edge of the Lake District. Named after another Norseman. (One begins to suspect they only really came to Britain to make names for themselves in the Lake District.) It has been enlarged by damming at the north end to turn it into a reservoir for Wigton. Not worth trekking a long way to see. Looks pretty from the road. A great pity it can't be used by the public.

Alcock Tarn

A small, part-artificial tarn on the fell to the east of Grasmere. There's a good path to it on the road to White Moss, above Town End. A good objective for an afternoon stroll. Not spectacular (quite the reverse, in fact, you tend to think it's something else until you read the sign board) but there are some good views from round about, taking in Coniston, Langdale and Helvellyn mountain ranges. It used to be called Buttercrags until a man named Alcock dammed it and stocked it with trout.

☆☆ Grisedale Tarn

One of the largest, deepest and set in splendid scenery. It is on the Grisedale route to Dollywaggon Pike and Helvellyn, so it is for dedicated fell-walkers only. The pass was once a packhorse route through to Penrith. The tarn is over 100 feet deep. Nearby is a rock bearing an inscription to commemorate the parting of Wordsworth and his brother John, who died five years later - without William ever seeing him again - when his ship, the Abergavenny, sank in 1805. The inscription was put there at the insistence of the energetic Canon Rawnsley.

☆☆☆ Easedale Tarn

As tarns go, it deserved three stars as it is one of the nicest and easiest to get to and it has one of the best approach marches, right alongside Sour Milk Ghyll, with its beautiful tumbling waterfalls and small ponds. (Great for a hot, summer day.) The tarn lies north west of Grasmere village; just opposite the green is a road which leads to Easedale car park. The walk is up the Easedale Valley. The tarn itself has a rather sombre setting, though there are repeatedly good views back down the valley. The mass of stones on the left as you come within sight of the tarn are the remains of an old refreshment hut. A painting, showing what it was once like, is hanging in Dove Cottage. William and Dorothy Wordsworth knew and loved this little hidden tarn.

☆☆ Red Tarn

On Helvellyn and one of the highest and most magnificently-sited of all the tarns in the Lake District. It lies in the depths of an immense bowl, formed by Helvellyn, Striding Edge and Swirrel Edge. Not as deep as it appears, it is only 85 feet. In the last century, a dam was built to supply the mines at Glenridding.

Loughrigg Tarn

On the west side of Loughrigg Fell, passed by the road from Grasmere over Red Bank. Wordsworth said it had "a margin of smooth green meadows, of rocks, and rocky woods, a few reeds here, a few waterlilies there", which just about sums it up. No public access to it. Nice to come across, not worth going to a lot of trouble to seek out.

☆☆☆ Blea Tarn

Say that you have been to Blea Tarn and the response is likely to be: "which one?" So we'll start with the prettiest and most accessible. It is in the Langdales, between Little and Great Langdale.

The easiest way to find it is to follow the B5343 along Great Langdale, until it becomes a minor road and begins to climb. At the top, there';s a car park on the left and one of the best tarns in Lakeland on your right. You can walk right round it and it has some of the best views in the area.

☆ Blea Tarn II

Above Boot in Eskdale and accessible only to those on foot. Rather a long way to get to it, but worth it because it is very pretty.

Blea Tarn III

Just south east of Watendlath, high up to the west of Thirlmere. Set in a bog and very boring. Only worth mentioning because it is higher than the other two.

Final Warnings - Lest You Forget.

Private powered craft are only allowed on the following lakes -

Windermere	Coniston
Derwent Water	Ullswater

Note: These are the only four lakes with regular steamers or launch services.

No private craft, either powered motors or sailing dinghies, are allowed on the following, however tempting it may look -

Ennerdale	Wastwater	Loweswater
Rydal Water	Haweswater	Tarn Howes
Bea Tarn	Overwater	Yew Tree Tarn
Lrigg Tarn	Little Langdale Tarn	

Chapter Eight

Mountains

Mountains and other Natural Features, including Fells and Dales, Passes and Waterfalls, with brief descriptions and recommended routes.

Mountains

There are four mountains in the Lake District over 3,000 feet, or three if you count Scafell Pike and Scafell as one, which they're not, as they have separate summits, but most visitors and many natives refer to having climbed 'Scafell' and mean in fact they've climbed Scafell Pike, ignoring or forgetting the twin peak of Scafell which is assumed to be part of the same, but is fifty feet lower.

Such a pity about metres. There was something satisfying and rather grand and important about getting above the magical 3,000 feet mark. Getting above 920 metres not only seems lower but not nearly as impressive. However, if only to give the printers more work, we will use both measurements in our Mountains guide.

The four big ones are:

Scafell Pike	3,210 feet,	978 metres
Scafell	3,162 feet,	964 metres
Helvellyn	3,118 feet,	950 metres
Skiddaw	3,053 feet,	931 metres.

Scafell Pike, Helvellyn and Skiddaw also happen to be the most popular mountains, climbed the most often, though figures are naturally non-existent. They haven't quite yet got to a turnstile on the top, though on busy days it could ease congestion as there is very often a queue to stand on the final cairn.

Note well: our routes are purely rough guides, to be used with a good map.

Top Three Mountains

☆☆☆ Scafell Pike 3,210 feet, 978m

England's highest, the hardest to get to of all the popular Lake District mountains, the one which has seen terrible accidents, but the one which you can boast most about - if you honestly get to the top. It's not really very difficult, but a long slow climb which means the weather is more likely to be different on top, usually worse, so be well prepared with stout footwear, some extra warmth and good rainwear.

Part of a range of peaks known as the Scafell Pikes which you have to work your way over or round before you finally start climbing the big one, hence the relatively long time needed to get up, compared with some other mountains which happen to be much nearer civilisation or parking. That's what makes Scafell all the more special. Samuel Taylor Coleridge did it in 1802, all on his own, without a guide or companion, carrying a pen and a bottle of ink with him. He wrote a letter on top, so his is the first *recorded* climb of Scafell, then he hurried down any old way, ignoring all the easy paths, which is not to be recommended.

A ravine called Piers Gill is about the most dangerous part. In 1921, someone fell down it, breaking both ankles, and lay at the bottom for eighteen days. He was finally found, having landed near a pool of water, which had kept him alive.

Routes The shortest and quickest but steepest route is from Wasdale Head, going up Lingmell Gill, but you have to get round and into Wasdale in the first place, which is a long drive for anyone in Central Lakeland.

From Seathwaite walk straight up the valley till you hit Stockley Bridge, then cut right up Sty Head Gill for Sty Head Tarn. You'll probably see hordes of walkers by the tarn, socks and boots off, resting or guzzling. Once over Sty Head Pass, you hit a long, open walk which takes you along the western flank of Scafell Pike, a route known as the Guides' Walk or the Corridor. It finally takes you straight up to the summit, over rougher, rockier ground, but still not too difficult.

The actual summit is not very exciting or pretty, being rather bleak and barren. But on a clear day the views are sensational.

On the way back, if the day is clear and you feel confident, try varying the route into Borrowdale by coming down via Sprinkling Tarn. The round trip should take about six hours. On a hot day, celebrate with a dip in the ice green, marvellous marble water at Stockley Bridge.

☆☆☆ **Skiddaw** 3,053 feet, 931m

There are clever folks, the real climbing types, who are rather scornful about Skiddaw, dismissing it as easy peasy, nowt more than a stroll, with no hairy or horrible bits where real men can break their legs. All true. It is rather a cuddly, rounded, modest sort of mountain, but it makes an excellent mountain walk all the same. How nice not to walk in fear and dread. How reassuring to think that even if the mist comes down or it grows dark, you should be perfectly safe. Just follow the crowds.

Skiddaw was the first popular mountain climb in Lakeland and that lovely open path from the Keswick side has been used by millions for over 150 years. You could probably take a pram up it. In the last war, motor bikes and army vehicles went up it. No bother.

In 1815, Wordsworth and Southey took their respective families for a bonfire party to celebrate Waterloo, with the servants carrying up roast beef and plum pudding. It's that sort of friendly, accessible mountain. Terribly handy for parking.

Skiddaw dominates the Northern Fells, Big Brother over its surrounding mountain mass, a landmark for miles around and people who live beyond it describe themselves as living Back O' Skiddaw.

Routes Several ways up. From the Bass Lake side, coming from Bassenthwaite village, you can get up it from Millbeck or from High Side.

Or you can approach it from the rear, the eastern side which is hidden from Keswick. It's an excellent approach, hardly used, though it means a long, but exciting walk from Dash Falls. If you do this route, look out for Skiddaw House, an amazing building, stuck literally in the middle of nowhere, once used by shepherds, and now recently converted into a youth hostel. Provides good shelter in bad weather.

Best route The famous one, from Keswick. By far the most popular and probably the most dramatic, as you rise very quickly and can get good views over your shoulder, looking over Keswick and Derwentwater, and pat yourself on the back for doing so well. Come out of Keswick and turn right just past the big roundabout, following the sign saying Skiddaw, heading up the little road towards Underscar. You eventually hit a rather rough road, Gale Road. Go right along it to the very end and you'll find car parking space probably already full, so come back and find some space on the road. This drive is a bit of a cheat, as you've saved almost 1,000 feet already. Real climbers start from Keswick and climb Latrigg first. But it means that you can come straight out of the car and can start climbing. You actually see children *running* to get up. That beautiful grassy slope, right in front of you, looks so attractive and tantalising almost like a grass ski slope. This takes you up Jenkin Hill, the first slope of Skiddaw, and it is in fact the steepest. After that, it's a long but easier walk to the summit. The top can be freezing, so take warm clothes. Can all be done in three hours, even with the children or a family dog.

☆☆☆ Helvellyn 3,118 feet, 950m

Often considered the finest of the Big Four by Lakeland experts, for its brilliant views and exciting summit. In some ways the most dangerous, at least it seems to have more accidents than any other Lakeland mountain. But Wordsworth climbed it safely aged seventy. Makes you sick.

Routes From the King's Head Inn, Thirlspot, follow the whitewashed stones, crossing over Helvellyn Gill to join the route up from Swirls car park, gaining Helvellyn via Lower Man.

Or from Grasmere follow the old packhorse road up Great Tongue to Grisedale Tarn. Fairfield is on the right and Seat Sandal on the left, in front Dollywaggon Pike. Climb up Dollywaggon Pike to Helvellyn. Steep at first but a good expedition, with fine views all round.

Or from the little church at Wythburn follow the path through the forestry plantation, up the side of Combe Gill onto Swallow Scarth and Helvellyn on your left.

Best routes From Glenridding car park, follow the lane on the other side of the beck until you reach a fork in the path. Take the left fork indicating Lanty Tarn. Follow the zig-zag path to Lanty Tarn, which is set amidst trees and is very pretty. Go down the hill, through a small plantation and up onto the ridge taking the right hand path up the fellside. Grisedale valley is on your left. Once on the ridge cross over the stile and take the left hand path onto Striding Edge. The edge is narrow and involves a bit of scrambling but this can be avoided by using the path a little lower down (approx 20 feet). Red Tarn is on the right. It gets its name because when the sun rises the tarn appears dark red in colour. Traditional to watch the sunrise from the summit on Midsummer's Day - always a lot of people there, but worth the trip.

Getting off the Edge and onto Helvellyn is interesting (more scrambling) and the path up Helvellyn is steep. Once on the summit you can rest on the seats in the shelter. Fantastic all round views.

Way down is by Swirral Edge and path down to Red Tarn. Follow the path back to the stile and take the left path down to Mires Beck, keeping the wall on your right. Good views down on to Ullswater and peaceful on a nice summer's day. When you reach the bottom keep right of the beck and follow it back to the car park.

Note: Only experienced walks should take this route in poor weather conditions.

Other Recommended Mountains

Eight other Big mountains, all worth attempting sometime.

☆☆ Great Gable 2,949 feet, 899m

Paths up from Wasdale, Seathwaite and Honister, the latter being the easiest over Brandreth and Green Gable.

Park at Seathwaite (parking neatly, nose to the wall) and walk up Sour Milk Ghyll onto Green Gable, across Windy Gap and onto Gable - quite steep. Good views into Wasdale Valley and of the Scafells. Westmorland Cairn is well worth a visit - probably the most spectacular view of the Lakeland crags, down into Great Hell Gate and to Tophet Bastion.

☆☆ Bow Fell 2,960 feet, 902m

Park in the National Trust car park in Langdale and walk up Mickleden, which is nice and flat, passing under Pike O'Stickle. Take the left path when you reach the guide stone, and up Rossett Ghyll. Go beyond Angle Tarn and turn left up Ore Gap which takes you onto Bow Fell.

On a clear day the views are fantastic, seeing as far as Ingleborough in the Pennines and even Snaefell on the Isle of Man.

For the return, head for the Three Tarns and take the left path down the Band back into Langdale.

☆☆ Pillar 2,927 feet, 892m

Possible from Ennerdale following a long path through the forestry plantations.

From Wasdale follow the bridleway up Mosedale and over Black Sail Pass and an easy walk up onto Pillar, noticing Robinson's Cairn on the right, which marks the climbers' traverse to Pillar Rock.

Pillar is part of the famous Mosedale Horseshoe walk which takes in Steeple and Yewbarrow. From Pillar it is recommended that you take the same route down as others are very steep and only for the sure footed.

☆☆ Blencathra 2,847 feet, 868m

Or Saddleback, as it's also known. For the more adventurous, follow the footpath along Sharp Edge - the best ridge walk in the Lake District (best not to undertake this route in the wet). Scales Tarn is down to the left and the path leads onto the summit. Return by Hallsfell which is quite steep.

An easier route is from the Blencathra Centre (may be marked as Blencathra Hospital on maps) which can be reached by taking Blease Road in Threlkeld. There is a public car park behind the Centre. Follow the footpath over Knowe Crag. Return the same way. This is really only a half day walk.

☆☆ Crinkle Crags 2,816 feet, 858m

The quickest and easiest route onto Crinkle Crags is from the Three Shire Stone at the top of Wrynose Pass, going over Cold Pike.

For a day's outing the best route is: Park in Langdale and follow the track to Stool End Farm, turning left up Oxendale. Go up Brown Gill and over Great Knott. An interesting walk providing easy scrambling. There is one difficult steep section which may be climbed if competent, otherwise take the footpath west (left) of this. Continue along the top of the crags, to Shelter Crags and down to the Three Tarns. Here take the path back down to Langdale, taking the right fork down Hell Gill, into Oxendale.

An interesting and varied route, providing excellent views all round.

Note: In misty weather it is easy to inadvertently descend Long Top (this is the next top after the awkward section) thereby losing several hundred feet and going towards the Eskdale Valley.

☆ High Street 2,718 feet, 829m

From Hartsop, park in the car park and walk up Hayeswater Gill to Hayeswater, onto the Knott and along the ridge to High Street. The cairn on Thornthwaite Crag is about 14 foot high, which must be one of the most remarkable in the Lake District. Only a short distance from the summit of High Street. Walk beyond here and down in Threshthwaite Cove, quite steep and a bit tricky, back to the car park.

From Kentmere - up the Nan Bield Pass, over Mardale Ill Bell.

From Troutbeck - up the Garburn road; a long walk.

Best route: Park at the head of Haweswater Reservoir, walk up the Gatesgarth Pass onto Harter Fell and along the ridge, crossing over the Nan Bield Pass. Small Water is the tarn down on the right. Over Mardale Ill Bell, onto summit. Descend by walking north a short distance and down Long Stile and Heron Crag, and a short walk by the lakeshore back to the car park. A fairly long but not difficult walk, providing views into the Longsleddale, Kentmere and Haweswater valleys. Good views over Lakeland fells, varying from where you stand on High Street.

☆☆ Fairfield 2,863 feet, 873m

Various ways to the summit.

From Grasmere take the path near Swan Hotel up Stone Arthur and onto Greatrigg Man and then across a short distance to Fairfield. Steep at first.

From Patterdale follow the bridleway up Grisedale to Grisedale tarn. Here take the very steep and not very pleasant path to the summit.

From Ambleside: The Fairfield Horseshoe is a long but easy mountain walk. After completing it there is a real sense of accomplishment. From the central car park go up the Kirkstone Road a little way, turn left up Nook Lane, right to the end, passing through a farm to Low Sweden Bridge. Follow the path onto Low Pike and then High Pike, Dove Crag and onto summit, which is a bit disappointing as it's a massive boulder-strewn area. Return by Greatrigg Man and Heron Pike, down to Rydal Mount. The footpath then leads through Rydal Hall back into Ambleside.

Best route: Park in Patterdale and walk up the road by Patterdale Hall. A few hundred yards on the left take the path eventually leading up onto St Sunday Crag. Return by the ridge off Hart Crag, over Hoggil Brow. This superb walk is only slightly spoiled by the short road walk back into Patterdale.

☆ Coniston Old Man 2,635 feet, 803m

Park in Coniston village and go across the old railway bridge up the steep metalled road onto the Walna Scar Road (not a highway). Bear right and follow the path to Goats Water. Dow Crag is the impressive rock face on the left. Follow the path past the tarn and out of the hollow and right onto the summit of the Old Man. An easy, very pleasant walk and the best way onto the summit.

Go down by the steep footpath down to Low Water and through the jumble of relics from the coppermines, down into Coppermines Valley. There are a few houses, mostly climbing club huts, and a YHA. Follow the track back into the village, finishing by the Sun Hotel.

Fells

Fells are mountains which didn't grow, but they can provide just as much pleasure, and even danger, as their big brothers. Here are eight, around 1,000 to 2,000 feet high, which are recommended.

☆☆ Castle Crag 980 feet, 299m

A small crag with old slate quarries, north of Rosthwaite, Borrowdale.

Park in Rosthwaite car park. (Travelling south, turn right just before Scafell Hotel, car park is on right a few hundred yards up the road.) Walk to the end of the road, passing through a farmyard and follow the track right of river, eventually crossing to the left. Follow the riverbank path through the wood to the campsite at Hollows Farm. Beautiful walk when river is full and on a sunny day. Turn left through a gate and up the track by side of Broadslack Gill to the old slate workings. Turn left up the track over the spoil heaps, up a steep path onto Castle Crag. Marvellous views all round, probably one of the best viewpoints in Borrowdale area.

☆☆ Cat Bells 1,481 feet, 451m

Off the road leading south from Portinscale to Grange-in-Borrowdale.

Park at Gutherscale car park on western side of Derwentwater, and follow the erosion control signs up the steep fellside to the summit. Very good views in all directions, especially into Newlands Valley. Descent by dropping down to Hause Gate and turn left down to the road at Manesty. Walk south a short distance and turn off left and take the path leading through the woods and beside Derwentwater, back to Hawes End. Very attractive walk beside the lakeshore. Good fun for a family walk.

☆☆ Harter Fell 2,129 feet, 649m

In the Dunnerdale Valley. Routes from Eskdale and Hardknott Pass
Best route: Park in the Forestry Commission car park at Birks Bridge, follow the track through the plantation to an old farm, turn right up the gill which eventually leads onto the summit. A fairly short trip (1/.2 day) steep but fairly easy. The summit is quite craggy and provides a good playground for children. Good views to the Scafells and Dow Crag range.

☆☆ Haystacks 1,959 feet, 597m

On south west side of Buttermere.

Easiest approach is from Honister. Park in car park at YHA, follow the track towards the quarries but turn left after a few yards, up the steep fell path. Follow this to Blackbeck Tarn and onto Haystacks.

Park at Gatesgarth, Buttermere, follow the Scarth Gap Pass, turn left at top and onto Haystacks. Nice gentle walk, with good views over Buttermere and Crummock Water and across to Gable and Ennerdale Valley. Several tarns, Blackbeck being the largest. Descend by Warnscale Beck.

☆☆ Helm Crag 1,299 feet, 396m

Park in the car park up Easedale Road on the north side of Grasmere village. Walk beyond Easedale House and up the steep path onto Helm Crag and climb both pillars on the summit before continuing along the ridge over Moment

Crag (pausing here) to the old boundary fence. The fence itself is no longer there but the posts remain and one stile. Cross over the stile (everyone does) and turn south to Codale Head, and down to Codale tarn and Easedale Tarn. Finish off by going down Sour Milk Ghyll. A nice walk with varying scenery and views.

☆☆ Lingmoor (Brown Howe), Little Langdale 1,530 feet, 466m

Park in the car park opposite Blea Tarn. Walk down the hill towards Langdale a short distance and follow the path onto Side Pike. Walk up the hill and onto Brown Howe. Good all round views of Langdale Valley and across the Coniston range. Lingmoor is a bit of a surprise, once you have gained height it can be seen that it opens out into a moorland type plateau, complete with tarn. Only a short walk from the car but interesting and well worth the trip.

☆☆ Loughrigg Fell 1,101 feet, 336m

Park in the car park on the A591 between Rydal Water and Grasmere. Cross over the River Rothay through the wood onto the Terrace. An easy plod with lots of seats. Good views over Grasmere and area. Follow the Terrace to the gate and turn left up some steep steps of strange proportions. Impossible to get a good walking rhythm on these. The real summit is the one with the trig point. Spectacular views.

☆ Walla Crag, Borrowdale 1,234 feet, 376m

Above the B5289 south of Keswick, the first craggy outcrop high on the left as you drive down the valley. Easy family walk.

Park in Great Wood car park south of Keswick; from the car park follow the signs, turning left through the woods towards the TV aerial, heading towards Rakefoot Farm onto the fellside. Pass through a gate keeping the boundary wall on your right hand side. Fine views over the Borrowdale Valley and higher fells; Grisedale Pike, Skiddaw, etc. Descend the same way or by Cat Gill, which is very steep and loose and should only be undertaken by the sure-footed.

Dales

And now eight dales to explore, by foot or car, which are attractive and interesting in their own right but which also offer fairly easy walks and explorations for those sensible people who want to leave their cars and strike out on their own.

☆☆☆ Langdale

The most popular valley in the Lake District. It consists of two dales, joining at Elterwater and separated by Lingmoor Fell, called Great Langdale and Little Langdale. Great Langdale is the more popular and the little, winding road which runs its length is sometimes crammed with cars in mid-summer. It has dramatic scenery, especially during the drive up the valley, the Langdale Pikes suddenly rearing up in front of you. Many walks onto the higher fells, with lower fells at the Elterwater end of the valley. Good walks in Little Langdale, which is charming, though not as spectacular.

For low level walks in Great Langdale, try Oxendale and Mickleden, both of which give a sense of being amongst the mountains. At the head of the valley, the Old Dungeon Ghyll hotel is a famous meeting place for climbers and walkers and the nearby Stickle Barn provides a good cafe and bar. Make an early start, if you want a decent parking spot. Avoid the new houses at Chapel Stile. Ugh.

☆☆☆ Borrowdale

One of the prettiest valleys in the Lakes with spectacular views, but gets very crowded. A southern extension of the Vale of Derwentwater with a variety of scenery and contrasts. A good area from which to walk, low-lying and higher fells are easily accessible and so are many valley walks. The drive around the west side of Derwentwater provides good views of the lake. Good low-level walks up the Langstrath Valley (visit Black Moss Pot) and Greenup Ghyll. Borrowdale seems to come to an end just beyond Grange, where the slopes of Grange Fell and Castle Crag come together to give barely enough room for the river and road to pass through. These are the famous 'Jaws of Borrowdale'. Don't be put off - the valley opens up beyond and continues a long way down to the village of Seatoller and then up to Seathwaite. Gets very busy in the summer.

☆☆ Duddon Valley

Also known as Dunnerdale, this is the valley of the River Duddon. Wordsworth wrote thirty-five sonnets on this charming river. The whole valley is lovely, with plenty of car parking and pleasant walks on the surrounding fells. Ideal for picnicking and swimming. At the northern end is Birks Bridge, a little packhorse bridge in a renowned beauty spot.

☆☆☆ Wasdale

The most inaccessible valley in the area, therefore one of the quietest, even at the height of the season. The Wasdale Head Hotel is famous for its association with the development of rock climbing at the turn of the century.

Good bar meals. Wast Water is the most foreboding of the lakes. The whole valley, though spectacular, has a brooding air about it. Just read the tombstones at the little church at the head of Wasdale.

Good climbing and walking base for Gable and the Scafell range.

☆☆ Eskdale

One of the most interesting dales in Lakeland and popular with tourists, though only the lower-half - from Boot - is really well known to visitors. A beautiful valley, its head lies at Esk Hause in wild and dramatic scenery, the foot is amongst the plains and sand dunes at Newbiggin. The road only traverses about four miles of the dale itself. To explore the foot of the valley at its best, leave the car at Ravenglass and take the miniature railway to the Dalegarth terminus and walk back, detouring to follow the River Esk through lovely woods and pastures.

☆ Ennerdale

One of the few Lakeland valleys not properly accessible by road. Wild and isolated (or it used to be - becoming increasingly popular of late), the head of the dale is spectacular with Steeple and Pillar rising above the dark conifer plantations. The road goes along the north shore of the lake as far as Bowness Point (a good viewpoint). Thereafter it is for walkers only. There are Forestry Commission trails amongst the woods. It helps if you like conifers.

☆ Swindale

Reached from Bampton or Shap, a lovely, long valley, usually forgotten by the hordes. Rolling fells provide plenty of interest with low-level and higher walks, especially onto the ridges, with good views down into the neighbouring valleys. No proper road up it; this is a walker's valley.

☆☆ Vale of Lorton

Not technically a dale, more a sequence of valleys, but the lushest, prettiest part of the Northern Lakes. It's best to explore it from Cockermouth to get the full shape and extent. Coming from Keswick, you can get into it over the Whinlatter Pass, hitting the village of Lorton, where you turn left and follow the River Cocker upstream, and very gently and subtly, three marvellous lakes carefully unfold themselves for your inspection. First there's Loweswater, then bigger Crummock Water and finally the most popular of the three, Buttermere. Go right to the end of the valley and you can get back towards Keswick, over Honister Pass this time. Excellent walks all the way, either round lakes or up the surrounding fells, with some nice hamlets and pubs to explore along the way.

Passes

Lakeland has several, dramatic mountain passes suitable for motor traffic. Some are famous. Two are notorious. All of them are exciting as for those lazy motorists who never leave the wheel but want to go home and boast that they have scaled the Lakeland heights . . .

☆☆ Hardknott Pass 1,291 feet, 394m

The Lake District's most exciting road. Hair-raising in places, with 1-in-3 gradients, sharp bends and a delightful sheer drop on the west hand side. It can also get very busy in summer, with numerous hold-ups as motorists shuffle about on the steep bits to get past each other. Cyclists are advised by a sign at the top to dismount and walk the descent (but you're allowed to cycle up it, if you've the stamina and the gears). At one time, you could regularly watch the 2CVs being pushed up by groups of students.

Just below the summit, on the Eskdale side, there are parking places and Hardknott Fort, which guards over this once Roman road, should not be missed.

Worth trying for the dramatic views alone, but only if your nerves, brakes and engine are in good shape.

☆ Wrynose Pass 1,281 feet, 391m

The second of the Big Two and probably the more famous, though staff at Tourist Information Centres frequently get asked the way to Rhino Pass or even Buffalo Pass. Goes from Little Langdale and heads west towards Eskdale. Notoriously steep and narrow (although the best is yet to come). There are places where it is impossible for two cars to pass. Special passing places provided. These are *not* laybys and anyone parking in them deserves to have their handbrake released. At the summit is a pillar of rock called Three Shires Stone which used to mark the meeting point of the boundaries of Lancashire, Westmorland and Cumberland. The place where traditionalists still shed a few tears. The pass ends down at Cockley Beck, where you can either continue up Hardknott or turn off for the Duddon Valley.

☆ Honister Pass 1,176 feet, 359m

From Seatoller, in Borrowdale, to Buttermere. There are 1-in-4 gradients in places and on the Buttermere side it can get narrow. Not a brilliant route for scenery. At the top is a green slate quarry. Not a difficult pass.

Newlands Pass 1,100 feet, 335m

The most direct route from Keswick over to Buttermere Village. Starts off yummy and easy looking, through Beatrix Potter type country, but gets steep and wild on the top.

Whinlatter Pass 1,043 feet, 318m

Goes from Braithwaite, near Keswick, to High Lorton. The easiest of all the passes, although there are occasional steep sections. Going up from the Keswick end, there are good views over Bassenthwaite, with parking places. A lot of the view is obscured, however, as you enter the Forestry Commission's Thornthwaite Forest.

A nice, easy route to Loweswater, Crummock and Buttermere.

Kirkstone Pass 1,489 feet, 454m

Connects Windermere and Ambleside with Ullswater. This is the pass all the TV crews rush to when snow begins and they want to show everyone that the Lake District is snowed in. From Windermere, the road is good, with a long, interesting descent to Patterdale. To get to the pass from Ambleside, you go up a very narrow, steep road, aptly called The Struggle (it is almost opposite the Bridge House). 19th century travellers used to have to leave their coaches and walk alongside the horses up this part. Not quite as bad as that today, but there are some sharp bends to trap the unwary.

Waterfalls

Most Lakeland becks or streams have a force or water-fall of some kind. Many of them are small, hidden and unsung. They do their own gentle singing. Tra la. Gurgle, gurgle. Here are some of the finest and most famous - but don't expect to see them at their best after a long, dry spell. Yes, that often does happen in a Lakeland summer. After a heavy rainfall, they're at their most spectacular . . .

☆☆☆ Taylor Gill Force

Above Borrowdale, at Stockley Bridge. This is what the experts generally consider to be Lakeland's finest water-fall. A spectacular setting with an ambling mountain stream transforming itself into a 140 foot cascade. Can be seen from below the bridge, but for the best views follow the path to the right of the falls.

☆☆ Scale Force

The Lake District's longest waterfall, at 172 feet. The path to the falls goes from Buttermere village and the falls are hidden in a narrow, tree-lined gorge. More for the real waterfall collector than the average visitor.

☆☆ Aira Force

Probably the most famous of the Lake District's falls. On the west side of Ullswater, near Dockray, the falls are a few minutes pleasant walk from the public car park. The main force falls 70 feet from below a stone footbridge. You also get a good viewpoint from the path which ends just below the falls. If the sun is shining, look out for the rainbow. Cafe beside the car park.

☆ Stock Ghyll Force

On the fellside behind Ambleside, this delightful little waterfall is easily reached by walking from the town centre up the road which runs behind the Salutation Hotel. A nice, wooded walk to a 90 foot cascade flowing under a stone footbridge. Not spectacular, but very pretty.

☆ Lodore Falls

At the southern end of Derwentwater, easily reached from the road but perhaps the nicest way to view it is by boat. This 40 foot cataract is in a chasm surrounded by woods and crags. You have to pay to see it and there is an honesty box, which must be unique for a natural feature of this kind. It is owned by the hotel, the Swiss Lodore.

Skelwith Force

Only a small waterfall, just a drop of 16 foot, but nicely situated on the River Brathay. Just above the Kirkstone Slate Galleries at Skelwith Bridge.

Best Views

Eight viewpoints, chosen because they're either good, brilliant or simply classics, in our own un-humble opinion.

☆☆ **Castle Crag, Borrowdale** One of the best viewpoints in the Borrowdale area. Marvellous views all round.

☆☆☆ **Border End** (At the top of Hardknott Pass.) A short walk up the fellside but providing spectacular views across to Scafell and Scafell Pike, over the River Esk.

☆☆☆ **Whinlatter Pass** From the brow of the hill, looking north across Bassenthwaite Lake.

☆☆ **Orrest Head, Windermere** Just above Windermere village. Brilliant views through all 360 degrees.

☆☆ **Corney Fell** From the summit, looking north west to the Isle of Man.

☆ **Loughrigg Terrace** Looking down into Grasmere Vale, with Helm Crag and Dunmail Raise in the background. A classic.

☆ **Ashness Bridge** Looking over Derwentwater. Another classic and in every postcard rack.

☆ **Gummer's How** At the south east end of Lake Windermere. Summit gives a view up Windermere and into the Lakeland fells.

Chapter Nine

WALKS

Where to put those feet, especially family feet, with not too much danger. Also some Forests and other Natural Wonders.

I like a walk to be round. I don't like dragging straight up, that's for fell runners, only to come straight down again the same way. A sort of circle is best, slowly up a valley, through a gap, easily on to the top, then round the other side, preferably near a lake, back to base, without repeating one step. I don't like it too steep, especially coming down. Hurts the old knees. I like variety, smooth bits and rough bits. I don't want any roads, but I do like paths I can find easily, especially those grassy swards which look as if the Great Gardener in the sky had got out his celestial lawn-mower to the side of the fell. I definitely want views, especially a lake, and I want to feel impressed by myself, look how far we've got, haven't we done well. I like a top that is a top, with a cairn we can crouch beside, scoffing the while. And back at the beginning, I like the thought of a pub or hotel nearby, for emergencies, such as more scoff.

My wife hates screes, so we are not allowed anywhere near them, certainly not. On family walks, the children have their own requirement - it must be a new walk, one we haven't done before. Oh the hours I have studied the OS and old Wainwright, getting further and further afield, trying to work out new routes which will keep us all happy. Many of those books of family walks you see are full of the obvious stuff, often lifted from each other, which any idiot can work out for themselves, such as round Grasmere, or Friar's Crag. I don't want them as easy as that, I like a walk which can spread itself across the day, with two hours up, a picnic and lots of rests, then two hours to stroll back. The joy when we find a new one, which we like to think we have created, carving it out of the contours, shaping it in our minds. And after all these years, we still manage to find them. So here's a dozen of them - all simple and fun. They make a pleasant change from the more arduous mountain and fell climbs of the previous chapter (and don't forget them, of course, when contemplating possible family outings). Right, best feet forwards.

Best Family Walks

Low-level walks, chosen for scenery and ease of walking, with a variety of pleasures and sensations, all possible with a relatively fit family party - and a good map.

☆☆☆ 1) Ullswater

Our all time favourite walking area is around the far shore of Ullswater, that section where there's no road. Everything is there, all the sights and sensations, and all in a fairly short space. There are two ways of doing it, either by driving round the lake to Howtown, then doing a round walk, ending back at your car; or by taking the steamer there and back across the lake. Either way, you are in for sheer pleasure.

(a) Park at the little church of Martindale, above Howtown, just on the top after the switch back road, then walk down the little twisting road and into Bore Dale. It starts off like easy Beatrix Potter country, all smooth and rounded, but as you proceed up the valley, the fields and farmhouses run out and it gets wilder and emptier. Climb up to the head of the valley, through the Hause or pass. The path is clear and the walking easy, though it gets a little steep towards the end. Once over the top, bear right, heading down towards Patterdale. Admire the views, then pick up the path which leads along the shore of Ullswater, underneath the flanks of Place Fell. The path twists and turns with the shape of the lake, giving a different but equally wonderful view at every angle. At Sandwick, you can carry on, if you're not tired, and take in the walk round Hallin Fell, or turn right up the little road, back up the hill to the car. About 10 miles in all. The perfect walk. Allow four hours.

(b) Leave the car at Glenridding and catch the steamer to Howtown. On leaving the pier, turn right through several gates and go onto the fellside track above Waternook. Continue along the footpath, descending to the water's edge before entering woodland below Hallin Fell. Cross the little road at Sandwick and walk up towards Townhead Cottage, where you should turn right and follow the wall before crossing Scalehow Beck. Descend to Long Crag and the lakeshore. The next mile is through attractive open and wooded slopes. Below Silver Crag, the bridleway divides. Keep to the path nearest the lake and follow it back to Patterdale, then follow the road to Glenridding.

A brilliant walk. Allow about four hours.

☆☆☆ 2) Buttermere

From Buttermere village car park, follow the path to the left of the Fish Hotel. Take the left-hand path through the kissing gate, cross the footbridge and follow the left-hand path around the lake's southern shore. At the head of the lake, go left across the fields and rejoin the road. As the road runs alongside the lake, watch out for a small car park on your left. Leave the road here and follow the shoreline once more, back towards the village.

A lovely, easy walk with good views. The walk takes about 2 1/2 hours.

☆☆ 3) Derwentwater

An easy, three mile walk along the west shore. Take the launch from Friar's Crag and get off at Hawse End. Follow the lakeshore footpath left (it goes through a field for a short while, leaving the shore). Keep to the path at the edge of the lake until it reaches the Brandlehow landing stage, then bear right until you reach a fork. Go left up some steps, through the kissing gate and then keep left between the cottage and boathouse. At the next fork in the path, go right across some rather boggy ground. Join another path going left to the shore. Follow the footpath until it joins the road, then go left to the Lodore landing stage, where you can catch a launch back to Friar's Crag.

Some good views on the walk, both of surrounding fells and of the islands, particularly St Herbert's. Watch out for the Floating Island at Lodore - you might be lucky.

☆☆ 4) Easedale

This one does go uphill a little bit, in fact it is quite steep in places, but it makes a good family walk if you take your time. Should require about 2 1/2 hours. From Grasmere village go along Easedale Road for half-a-mile until you come to a bend and a footbridge signposted 'Easedale Tarn'. Go through the woods along an obvious track and at the small, iron kissing gate take the path directly in front of you up the hill. This follows Sour Milk Ghyll (which has some nice little waterfalls and pools) up to the tarn. You can walk around the tarn, though it gets a bit boggy at the head.

Follow the beck back down the hill, this time on the opposite bank. Watch out for a footpath on your left waymarked with white dots and small cairns. This leads down to Far Easedale Gill. Cross by the footbridge, and follow the stream. Keep straight and ignore the farm on the right. Eventually you'll come to a gate and can follow the track as it becomes a road and takes you back into Grasmere.

☆☆ 5) Rydal Water

Park at White Moss car park, between Grasmere and Rydal on the A591. Cross over the Rothay via the footbridge and go south along the western shore of Rydal Water. Where the path splits, the lower path goes alongside the lake, the upper takes you a little way up the fellside and past Rydal caves (two disused mines, carved out of solid rock and perfectly safe - although you can only easily get into the larger of them). The path rejoins the A591 at Pelter Bridge. Cross up to Rydal Mount and, just beyond, turn left and follow the old packhorse route back to White Moss.

Good for Wordsworth buffs as you can take in Rydal Mount. Allow three hours. Can easily be extended into four to five hours by heading up to the top of Loughrigg Fell, rather than hugging Rydal lakeshore. But it is very popular walking country in the high season.

☆☆ 6) Mirehouse

Park at Dodd Wood car park and leave via the path which crosses the stream behind the Old Sawmill cafe. Join a tarmac forestry road and turn left for a few yards before turning right and walking uphill along a narrow track. This levels out and descends through the trees to bring you out on the A591 beside the Ravenstone Hotel. Turn right, in front of the hotel and cross the road just past the white bungalow on your left. Take the footpath beside the bungalow, down some steps and across a series of fields until you reach a minor road. Go straight across and follow the path through the fields to St Bega's Church. This may once have been a pagan site - notice the circular graveyard. It is certainly spectacular, set right on the shores of Bassenthwaite.

From the church, follow the stream towards Mirehouse, with Dodd rising impressively in the background. The right of way goes through Mirehouse's grounds, behind the house and back to the A591, near the car park.

A lovely, easy walk. Only three miles and easily done in a couple of hours. Go on Wednesday or Sunday during the season and visit the house.

☆ 7) Muncaster Castle

Park at Ravenglass railway station and leave via the footpath at the back, behind the Ratty terminus. This track takes you past Walls Castle, an amazing Roman ruin - once a bath house and now the tallest standing Roman building in the north of England. Continue along the track to Walls Mansion (not a Roman anything) and then turn left to Newtown House. Bear left again here and just past a small cottage look for a gate in the fence on your left. There is a permissive path across the conifer plantation which takes you up to a field. Cross the stile and once in the field, the path disappears. Use this as an excuse to run to the top of the hill in front of you for superb views across the valley to the fells of Lakeland. Look a little to your left and you'll see a wood at the far side of the field. Head towards it - but first turn round for the view out to sea where, if you're lucky and it's a clear day, you might see the Isle of Man.

As you approach the wood, you'll see a gate in the stone wall. Go through and into Muncaster Castle grounds (don't worry - it's a right of way). Go downhill through an amazing bamboo plantation until you arrive at the Castle. The right of way goes straight across and up the drive to the main road. You should stick to this if the grounds are closed, but if open detour right for more wonderful views (you may also spot a few wallabies - bet you haven't seen many of those elsewhere in the LD).

Go out to the main road and turn left for 3/4 mile until you reach Home Farm. Cross here and follow the footpath through the farmyard and across fields to bring you back to the track leading to Walls Castle. Retrace your steps to the station.

3 1/2 miles, allow two hours; a super walk well away from the crowds.

☆ 8) La'al Ratty

Opportunities to cheat on this walk and use the miniature railway to ride back.

Park at Dalegarth Station in Eskdale and walk back along the road towards Hardknott. Turn right at the crossroads, beside Brook House, and follow the lane to St Catherine's Church and the River Esk. Turn left along the riverbank and follow this very pretty route for about 3/4 mile you come to a hump-backed stone bridge. Cross over and head back towards Dalegarth. The track climbs away from the river, through a farm and then meanders across several fields. Ignore the path signed 'St Catherine's Church' (unless you want to cut the walk short) but continue through a wood and across a campsite, via a rather impressive footbridge across Stanley Gill. Cross the track and into the next field (signed 'Force Bridge') and through more woods until you enter an attractive park. Follow the tarmac track to the minor road at Forge Bridge. Cross the bridge and continue to the road junction (beside the George IV pub). Turn left and walk to the railway station at Eskdale Green and enjoy the train ride back to Dalegarth.

A beautiful riverside walk, covering about 3 1/2 miles in total. Good for children, who will love the train ride. Allow about two hours.

☆☆ 9) Loweswater

One of Lakeland's forgotten lakes - a good place to escape the mid-summer hordes.

Start at the Kirkstile Inn and follow the road past the church, towards Loweswater lake. Turn left at the road junction and then straight on, signposted Ennerdale and Mockerkin. Follow the narrow, twisting road (beware boy racers) until you reach the fell road. Turn right up here and follow this uphill, towards Mosser. Good views from the top. At a prominent footpath sign, turn left and go downhill to a farm gate. Follow the track to Grange Road. Turn right and then, just past the second entrance to the Grange Hotel, left and follow the bridleway to Hudson Farm.

Keep to the main track. By the farm, turn onto the gravel track and then through the left-hand of two gates. This track takes you down to the lake. A nice, grassy path follows the shore, through Holme Wood and brings you to Watergate Farm. Follow the track left, across several fields, and it brings you back to the road. Turn right and go back to the inn.

Four miles, 2 1/2 hours - dead easy. Good views of Mellbreak and - from the fell road - the Isle of Man.

☆☆ 10) Arthur's Pike, Ullswater

A quiet, unusual way of seeing a familiar view.

Park at Howtown, if you can, which means getting to the pier before the crowds or, if you're cheeky enough, park at the hotel, telling yourself you are going to be a guest, once you've done the walk. Go through the hotel grounds to Mellguards, then left through a gate and onto a long, very easy grassy path which hugs the side of the hill, almost parallel with the road to the left below. Just after the little reservoir thingy, cut up steeply through some ferns and climb up to White Knott, which is the first cairn. All very easy. It looked hard from below, but come on, you'll be on top in no time. Carry on to Arthur's Pike itself - then continue to Bonscale, a lovely ridge walk, but take care not to come down into Swarthbeck Gill. When you're above Fusedale, then cut right, zig zagging down the grassy slopes, heading back to Howtown Hotel. If the bar is closed, try their afternoon teas, especially the hot scones.

Perfect round walk, about three miles, takes 3 1/2 hours, with lots of stops on top to admire the brilliant views of Ullswater. Nice, easy beginning, just to warm yourself up, then the satisfaction of a brisk climb. Always uncrowded. Not many know this walk.

☆☆ 11) Barrow

No, not that beautiful town, but another relatively unknown fell, yet right within top tourist country. On a bank holiday, when the world and his wizened grandad is doing Cat Bells, try Barrow instead.

Park in Braithwaite village, then leave as if heading for Newlands, turning right off the road at Braithwaite Farm. It looks private, but head straight up to it and then on and upwards, trying to ignore the sound of the A66 below in the distance as it will soon disappear. Having reached the top of Barrow, where the views of Derwentwater are magnificent, you can either head back by going right, down on the path to High Coledale, that's if the weather is bad or the party is lazy (which would give a two hour round walk), or better still, carry on, veering to the left of Stile End, which there is no need to climb, round Outerside (no need to climb that either) and you'll emerge above Coledale. Cut right down the grassy slopes to the valley bottom, heading for the old mines, then straight along the very good Coledale Beck track, back to Braithwaite. Time perhaps for tea in Book Cottage, or drive straight to Keswick and lash out at Maysons on something nourishing.

Very satisfying, really round walk, impressive views, no hard climbing. About four miles. Allow four hours.

☆☆ 12) Gowbarrow

Yes, another Ullswater stroll, but this time on the main road side, where it is very attractive, but hard to work out a decent family amble without hitting millions of other families, or the dreaded road. Park at the Aira Force car park, which has smart toilets and a cafe nearby, and usually hordes of coaches. Depending on the crowds, go up and explore the waterfall at once, or save it for later. The walk proper begins by heading right over a stile, aiming for the towers of a house called Lyulph Tower. As you climb the flank of Gowbarrow Fell, there are excellent views of Ullswater. Eventually start going up above a stream, following a wall, to the top of the fell. It's usually empty on top, as the softies have all stuck to Aira Force. Back along the top and then descend by a steep but easy grassy path, which children usually try to slide down, the fools, to Aira Force.

Easy, satisfying three hour family stroll, with great views, the famous waterfall to take in, Wordsworth's daffodils to look out for in season, and a caff at the end.

Forest Walks

Forests and woodland cover about 8.5% of the National Park, over half of them belonging to the Forestry Commission. These aren't, strictly speaking, natural features of the landscape and the Commission has earned itself some bitter enemies with its policy of covering the fells with dark, regimented conifers. To balance this, they have of late taken to opening up some of their plantations to the public, providing waymarked walks and setting up centres to explain what they are doing. The Forestry Commission has three main forests where this has taken place:

Forestry Commission Forests

1) Grizedale

The best known and one the Forestry Commission apparently feels terribly very proud of.

The forest lies between Esthwaite and Coniston. The main access points have car parks and toilets and there is a visitor centre just north of the village of Satterthwaite. This area was one of the first to be opened to the public. Perhaps for this reason it is not as good as its northern counterparts. The forest trails are often poorly marked and the paths can be confusing. The sculptured trees are fascinating, if you can find them. There are now mountain bike trails through the forest - a good way of keeping them off the fells. Don't miss the shop, which sells haunches of venison, and the little nursery where you can buy small trees very cheaply.

☆ **Grizedale Visitor Centre** contains a forestry exhibition and displays relating to the industry and how it affects the area. Refurbished £1/4 million visitor centre recently opened by Lord Whitelaw. Vastly improved over the previous effort with fascinating computer displays where you can try your hand at forest management.
Open (Visitor Centre only) April to October, daily 10.00-5.00. Very small admission charge. The forest itself is open at all times. Tel: Satterthwaite 272.

2) Thornthwaite Forest and Dodd Wood
Two separate plantations, though usually publicised on the same leaflet, so we'll treat them as one.

☆☆ **Thornthwaite Forest** lies over to the west of Bassenthwaite Lake, and Whinlatter Pass goes through it. At the top of Whinlatter is a car park, the starting point for a number of good walks which give some great views over Derwentwater and Keswick.

☆ **Whinlatter Visitor Centre** is based at the top of the Whinlatter Pass. It is set back from the road, at the edge of the forest, so it is easy to miss. It is an excellent little centre. Open: Easter to October, daily, 10.00-5.00. Admission free. Tel: Braithwaite 469.

☆ **Dodd Wood** is leased from the Mirehouse estate and lies on the east shore of Bassenthwaite Lake. There is an excellent walk which leads you to the top of Dodd, giving a good view over Bassenthwaite and the fells. The car park down at the start of the walk also has the excellent Old Sawmill cafe.

☆☆ 3) Ennerdale
One of the most dramatic Lakeland forests. Cars must be left at Bowness Knott car park. The main forest trail - Smithy Beck - goes along the edge of Ennerdale Water and is clearly waymarked. Openings in the trees reveal fine views.

Forestry information Walk sheets are available from most Tourist Information Centres, or direct from the Forestry Commission. For Grizedale, write to District Officer:

> South Lakes District
> Forestry Commission
> Grizedale, Ambleside. Tel: Satterthwaite 373.

For Thornthwaite and Ennerdale:

> North Lakes District
> Forestry Commission
> Peil Wyke, Bass Lake. Tel: Bass Lake 616.

National Trust Woodlands

The National Trust also owns some major woodlands. Good walks can be found at the following:

Windermere North west shore (Claife shore); a nature trail with an illustrated guide available (from National Trust information centres).

Coniston Park-a-Moor and Nibthwaite Woods on the east shore.

Derwentwater Great Wood (east shore), Manesty and Brandlehow (west shore) and Friar's Crag.

Specialist Walks

Nature Trails Many authorities in Lakeland have them these days, apart from the Forestry Commission. Enquire at local TICs for leaflets, but some of the best include: Ambleside (round Loughrigg and White Moss); Appleby (Castle Nature Trail); Barrow (South Walney Nature Trail); Carlisle (Kingmoor Nature Trail); Coniston (Brantwood Nature Trail); Dalton-in-Furness; Eskdale (Stanley Ghyll Nature Trail); Glenridding (guided walk); Grasmere (guided walk); Hutton-in-the-Forest (Woodland Walk); Kendal (Serpentine Woods); Keswick (Friar's Crag); Ulverston (Hay Bridge Nature Reserve); Nether Wasdale.

Town Trails These are often marked or guided walks round towns and larger villages, or do-it-yourself trails with the appropriate leaflet. They include: Appleby; Furness Abbey; Carlisle; Cockermouth; Dalton-in-Furness; Grasmere; Hawkshead; Kendal; Kirkby Lonsdale; Maryport; Pooley Bridge; Sedbergh; Whitehaven.

Industrial Trails Don't mock. Carlisle had its industrial revolution before Lancashire, and those West Coast towns led the nation at one time in coal and shipping and town planning. Lots of interesting Victorian industrial stuff to be seen, especially in Carlisle (Industrial Trail); Barrow (Vickerstown Town Trail); Whitehaven (Town Walkabout); Maryport (Harbour Walks).

Eden Valley Although we're mainly concerned with Lakeland proper, the good folks on the other side of the M6, still in Cumbria, have recently been setting out many fine walks in the Eden Valley and the Pennines. Leaflets available from Eden District Town Hall, Penrith.

Farm Walks Another recent development. There are now regular Open Days on Lake District farms, mainly upland farms, on the hills, the sort peculiar to Cumbria. Most start around 2 o'clock, and the farmer usually does the guided walk. Get a leaflet from the National Park people, or a TIC.

Wildlife The Cumbrian coast is especially rich in wildlife, thanks to the mudflats and saltmarshes. Large numbers of wintering waders and wildfowl can be seen, in some cases more than in any other spot in the world. You might also see rare animals, such as natterjack toads.

For information about Cumbria's trees, flowers, birds and mammals, and about the conservation work going on, contact - Cumbria Wildlife Trust, The Badger's Paw, Church Street, Ambleside.

Geology After Cornwall, Cumbria is probably the most interesting county in England, geologically speaking. In fact, American geologists come all the way here for things they can't get at home, such as fluorites. Even an amateur, with no knowledge, soon can spot bits of the stuff, scattered over the fells. The two most popular Lakeland areas for finding specimens are:

Northern Fells, just south of Caldbeck, especially Roughton Gill, Carrock Fell and Driggeth. Beware the old mine workings. They can be dangerous. Very good for pyromorphites, malachite, pyrite. You might even find campylite, if you're lucky.

West Coast, round Beckermet, Frizington, Egremont. Good for haematite, barytes. I met a man from Sussex who found a piece of Pallaflat Calcite at Egremont, which he sold for £450. Lucky.

Walking Books and Leaflets

In addition to the general guide books listed already in Chapter 1, there are a number of others which give good low-level walks.

☆☆☆ Walks in the Countryside
The National Park people publish an excellent series of walk sheets, 14 in all, each based in a particular area and offering two or three fairly easy walks, with a description and sketch map. They only cost 12p each, so are great value. Or you can buy the set in a special pack for £1.25. Highly recommended, because you don't have to take a whole book out with you.

Cheap to replace if lost or damaged. The maps, I mean, not you. You are irreplaceable . . .

Enjoy the Hills in Safety - free. Leaflet published by the National Park Authority is worth a mention. Gives advice, safety hints, suggested equipment and - best of all - fell ascent times.

Nature Book Best book which covers Cumbria's mines, soils, animals, plants and such like is *A Field Guide to the Lake District*, by Jim Taylor Page, published by Dalesman, 1984. Rather school masterly, so it would be very useful if you are a teacher, or in charge of a group, but comprehensive and fairly easy to read.

Long Walk Book Just in case you've exhausted all those short family ones, or even those quick mountain climbs, why not try the Cumbria Way, a 70 mile walk from Ulverston, on the shores of Morecambe Bay, right through the heart of the Lake District, up to Carlisle in the north. You could do it in a week, taking in bed and breakfast places or youth hostels along the way. It's a Ramblers' Association enterprise and easily followed. Good booklet all about it called *The Cumbria Way* by John Trevelyan, published by Dalesman in 1987.

Guides

If you now feel you've got the hang of it, managing to place one foot in front of the other, or walking as we normally call it, you might want to venture up onto the hairy stuff. In that case, a proper mountain guide might be useful, one who knows the terrain and has reached the professional standards set down by the Association of British Mountain Guides.

There are a dozen or so professional ABMG guides in Lakeland. Contact their regional rep, Stewart Miller of Eel Crag, 5 Melbecks, Braithwaite, Keswick, tel: Braithwaite 517. If he can't take you, he should be able to recommend someone.

Hugh Walpole at Skiddaw House

Chapter Ten

Museums and Galleries

The Lake District has a large number of museums and galleries for such a small area. And not all of them are simply about Lakeland fells and sheep. I bet you didn't expect to find the largest collection of Laurel and Hardy possessions here, or a five hundred year old cat, or a seven foot pencil.

A lot of museums are now transforming themselves into highly imaginative interpretative centres, with up-to-date audio-visual displays and light, airy buildings. But in some ways the ones which are being left behind can be the nicest - old fashioned and badly displayed, but ideal for just pottering.

Admission charges

A - under £1
B - £1-£2
C - over £2.

Children are normally half price. Last admission time is often 1/2 hour to an hour before closing time. Opening months are inclusive - ie 'March-October' means 1st March to 31st October.

We have arranged them alphabetically, according to the nearest town or village. Note those which offer tea facilities - very few of them do.

Warning: Museums are obvious places to go in rainy weather, so if there's one you really want to see at its best, take a day off from the fells and go when it is sunny. Particular ones to avoid when wet are those in areas where there is little else to do when the weather is bad (e.g. Grasmere and Hawkshead).

We have tried our very best to give correct opening times, but they can change, so ring in advance if it's a vital visit.

Note: Literary Homes are in Chapter 11; Stately Homes in Chapter 13.

Ambleside
Armitt Collection
Mill Cottage, Rydal Road, Ambleside.

It all began with three Bronte type sisters, Marie Louisa, Annie Maria and Sophia Armitt, who devoted themselves to writing and the arts. They founded a library in 1912, subsequently supported by the great and the good of the times, such as Canon Rawnsley, Beatrix Potter, Arthur Ransome, G. M. Trevelyan.

Best things: The Armitt Library now owns the largest collection of fungi water colours done by Beatrix Potter (that was an early passion, before she wrote Peter Rabbit); early Lakeland photographs; rare books of literary and Cumbria interest; archaeological relics; literary manuscripts.

They have recently converted Mill Cottage, next to the Stock Ghyll car park, and plan public displays from the autumn of 1989, while students will be able to use the reading room upstairs for research purpose, or the old premises, above Ambleside Public Library.

Open: Very soon, to the general public. In the meantime, you can use the public library facilities if you become a Friend of the Armitt Trust, just £5 a year. Write to Armitt Trust, Ambleside, Cumbria LA22 0BZ. Enquiries, telephone the Librarian, Ambleside 33949.

Appleby
Dyke Nook Farm Museum
Barn End, Dyke Nook, Warcop, Appleby. Tel: Brough 207.

Miles from anywhere. Come off the Appleby bypass and head towards Warcop until you see the sign marked 'Farm Museum'. Parking on site. This is actually a working farm, with a museum bit added on.

Best things: Lots of old agricultural tools and implements, some of them used on the farm itself. The Clydesdale horses are still working on the farm. There are also some Highland cattle, plus some Jacob and Soay sheep, partly for the kiddies to look at. Not really worth trailing a long way out of your way to find, but an odd museum, a lot of it in the open air. There is also a steam threshing machine in operation on selected days.

Open: Mid-summer only, 1.00-5.00. Closed Thursday and Saturday. As it is a family concern, they will sometimes open by arrangement at other times. In any case, it is always best to ring first to make sure they are open, if you are making a special journey. Admission - B.

Barrow
Furness Museum
Ramsden Square, Barrow-in-Furness. Tel: Barrow 20650.

It's up towards the docks, by the roundabout at the junction of Duke Street and Abbey Road. About five minutes walk along Duke Street from the shops. The museum is in the Library building. Park in town.

Best things: The museum is very small - it is actually a room in Barrow Public Library. The County Archive and the local book collection are in the same building so it offers good research facilities. There are some nice ship models and it has changing temporary exhibitions. They can also arrange tours of Furness villages and industrial sites for groups and parties. (Could be one to watch as the Furness Maritime Trust is about to embark on the largest museum development in Cumbria - a large Maritime museum to be built on a dockside site.)

Open: All year. Monday to Saturday 10.00-5.00, Thursday 10.00-1.00. Closed Sunday. (The opening times are the same as the library.) Free admission.

Carlisle
☆☆ Carlisle Museum and Art Gallery
Tullie House, Castle Street, Carlisle. Tel: Carlisle 34781.

Right beside the Cathedral, just before the Castle. Nice and centrally positioned, handy for Carlisle's many other wonderful tourist attractions, but rotten for parking. The best car park is at West Walls, if you can find your way into it. Best to park elsewhere and walk to it. The building has frequent special exhibitions in both the Museum and Art Gallery. Needs to be carefully explored as bits are tucked all over the place and you can easily miss some rooms.

Best things: For a start, the building itself. Stand out at the back and admire it, especially the ornate lead drainpipes. It's Carlisle's only Jacobean building. Inside, the museum part, the Roman remains are outstanding, some of the best bits found on the western end of Hadrian's Wall, though not very excitingly displayed. (The building is on the site of Carlisle's Roman fort.) In the Art Gallery, upstairs, and on the staircases and landings, look out for the pre-Raphaelite paintings. Carlisle has an amazing collection of them for such an out-of-the-way provincial town - works by Burne-Jones, Millet, Pisarro, Whistler, Augustus John, Paul Nash, Stanley Spencer. (They got many of them fairly cheaply in the 1930's when Sir William Rothenstein became their London art advisor.)

Open: Well, not very. The above is what you used to be able to see. The bad news is that from May 1989 to December 1990, the Museum and Art Gallery will be closed. That's the bad news. The good news is that it is all part of a £3.6m refurbishment scheme. When it reopens we are promised new displays, new facilities, new exhibitions. Plus a shop, refreshments and facilities for education groups. Look out for the next edition ...

☆ Prior's Tower

The Cathedral, Carlisle. Tel: Carlisle 35169.

Part of Carlisle Cathedral, so finding it shouldn't be any problem. Parking is a different matter. Park elsewhere and walk.

Best things: Prior's Tower is a 13th century pele tower and contains a lovely little museum display. There are guided tours on request (the last one goes round at 7.00). Nice just to wander round on your own, though. A new Treasury was being built at the time of writing, with plans to open it as a small museum in the summer of 1989.

Open: All year - May to September, 8.30am-9.00pm (closed Sunday); October to April, 8.30-5.30 (closed Sunday). No admission fee.

☆ Border Regiment Museum

Queen Mary Tower, Carlisle Castle. Tel: Carlisle 32774.

Part of the Castle, which is well worth a visit in itself. Free parking on the Castle's parade ground which is a great help.

Best things: The Border Regiment has served in battles all over the world for the last 300 years - from the Duke of Marlborough's days, the Napoleonic Wars to the last two World Wars. Of great fascination to all those with local connections, as the regiment's roots are well explained, but still of interest to all military fans. Good displays of regimental trophies and uniforms.

The full name, by the way, should be the Border Regiment and King's Own Royal Border Regiment Museum (making it the Longest Museum Title in Cumbria).

Open: Easter to mid-October, daily 9.30-6.30; Winter, Mon-Sat, 9.30-4.00, Sunday, 2.00-4.00. Admission - A (entrance to the Castle also gets you into the Museum).

Carnforth

☆ Steamtown Railway Museum

Warton Road, Carnforth. Tel: Carnforth 732100.

Rather out of the way, though it tends to get advertised in the Lake District and they do promote Carnforth as 'The Gateway to the Lakes' (they'll be saying that about Manchester soon). Go down the A6 to Carnforth, then follow the signs to 'Railway Museum' - it's behind the British Rail depot (recognise it from 'Brief Encounter'?). Parking on site. Carnforth has few other attractions (apart from a superb secondhand book shop) so it is unlikely that you'll be walking from anywhere.

Best things: Thirty diesel and steam engines. It boasts that it's Britain's largest steam loco depot. (There are now so many exhibitions of old industries in Lakeland - what with bobbin mills, water-mills and steam engines - you sometimes get the feeling that if the rest of industrial civilisation collapsed, the Lake District could just turn the clock back 100 years and carry on as normal).

Look out for a miniature railway (NB it doesn't run every day, so ring to check first), a Midland Railway signal box (how did that get there?); they used to have the Flying Scotsman, but it has now gone elsewhere (shame). Steamtown is often visited by mainline locomotives, so it could reappear. Full steam days are public holidays and Sundays in April, May and June. Wednesday, Saturday and Sundays in July and August. Also Sundays in September and October. Well worth a visit for railway buffs.

Open: Easter to September, daily 9.00-5.00; winter, 10.00-4.00. Closed Christmas Eve to Boxing Day. Admission - B/C - depending on whether it is a steam day or whether the miniature railway is running (why does anything to do with British Rail have to be complicated?). There's a small tea shop on site which is OK for snacks.

Cartmel
☆ Cartmel Priory Gatehouse
Cartmel, near Grange-over-Sands.

Cartmel is a lovely little village, best reached from the north by coming down to Newby Bridge and turning left, then taking the turning for Cartmel about a mile further on. You can park in the village square, but if full (which it always is if the pubs are open), carry on through the square down the little road on the left of the post office and park by the racecourse. The Gatehouse is under the arch, just opposite the pump in the centre of the square.

Best things: The building itself dates from around 1330 and is owned by the National Trust. It is now let to a local artist, who has a display of work on show, often painting whilst visitors look around.

Open: April to October, daily 11.00-5.00 (closed Monday). Admission free.

Cockermouth
☆ The Toy and Doll Museum
Bank's Court, Market Place, Cockermouth.
Tel: Cockermouth 85259.

A welcome addition to the more eccentric Lakeland museums. Barbara Pickering, German born, has put her own collection of 300 ethnic dolls on show, from over 60 countries. By ethnic she means they are in regional costumes. She says it's the only one of its type in the UK.

Best things: Nice display of 80 years of toys, including a working tinplate model railway. There's also a model of a 15th century Kentish House which took Mr Pickering 2,900 hours to build. So that's what they do in Cockermouth in winter nights.

Open: Summer, daily 10.00-5.00; winter, daily (except Thursdays) 11.00-4.00. Admission - B.

☆ Castlegate House Gallery
Cockermouth, Castlegate. Tel: Cockermouth 822149.

A newly opened commercial gallery, specialising in Cumbrian paintings by living, local artists. You don't have to buy of course, just admire the art, savour the ambience.

Best things: Depends on the current show, but the house itself is worth a peep, as it's one of Cockermouth's larger Georgian gems, just opposite the Castle, with a surprising garden. (Ask to see it, and the inscription over the back door. It's private, but you could be lucky.)

Open: March to October, Monday-Saturday 10.30-4.30, except Wednesday, which is open 10.30-7.00. Closed Thursdays. Admission free.

Coniston
☆ The Ruskin Museum
The Institute, Yewdale Road, Coniston. Tel: Coniston 41541.

Right in the centre of the village, so parking is pretty hopeless. Use the main car park and walk back. You have to look carefully for the museum as it's only tiny.

Best things: Once inside there are some interesting displays relating to Ruskin and his circle. There are also some fine mineral specimens. A good example of a typical, old fashioned museum. The recent BBC film of the Donald Campbell record attempt on Coniston has aroused a lot of interest, so the Museum is now trying to display more of its collection of photographs of Campbell and Bluebird.

Open: March to October, daily 9.30-5.30. Never terribly busy so no particularly good times to go - best to avoid it on wet days, though. Admission - A.

Finsthwaite
☆☆ Stott Park Bobbin Mill
Finsthwaite, near Newby Bridge. Tel: Newby Bridge 31087.

On the west side of Lake Windermere, just north of Lakeside on the Hawkshead Road (about a mile away), at the Finsthwaite road junction. Free car park on site.

Completely out of the way and set in wooded country-side. Can sound like any other little craft gallery, but is actually a major site of what used to be one of the Lake District's most important industries. Can be combined with a pleasant walk through the woods to Finsthwaite High Dam.

Best things: The place itself - this really *is* a bobbin mill, not a reconstruction. It was built in 1835 and was turning out bobbins right up until 1971. After it closed down, English Heritage bought the property and reopened it as a museum in 1983. It is now run by the Abbot Hall people. The massive mill building houses much of the original machinery, including the old water turbines and steam engines. The two resident curators, Mr Dixon and Mr Steeley, will give guided tours and demonstrations. They have both worked in the industry (though not at Stott Park) and are full of stories. There are also static displays and a small exhibition. A fantastic place, unique and well worth leaving the beaten tourist track to find.

Open: Easter or 1st April to October, Mon-Sat 9.30-6.30. Sunday 2.00-6.30. During October, closing time is 4.30. Admission - B.

Grasmere
☆☆☆ Grasmere & Wordsworth Museum
Town End, Grasmere. Tel: Grasmere 544.

Next to Dove Cottage, just off the A591, opposite the southern turning to Grasmere village. The museum is in a converted stable block which used to belong to The Prince of Wales Hotel. Limited parking if you're early, but impossible later in the day during the summer. Best to park in the village and walk up.

Best things: After Abbot Hall, this is probably the best and most 'professional' museum in the Lake District. They are very proud of the fact that it is the only 'Grade A' museum in the North-West, which means it has its own internal climate and air-conditioning. (Very refreshing on a sweltering summer day. You can wander about inside and get cool.)

The museum houses the best collection of original Wordsworth manuscripts in the entire known universe. Look out, too, for a copy of Dorothy's notebook, where she kept her famous journal. Not all the manuscripts are in William's own hand - he used to get his wife, Mary, or sister to write out his poems for him and would then go through and make corrections. It is fascinating to compare his handwriting later in life with a handwritten poem composed when he was at Hawkshead Grammar School - it got much worse. The display is brilliantly presented and it's all in chronological order, telling the poet's life story, so don't worry if your knowledge of Wordsworth is confined to a single poem about daffodils. There are many of Wordsworth's possessions on display, including a coat and waistcoat mounted on a dummy torso so that you can get an idea of his size. There are also paintings of many of his contemporaries. Each summer there is a special exhibition in the downstairs gallery.

It's not all Wordsworth and there are two rooms devoted to local history. Downstairs is a display showing the history of tourism in Grasmere, including some wonderful old optical instruments. Upstairs is a reconstruction of a farmhouse interior, as it might have been around 1800.

The Museum host three residential courses each year - a Winter School (Feb), Book Collectors Weekend (March) and the Wordsworth Summer Conference (August). More details in chapter 14.

There is now a restaurant, just on the main road (well, there's always been one there but now the Dove Cottage lot actually own and run it). Open during the day and for evening dinner. Tel: Grasmere 268.

There is quite a lot of reading to be done in this museum, so it is best to get there early in the day to avoid the crowds. It is often quiet around lunch time.

Final tip - do the museum before you do Dove Cottage. You'll appreciate it more.

Open: Now almost all year (they're closed from mid-Jan to mid-Feb), daily 9.30-5.30. Last admission - 5.00. Admission - C (includes Dove Cottage and special exhibitions). Special rates for families and groups.
Warning: It can get very crowded during wet weather, especially during school holidays.

Hawkshead
☆☆ Hawkshead Grammar School
Hawkshead, near Ambleside. No telephone.

Dead easy to find - it's opposite the main car park. Leave the car in the car park, visit the grammar school, then walk into Hawkshead via the path round the back of the grammar school. This brings you into the centre of Hawkshead and avoids all the crowds panting to get into the sheepskin and gifte-shoppes.

Best things: The school is a lovely old building, though now painted up and looking somewhat different than in

Wordsworth's day. It is famous, of course, because the young William Wordsworth went to school here. Inside you can see the desk where he carved his initials. (Or at least, that's what they tell you - very hard to find.) The main room is a school room set out as it was in the late 18th century. The curator is always on hand to answer questions about the school or Wordsworth. (Go early and catch him when few visitors are about and make the best of his local knowledge.) Upstairs there is a small library and a small exhibition on the history of the school. If you want to know how they made quill pens, there's a display which tells you. There is also a new room recently opened - the headmaster's study (potential for an exhibition of canes through the ages?). A nice, relaxing little museum, quiet even in summer.

Open: March to October, Monday -Sat. 10.00-5.00 (closed for lunch 12.30-1.30), Sunday 1.00-5.00. Admission - A.

☆☆ Beatrix Potter Gallery
Main Street, Hawkshead. Tel: Hawkshead 355.

For several years now, visitors to Hill Top have been disappointed to find that the original water colours from the Beatrix Potter books have not been on show. Taken, and hidden away, or so it seemed. Now they have reappeared, and in a marvellous setting. The National Trust have converted the original legal offices of William Heelis, BP's husband, and turned it into an excellent little gallery.

Best things: The Potter paintings of course. Don't miss them. Especially if you were amongst the thousands who couldn't see a thing for the crowds at the Tate show of Potter stuff. It is nice to be able to compare the printed illustrations with the early sketches and paintings. A shame the NT have concentrated on Peter Rabbit et al, to the exclusion of Beatrix Potter's other watercolours (such as her flower paintings which are exquisite). There's also a recreation of Mr Heelis's office, complete with his desk ledgers and period files.

Open: March to November, Wednesday -Sun. 11.00-5.00. Admission - B.

Holker
☆☆ Lakeland Motor Museum
Holker Hall, Cark-in-Cartmel, Grange-over-Sands. Tel: Flookburgh 509.

Holker Hall is on the B5278 between Haverthwaite and Cark. The easiest way to get to it is turn right at Newby Bridge along the A590 and turn onto the B5278 at Haverthwaite. It's about 7 1/2 miles from Newby Bridge and the Museum is in the grounds of Holker Hall. Parking in the grounds.

Best things: A northern Beaulieu in many ways - it even has Campbell's Bluebird, though this one is a replica, made for a BBC television play. There are over 80 historic vehicles - cars, motorbikes, cycles, engines, as well as various motoring bits and pieces (otherwise known as 'automobilia'), such as Princess Margaret's scooter, illuminated petrol pump signs, toy cars and a walk-round 1920's garage. Fascinating stuff. Favourite exhibit is likely to depend on your particular mechanical bent, but their prize exhibit is the 1922 Bentley. An excellent 'fun' museum, but it is expensive. Friendly manager though who will lift up the bonnet of their 1938 Lagonda, if you ask nicely.

Open: Easter Saturday to October, daily (closed Saturday) 10.30-5.30. Last admission 4.30. Life is too short to explain Holker's very complicated admission rules and charges - let's just say - B/C.

Kendal
☆☆☆ Abbot Hall Art Gallery
Abbot Hall, Kendal. Tel: Kendal 22464.

Situated in Kirkland, at the southern end of Kendal. It's just behind the Parish Church and has one of the loveliest settings in town - right by the river and looking up towards Kendal Castle. Free car park - get to it by going through the Council car park.

The Gallery is in an immaculate Georgian building, set in a small park along with some of the oldest buildings in Kendal. Just because Kendal is not a major city, don't expect another small, provincial gallery. It is generally reckoned to be the finest art gallery in the North WEst and one of the top 20 in the whole country.

Best things: Abbot Hall itself, for a start. Built in 1759 for Lt Col George Wilson (at a cost of £8,000) it has been open as an art gallery since 1962. Downstairs houses a small but impressive collection of 18th and 19th century paintings, displayed along with period furniture, porcelain and glassware. It's set out in such a way that you feel as if you're wandering around someone's stately home - only without all those ropes. Upstairs the house becomes a more traditional art gallery setting to display the contemporary collection, works by Barbara Hepworth, John Piper, William Johnstone, Norman Adams, Elizabeth Frink. There are also changing exhibitions each year which are well worth looking out for.

Open: May to October, Monday-Saturday 10.30-5.00, Sunday 2.00-5.00; rest of year Monday-Friday 10.30-5.00, Saturday & Sunday 2.00-5.00. Admission - B, or you can save money by buying a combined ticket for the Art Gallery and the Museum of Lakeland Life and Industry.

☆☆☆ Museum of Lakeland Life and Industry
Abbot Hall, Kendal. Tel: Kendal 22464.

A separate establishment in its own right, housed in what used to be Abbot Hall's stable block. Part of the collection spills over into the adjacent 17th century grammar school, so watch out for the diversion sign as you go round the upstairs part of the museum. Small but prestigious, it won the first ever Museum of the Year Award in 1973.

Best things: Definitely the lack of glass cases. Most of the exhibits are on open display - you can touch them, walk round them, peer under them, even sniff them if you want to. Some of the drawers are worth opening, too. It's a fantastic little museum, full of reconstructed workshops with genuine, hand worn tools and instruments. There's a beautiful old 19th century printing press, made of cast iron and once used by the Westmorland Gazette; a hundred year-old weaving loom (sometimes used to give demonstrations by local experts); engineering and wheelwright's workshops; massive old clocks and signs; there's even a bedroom and living room, a delight to walk round, fully furnished as they might have been around 1900. This is definitely the best museum for anyone interested in Lakeland and its people. One of the nicest things about it is that many of the tools and exhibits came from local people. It is all so well done that it looks as though the people who used these tools have just knocked off for lunch and might be back at any minute to carry on working. Look out for the paint shop door upstairs, covered in 'stalactites' of paint where the brushes used to be worked out.

In the tower upstairs (at the top of the old iron spiral staircase) is a replica of Arthur Ransome's study, with many of his possessions, including his desk and chair. But to get up here you have to be accompanied by one of the staff, so ask at the desk downstairs.

Part of the success of the display relies on its minimal use of labels and text, but this has its drawbacks - quite often you find yourself wondering what on earth you're looking at. The only remedy is to arm yourself with the guide book before you go in and think of it as part of the admission fee.

Queens Gate is the new replica of a Kendal street scene, circa 1890, along the lines of the Castle Museum at York. Excellent chemist's shop and perfumery but were streets really this dark 100 years ago? Opened in 1985 by the Queen, which may explain the tacky paper Union Jacks.

There is also a farming gallery which is easily missed as you have to go through the new Craft Shop to enter it. A nice, airy display of wonderful old farming implements, complemented by a refreshingly witty text (some of which is displayed actually inside the machines). A sign reads:

"Cumbria contains two million sheep and half-a-million people". Some might say it doubles to four million on a Bank Holiday.

Open: May to October, Monday-Saturday 10.30-5.00, Sunday 2.00-5.00; rest of year Monday-Friday 10.30-5.00, Saturday & Sunday 2.00-5.00.

☆☆ Kendal Museum of Archaeology and Natural History

Station Road, Kendal. Tel: Kendal 21374.

It's up by the railway station, about 10 minutes walk from the town centre. Limited parking at the museum.

Owned by the Town Council but administered by Abbot Hall, it is gradually changing from a typical municipal museum of the old school, into an imaginative 'interpretative' centre. Don't let that put you off though . . .

Best things: Kendal is full of surprises. Not only does it contain one of the best art galleries in the country, it also has one of England's oldest museums. Kendal Museum was first opened in 1796 when a gentleman by the name of William Todhunter staged an exhibition of 'curiosities'. Admission was 'one shilling per person; children, workmen and servants 6d each'. (The rate of inflation for museum admissions isn't bad - it has only gone up 20 times since then.) The museum has three main galleries, all designed to involve rather than simply explain. The dioramas are excellent; you can wander back and forth in time in the Westmorland Gallery, go on a nature trail around Morecambe Bay in the Natural History Gallery and wonder what on earth big-game were doing in the Lake District in the World Wildlife Gallery. This last gallery is fun, but doesn't have a lot to do with the area - the museum inherited a massive collection of stuffed animals and had to make a special gallery to display them in.

A new Wildlife Garden is under construction, opening in early 1989.

Open: Spring Bank Hol to October, Monday-Saturday 10.30-5.00, Sunday 2.00-5.00; rest of year Monday-Friday 10.30-5.00, Saturday & Sunday 2.00-5.00. Admission - B. Closed Good Friday, Christmas, Boxing and New Year's Day.

☆ Hall House Historic Collection

New Hutton, Kendal. Tel: Kendal 21767.

Situated on a farm, just to the east of Kendal on the A684. One of Cumbria's newest attractions, and possibly one of the oddest.

Best Things: This is another farm machinery and steam-driven implements museum. In addition to tractors, engines and vehicles, there are also musical instruments (played daily) and, the star of the exhibition, a fully-restored Churchill Tank. The restoration and transport to this Museum must have been a real labour of love.

Open: March-September, Sunday-Thursday, 11.00-5.00. Admission - B.

Keswick
☆☆ Keswick Museum and Art Gallery
Fitz Park, Keswick. Tel: Keswick 73263.

Beside Fitz Park, on the left on Station Road, going up the hill towards Keswick Spa. Parking usually quite easy.

One of Cumbria's oddest museums, more an idiosyncratic collection of strange objects than a normal little municipal museum. Almost gets three stars, just for not trying, but that would be unfair on the really professional ones at Kendal and Grasmere. Often referred to as Fitz Park Museum.

Best things: Excellent collection of letters and documents to do with Wordsworth, Southey, Coleridge and Walpole. Look out for an original copy of The Three Bears. Did you know that Southey wrote it? Bet you didn't. (In his original version it's an old woman who eats their porridge - Goldilocks is a later addition.) Of the dafter exhibits, there's a box marked '500 year-old cat - lift lid carefully'; and a set of 19th century musical stones, probably the best loved item in the museum, though the literary letters are much more valuable. Each stone gives out a different note when struck, so musical visitors can play tunes - and are allowed to, but using hands only. Can be very tiring. They were played before Queen Victoria in 1848. She was not amused.

There's a small art gallery, where exhibitions are changed each month. The Museum will also open in winter, but only for groups of ten or more.

Open: April to October, daily except Sundays, 10.00-12.30 and 2.00-5.30. Admission - A.

☆ Cumberland Pencil Museum
Southey Works, Keswick. Tel: Keswick 73626.

In the north west part of Keswick. Follow the main road out of town and it's beside the river, just before the A66 turning to Cockermouth. Plenty of parking on site. It is about 10 minutes walk from the centre of Keswick.

The museum is part of the pencil factory, now owned by Rexel.

Best things: A good museum for children - and fantastic if you happen to be a pencil freak. It has been billed as 'the story of the pencil brought to life'. (You could also call it a museum to industrial inertia, since the graphite for the pencil works now comes from abroad.) They have pencil making machines, a video display about pencils, a drawing competition, and a shop. (Where you can buy, wait for it ...pencils.) There's even a replica of a graphite mine, so you can see where the stuff comes from. Don't miss the very clever Wartime Pencils - with a secret compartment, containing a compass and a map of Germany. The museum also boasts the World's Largest Pencil (it's in the Guinness Book of Records) - 7 feet long, over 15lbs in weight, with a 1-inch diameter lead core. It was made in 1978 to raise money for Keswick Mountain Rescue. Nowadays it's a celebrity and often out and about, raising money for charity. So if you particularly want to see it, ring in advance to make sure it's in residence.

Open: All year, seven days a week, 9.30-4.00. Admission - B.

Keswick Railway Museum
1st Floor, 28 Main Street, Keswick.

One fortunate fallout from the arrival of the Timeshare johnnies into Keswick's old railway station was that the Derwent Railway Society, who have been crouching inside for some years, were forced to find new premises. They've now moved into the centre of the town, very handy for visitors, and gone properly public, which is lucky for us, opening a little museum. The only trouble is you can easily miss it, as it's upstairs above the Nat West Bank, and they're not on the phone. (I rang the bank, before I visited, to check I'd got the right address, but I don't advise it, as the bank is fed up answering calls from railway freaks.)

Best things: The main aim is to illustrate Cumbrian railway history, which they do very well, with bits of railway memorabilia, lamps, signals, instruments, buttons, photos, maps and even a video show. Small book stall, run by volunteers. Most fun thing is a working model railway of the Canadian Rockies. Don't worry about what that's got to do with Cumbria. Just enjoy it. It came from the bedroom of one of their members who died in 1982. Look carefully and you'll see how it was sculptured into the chimney breast of his bedroom. It had to be sawn up in chunks, before they could get it out of his window.

Open: Summer only, 2.00-5.00. Admission - A. Further details from the Secretary, Derwent Railway Society, 5 Manesty Rise, Low Moresby, Whitehaven CA28 6RY.

Maryport
☆ Maryport Maritime Museum
1 Senhouse Street, Maryport. Tel: Maryport 813738.

Easy to find as it's right beside the quay. Park beside the quay.

Best things: Typical in many ways of Lakeland's small museums, but neat and attractive. It is devoted almost exclusively to the history of Maryport as a maritime centre. Very important at one time. It is small, but well run on a shoestring budget using enthusiasm and invention rather than the latest wonder display techniques. A nice change from the Heritage Interpretative Visitor Centres of this world. Houses collections of photographs of old Maryport and of general maritime interest. There are also items relating to Fletcher Christian (remember Mutiny on the Bounty?) and to Thomas Henry Ismay, the founder of the White Star Line. Both local lads. The museum houses a small tourist information centre and shop.

Open: Easter to September, Monday-Saturday 10.00-5.00, Sunday 2.00-5.00. Rest of year Monday-Saturday (closed Wednesday) 10.00-12.00 and 2.00-4.00. Free admission.

☆ The Flying Buzzard

Elizabeth Dock, Maryport Harbour, Maryport.
Tel: Maryport 815954.
Now this a real novelty, more the sort of thing you'd expect to find in Liverpool or Portsmouth than a Cumbrian town. A real, genuine, Clyde tug, built in 1951 and now fully restored, and painted a foul orange colour to match Allerdale District Council's corporate colours. All done with the help of MSC volunteers.

Best Things: Well, the engine room is pretty neat, but it's hard to separate out any one item. That anyone bothered to do it all is the main wonder.

Open: March to October, Thursday 12.00-6.00, Friday-Sunday 10.00-6.00. Admission - A.

Millom
☆ Millom Folk Museum

St George's Road, Millom. Tel: Millom 2555.
If you can find Millom, finding the museum should be easy, though it is very tiny. Park in the town.

Best things: Another small museum, 'intimate' is the best description. It's a bit overcrowded, but visitors are encouraged to handle the exhibits. Pride of place goes to a reconstruction of an authentic mine drift, with a real lift cage from one of the local mines, complete with a tape recording of the lift's last journey down the mine (I wonder if the miners came up again before they took the lift away?). You can crawl round the mine drift and get an idea of what working underground must have been like. There is also a reconstruction of a miner's cottage kitchen. It is one of those places where they try to get you interested, rather than just looking at objects. Good fun. There is also a

recently-introduced exhibition about the life and work of
local poet, Norman Nicholson.

Open: Easter week, May Day weekend and Whitsun to
September, Monday-Saturday 10.00-5.00. Admission - A.

Penrith
☆☆ Penrith Steam Museum
Castlegate Foundry, Castlegate, Penrith. Tel: Penrith
62154.

It is down Castlegate from the railway station. (Or up
Castlegate towards the railway station, if you're coming
from the centre of town). Can sometimes park outside the
museum, but it is probably best to park at the station and
walk back.

The outside of the museum is a bit unimpressive - it
looks rather like a shop - but it conceals all manner of
wonders inside.

Best things: This is one of the Lake District's best 'fun'
museums - a good place to take the family. On display are
several massive steam engines, plus various agricultural
and engineering exhibits. The engines are all in working
order and most days are in operation. (But ring in advance
to make sure if you want to see them in steam.) It's a
specialist museum but it doesn't take itself too seriously
and there's enough going on to interest the casual visitor as
well as the enthusiast. One of the best museums in Lakeland and highly recommended by all the experts. Look out
for the period cottage and works office.

Open: Easter weekend and Spring Bank Holiday to September, Monday-Friday 10.00-4.30. Open Saturday and
Sunday at Bank Holidays only. Admission - B. Small tea
shop on the premises, often closed, so try pub next door.

Ravenglass
☆ Ravenglass Railway Museum
Ravenglass. Tel: Ravenglass 226.

Not hard to find as it's at the Ravenglass end of the
Ravenglass and Eskdale Railway. Parking easy.

Best things: The museum tells the story of the miniature
railway and its place in the valley. There are relics, models
and slides - all quite interesting. The best exhibit is the
Synolda engine - a twin of the original Ravenglass railway
engine which was built in 1915. It was rescued from
Bellvue Zoo and is smaller than the current railway engine.

Open: Same opening times as the railway; mid-March to
October, daily; 9.00am-6.00. Visits by appointment at any
other time. Admission - free, but donations asked for. Tea
shop on site.

Seascale
☆☆ Sellafield Visitor Centre
Seascale. Tel: Seascale 27027.

Yes, this is Windscale, the atomic place. Seascale used to be a little fishing village, right out on the west coast of Cumbria, miles from anywhere. Rail (either from Barrow or Carlisle) is probably the easiest way to get to it. There are also combined trips to get here, tying in with the Ravenglass and Eskdale Railway. Once you're within 10 miles, you can't miss it by road. (Local wits suggest you go by night and follow the glow.) Parking on site.

Best things: One of Lakeland's most biased exhibitions (probably rivalled only by the National Trust), this is basically a public relations job for British Nuclear Fuels. The present exhibition opened in June 1988 in a new, purpose-built building. The first thing which greets you as you drive in is a sign reading "Overspill Parking", which seems ominous until you realise what they're on about.

Once through the sliding doors and past the carpeted reception area, it is all very slick and impressive, with great use made of multi-slide and video presentations. Safety and the effects of radiation are dealt with straight away, though Chernobyl gets dismissed in a line (are people really soothed to learn that the average person received the same amount of radiation from Chernobyl as you'd receive from cosmic rays whilst on an airliner?). The simulated reactor interior is fairly stunning (the floor used to shake as part of the effect, but it had to be turned off because the first lot of visitors panicked). Plenty of interactive displays and buttons to press at the end of the exhibition. Ultimately, however, it is difficult not to get the impression of a controversial industry selling itself very professionally. You can easily spend a couple of hours on the exhibition itself, and there are regular bus tours of the site itself.

Hard not to recommend a visit, whatever your feelings about nuclear power. It is a great place to wander around if the weather is foul and if it encourages visitors out to the West Coast, so much the better. The easily impressed will be instantly converted by the exhibition's high tech displays, suave men in suits and the attractive ladies behind desks. Sceptics are liable to come out feeling vaguely unsatisfied.

Good cafe on site and there's a shop where you can buy rock with 'Sellafield' printed all the way through.

Open: April to October, daily 10.00-6.00; November-March 10.00-4.00. Closed Christmas Day. Free coach tours round the site available throughout the day. Day and half-day trips can be arranged by ringing Seascale 27735 (note that there is a long waiting list for these). Free admission. Of course.

Ulverston
☆ Laurel and Hardy Museum
4c Upper Brook Street, Ulverston. Tel: Ulverston 52292.

Tucked in a little side street, between King Street and The Ghyll. Easy to miss, as it's in a private house. Park at the Ghyll and walk down.

Best things: Ulverston seems an unlikely place to have 'the world's largest collection of Laurel and Hardy memorabilia', but that's because you didn't know that Stan Laurel was born in Ulverston. This museum was set up by L & H fanatic (and one-time Mayor of Ulverston), Bill Cubin. There is tons of stuff; posters, letters, portraits, possessions. You can even see L & H films - the museum has virtually every one available and shows them continually.

A definite curiosity (and not a little bonkers) but worth seeing. If you're really keen, Stan's birthplace is on the other side of town - the curator or his wife can direct you there, but all there is to see is a plaque.

Open: All year, daily except Christmas Day, 10.00-5.00. (Genuine fanatics can get in almost any time by ringing Bill Cubin at home on Ulverston 86614.) Admission - A.

Note - the Museum is hoping to stage a large celebration in 1990 to celebrate Stan's 100th birthday.

Whitehaven
☆ Whitehaven Museum
Civic Hall, Lowther Street, Whitehaven. Tel: Whitehaven 67575 (ext 307).

Best things: Used to be an excellent little local museum when it resided in the Market Place. Unfortunately its new home is less sympathetic. It has the air of a temporary exhibition staged in a local library. Attendants who have Radio 2 playing in the background don't help much. That said, the displays are good with lots of information about the town and its industries - especially mining. There are some great model ships and a fascinating bird's eye view of the town painted by Matthias Read in 1736. Look out for the St. Bees Man, the story of a 600 year old local, unearthed in 1981.

A society called the Friends of Whitehaven Museum publishes an excellent series of leaflets about the area, which are available from the Museum. They also give lectures which anyone is welcome to attend.

Open: Throughout the year (except winter Wednesdays, Sundays and Bank Holidays), Monday-Friday 9.00-5.00, Saturday 9.00-4.00. Admission free.

☆ Michael Moon's Bookshop and Gallery

41-43 Roper Street, Whitehaven. Tel: Whitehaven 62936.
Can be tricky to find, as the bookshop lurks in a side street,
away from the shops and Whitehaven's endearing one-
way system. No parking outside the shop.

Best Things: Once again, Michael Moon sails in where
others fear to tread. Whilst Whitehaven Museum lan-
guishes in the anonymous surroundings of the Civic Hall,
our intrepid bookseller has opened up a small, one room
gallery at the back of his large, second-hand bookshop. It
is liable to exhibit anything which takes his fancy, from
bookmarks to paintings. The main problem is getting past
all the books without spending all your time browsing.

Open: All year round, daily (closed Weds) 9.30 - 5.00.

Windermere

☆☆ Windermere Steamboat Museum

Rayrigg Road, Bowness. Tel: Windermere 5565.
Just out of Bowness, on Rayrigg Road. In its own
grounds by the lake and finding it is easy. Car park on site

Best things: Virtually anything set so close to a lake is
bound to be nice. This is another fairly recent museum.
There are 12 antique and vintage steamboats, well displayed but not always in steam. The best thing is undoubtedly the steamboat Osprey, which takes passengers out
onto the lake. As anyone who has been on the Gondola will
know, steamboat is the only way to travel. It is only
operating on fine days, running six or seven trips a day,
and it can only take 12 passengers. Ring in advance to
check if it is running. The museum has one of the finest
collections of steamboats in Europe. Still no proper tea
shop.

New for 1989 - a model boat pond, so you can take your
own model boat (is the Lake District really ready for this?).
The Museum hosts a couple of model boat weekends, in
May and August, plus a Steamboat Association Rally in
August.

Open: Easter to October, daily 10.00-5.00. Admission - B.

☆ Lake Windermere Aquarium

Glebe Road, Bowness-on-Windermere. Tel: Windermere
4585.
On the lakeshore on Glebe Road, about 200 yards past
Bowness Bay Information Centre and the steamer piers.
The Aquarium itself is quite small and is accompanied by
an even smaller shop, selling fishing tackle, bait and a
range of exotic shells and coral jewellry. Good for local
advice on fishing and they now hire out fishing tackle.

Best things: Amazing variety of freshwater fish, all in separate small tanks. Everyone has their favourites; the bullhead and the crayfish are fun. As you walk round the tiny, dark gallery you hear squeals as kids encounter the pike. Display itself is quite amateurish, but the fish steal the show.

Open: March to end of Autumn Half-Term, daily 10.00-6.00. Admission - A.

Workington

Helena Thompson Museum
Park End Road, Workington. Tel: Workington 62598.
Yes, even Workington has its own little museum, set in an eighteenth century house near Workington Hall. It has been here for a number of years, but only has a minuscule budget, so it doesn't go overboard on the advertising (unlike its neighbour, a few miles down the coast).

Best Things: Probably the house itself, plus the gardens. One or two nice costumes and some interesting examples of decorative art.

Open: April-October, Monday-Saturday, 10.30-4.00. November-March, Monday-Saturday, 11.00-3.00. Admission free.

Best Museums
To sum up, here in brief are our top recommendations:

Best Museum in the whole Lake District
If you can only see one, go to the Museum of Lakeland Life and Industry, Kendal. Good for museum buffs and the general public, but to make sense of the displays you really need to buy the guide when you go in.

Best Specialist (one-subject) Museum
Grasmere and Wordsworth Museum, Grasmere. The place to go if you want to learn about Wordsworth and his contemporaries.

Most Entertaining
Penrith Steam Museum, Penrith. You don't have to be a steam engine enthusiast, although it helps.

Most Idiosyncratic
Keswick Museum, Fitz Park.

Chapter Eleven

Literary Lakes

On the trail of Wordsworth and the Lake Poets, plus Miss Beatrix Potter, Mr John Ruskin and some other Literary Notables.

Admission Charges
A under £1
B £1-£2
C over £2.

Wordsworth

William Wordsworth gave us the Lakes and the Lakes gave us Wordsworth. No one should leave Lakeland without communing with Wordsworth, either by visiting one of his homes in person or remembering in spirit some of the things he wrote. As well as his poetry, he also wrote a Guide to the Lakes, a best seller in its time and still on sale today in a facsimile version. At the height of his literary fame, Poet Laureate and all that, a vicar is said to have asked him, "Excuse me, Mr Wordsworth, have you written anything else, apart from your Guide Book ? . ."

It is possible today to do a tour of the Lakes, following his life biographically. There are people, such as American and Japanese scholars, who come to the Lakes for this sole reason.

Cockermouth (born 1770)

☆☆ Wordsworth House

Main Street. Tel: Cockermouth 824805. Owned by the National Trust.

Wordsworth was born here in 1770, the second of five children of a lawyer who was an agent for the Lowther family. The house, which went with the job, is still the handsomest in Cockermouth. He wrote about it in his long poem the Prelude, bathing naked in the local river, chasing butterflies with his beloved sister Dorothy. The house and fine garden is structurally as it was, though the furniture is not Wordsworth's. Interesting china collection. A painting by Turner. Excellent coffee kitchen.

Open: Easter to Autumn Half-Term, daily 11.00-5.00 (closed Thursday), Sunday 2.00-5.00. Admission - B.

Penrith (1775-78)

Wordsworth's parents, on both sides, came from Penrith and he spent some time there as a young boy. His mother's parents had a draper's shop in the market square, though there is nothing of it now to be seen. His Penrith days were not happy. His mother died when he was eight and his father when he was 13. There was no money, as it turned out the Lowther family had not paid his father's wages. His guardians did not like him, considering him wild and unruly, and they separated him from his sister Dorothy. She was sent to live with relations, while William went to board at a little grammar school on the other side of the Lake District.

Nothing Wordsworthian can be seen in Penrith today, though you can climb the Beacon, a hill just outside the town, mentioned in the Prelude, which has good views of the Lake District. St Michael's Church, Barton, Pooley Bridge, has his grandfather's grave.

Hawkshead (1779-87)

☆☆ **Hawkshead Grammar School** No longer a school but open as a museum. The desks and books are laid out, just as they were in Wordsworth's time. (See Chapter 10.)

St Michael's Church Wordsworth described it as snow white, but it has now been un-whitewashed. Interesting church. Fine situation.

Anne Tyson's Cottage Wordsworth boarded with a 'dame', or landlady, who became a substitute mother. Now a private dwelling, called Wordsworth Lodge, but you can admire it from outside.

Old Windebrowe (1794), Brundholme, Keswick.

William and Dorothy lived here for a short time in 1794, after he had been to Cambridge and returned from France. (He had an illegitimate daughter by a French girl, a fact which was kept a secret in his own life time.) This was William and Dorothy's first home in the Lakes since childhood. Here, William nursed his friend, Raisley Calvert, who subsequently died, leaving William enough money to be able to concentrate on a career as a poet. The Wordsworth room was once open to the public, but in recent years it has been closed down. No plans to reopen in the foreseeable future, which is a shame.

(There is a small plaque outside the Robin Hood Inn, in King Street, Penrith, where Raisley Calvert died.)

Grasmere (1799-1813)

☆☆☆ Dove Cottage
Town End, Grasmere. Tel: Grasmere 544.

This is the Wordsworth shrine and the main pilgrimage centre for tourists and scholars alike. It has come to symbolise Wordsworth's philosophy of 'plain living and high thinking'. He lived longer at Rydal Mount, but by that time he was past his best as a poet. It was at Dove Cottage that his greatest works were written.

He moved in at Christmas time, 1799, with his sister Dorothy. Later he married Mary Hutchinson and three of their children were born here. He was also joined by Sarah Hutchinson, his wife's sister. Add to that a frequent flow of friends staying at this tiny, seven-roomed house and things became pretty crowded. They moved out in 1808 to a much-larger house, across the valley, but still in Grasmere.

Dove Cottage is much as it was in Wordsworth's day and is very lovingly cared for. The garden has been restored and even the old summer house rebuilt. Except during the height of summer, log fires are usually kept burning in the grates and visitors are offered a chatty and well-informed guided tour. Inside, most of the furniture is Wordsworth's and the general aim is to keep it the way it was when he lived there; the only jarring note are a few items which belonged to Wordsworth later in life, but Dove Cottage got them first and rivalry between the Wordsworth places can be fierce.

Next to the Cottage is the excellent Wordsworth Museum. Go there first, if you can. During the summer, you have to visit the Cottage early in the day as it can get very, very crowded (though even then you might run into the early morning coach parties, fresh from their hotels and wanting to blast round the cottage before heading off to Gretna Green). Wander around on your own and it's easy to imagine what it must have been like to have lived there.

Open: Now almost all year (they're closed from mid-Jan to mid-Feb), daily 9.30-5.30. Last admission - 5.00.

Admission - C (this includes Dove Cottage and special exhibitions). Special rates for families and groups.

Warning: It can get very crowded during wet weather, especially during school holidays.

Wordsworth has two other homes in Grasmere, neither of them open to the public. **Allan Bank**, where he moved in 1808, is a large house, easily seen from down by the lake as it is above the village, directly under Helm Crag. Quite a nice old house, with magnificent views over Grasmere. It is owned by the National Trust, but rented privately. Used to be white, but was repainted buff for Ken Russell's Coleridge film.

The second house is the **Old Parsonage**, opposite St Oswald's Church. Wordsworth moved there in 1811, because the chimneys at Allan Bank smoked too much and he fell out with the landlord. By 1813, two of William's children had died at the Parsonage, so he and Mary decided to quit Grasmere Vale altogether and move to Rydal.

Grasmere valley seethes with Wordsworth associations. William, Mary and Dorothy are buried in the churchyard, and they also left some of their 'pet' names on the surrounding landscape. On the road above Town End, walking towards White Moss, there is a field gate which Wordsworth used to call the 'wishing gate'. Now it is somewhat unromantically covered in barbed wire. Behind the Swan Inn, at the foot of Dunmail, is Greenhead Ghyll - the setting for Wordsworth's poem, *Michael*. Down in the village, there are no Wordsworth cafes, though it is probably only a matter of time. There is the Wordsworth Hotel, emblazoned with a facsimile of his signature, and featuring various horrors such as 'The Dove and Olive Branch Bar' (Dove Cottage was originally an inn, called the Dove and Olive Branch), the Prelude suite, etc. The hotel has no connection of any sort with Wordsworth. The same might be said of the portrait - supposedly of the poet - which hangs in the entrance hall. The whirring noise you can sometimes hear in Grasmere churchyard is Wordsworth spinning.

Rydal (1813-1850)

☆☆☆ Rydal Mount

Rydal, Ambleside. Tel: Ambleside 33002.

Rydal Mount was William's final home, until his death in 1850. In his own lifetime, it became a poetical shrine to his fans - he would sometimes receive as many as a hundred visitors a day, flocking to the gate just in the hope of a glimpse of the great man. He became Poet Laureate and would issue great pronouncements on the purpose and structure of poetry. (He has the distinction of having been a Poet Laureate who never wrote a line of official verse.) It is a somewhat grander house than their previous homes and William and Dorothy both thought they had gone up in the world. Once something of a rebel, by now William was a staunch supporter of the old order. The cuckoo clock that now hangs in Dove Cottage was once at Rydal Mount and its ticking used to soothe him to sleep. One night in 1850 it struck midnight and on the twelfth stroke, William died.

Originally a 16th century farmhouse, the house is still owned by a descendant of William's. Rather unimpressive from the outside, it is set in beautiful grounds - originally landscaped by William - and contains a lot of his furniture, manuscripts and possessions. When William died, most of his effects were sold off and bought by local people. Over the years, they have gradually been returned to their former homes.

On a fine day, Rydal Mount can be lovely and the magnificent view from the garden has hardly altered since William last saw it.

Open: March to October, daily 9.30-5.00. November to February, 10.00-4.00 (closed Thursdays during winter). Admission - B. (Groups can book evenings, complete with wine and poetry.)

At the bottom of the lane to Rydal Mount, just behind the church, is an area of land now owned by the National Trust and called Dora's Field. This has nothing to do with the daffodils of William's poem, as some visitors assume, but was a field given to his daughter by the poet. The real site for those notorious daffodils is on the west shore of Ullswater, in Gowbarrow Park (also owned by the National Trust and accessible). William and Dorothy passed through the park in 1802, when on their way to visit their friends, the Clarksons, at Eusemere, near Pooley Bridge.

The Lake Poets

Wordsworth gathered about himself quite a circle of other literary notables of the period. They became known as the Lake Poets, though in style there was little connection between them.

Samuel Taylor Coleridge was the first. As soon as the Wordsworths were installed in Dove Cottage, he moved up to Greta Hall, in Keswick, just to be near them. He would often walk over to Dove Cottage for the evening, often coming via Helvellyn. Coleridge was a notable walker and toured the Lakes extensively. In 1802, he made the first recorded ascent of Broad Stand on Scafell - a walk which has since become too dangerous to follow without ropes.

Greta Hall is now part of Keswick School and is not open to the public. Details of Coleridge's life and work can be found in the nearby Fitz Park Museum. He eventually left his family, took to drugs, lived abroad then moved to London where he died in 1834.

Robert Southey joined Coleridge at Greta Hall in 1803. They were brothers-in-law and Southey eventually ended up supporting Mrs Coleridge when her husband was pursuing Sarah Hutchinson (Wordsworth's sister-in-law) - which perhaps explains his frequent visits to Dove Cottage. Southey wrote hardly any verse directly connected with the area, but he wrote the original version of the Three Bears, a good piece of children's verse about the Lodore Falls and a fine biography of Nelson. He also wrote the first official history of Brazil and the government of that country paid for the memorial to him which is now in Crosthwaite Church, Keswick. He never went to Brazil.

Southey spent almost all his adult life in the Lakes. He became Poet Laureate in 1813 and between them, Southey and Wordsworth made the Lakes the centre of English poetry for several decades. Southey died at home in Keswick in 1843 - and Wordsworth took over as Laureate.

Thomas De Quincey is now most famous for writing a book called *Confessions of an English Opium-Eater*, but he also wrote a wonderful book of gossip and memories of the Lake Poets, called simply, *Recollections of the Lakes and Lake Poets*. He was an early fan of Wordsworth - although the great man treated him rather badly later in life - and made three separate attempts to visit his hero at Dove Cottage, coming up all the way from Oxford. Each time his nerve failed him and he retreated. He finally got there in 1807 and eventually took over the lease when Wordsworth and family moved out. Dorothy made him some curtains and was amazed at the huge quantities of books he installed in the house. He upset the family almost at once by knocking down their summer house and cutting down the orchard to let more light into the Cottage. Dorothy refused to speak to him after that. The Wordsworths further snubbed him when he began an affair with a local farmer's daughter, whom he eventually married. She came from Nab Cottage. It is beside the A591, looking over Rydal Water. it is not strictly open to the public, but they still have De Quincey's desk there. He moved into The Nab in 1829, though he still kept on Dove Cottage to house all the books. In 1835, he tried to buy it for £130.

De Quincey became the second editor of *The Westmorland Gazette* but got the sack for not going to the office. He was a tenant of Dove Cottage for 27 years, though only lived there for 15 years. He died in Edinburgh in 1859.

Dove Cottage still houses several items of interest to De Quincey enthusiasts, including his opium balance (he wrote *Confessions* whilst he was there) and some fascinating portraits. The house is described very well in *Recollections*.

Sir Walter Scott, the novelist, was a frequent visitor to the Lakes and a friend of the Lake Poets. He first came as a guest of Wordsworth and stayed with him at Dove Cottage. He was so put off by the meals (too much 'plain living' for his tastes) that he used to climb out of his bedroom window every morning and go to the Swan Inn in the village for a proper breakfast, before returning and getting back into bed as if nothing had happened.

He used Castle Rock in St John's-in-the-Vale as the setting for 'The Bridal of Triermain'.

William Hazlitt, the writer, visited Southey at Greta Hall, but left in a rush, pursued by villagers, having got himself rather too involved with one of the local girls.

Keats came to the area in 1818, visited Rydal Mount to see Wordsworth and climbed up to the waterfalls at Stock Ghyll in Ambleside. He also climbed Skiddaw and described Castlerigg Stone Circle as:

> like a dismal cirque
> 'Of Druid stones, upon a forlorn moor'.
> *(Hyperion II, 34-5)*

John Ruskin
☆☆☆ Brantwood
East of Lake, 2 miles from Coniston Village. Tel: Coniston 41396.

John Ruskin, art-critic, writer, philosopher and champion of many social causes, first came to the Lakes as a young boy in 1824. In 1871, at the age of 52, he decided to settle here and bought Brantwood on Coniston for £1,500, without even first seeing the place. "Any place opposite Coniston Old Man *must* be beautiful", he said. In the event, he got "a mere shed of rotten timbers and loose stone", but he transformed it into a beautiful home, stocked it with are treasures (particularly the paintings of Turner, of whom he was an early champion) and lived there for the last 30 years of his life. Today, Brantwood is open to the public (which was Ruskin's original wish) and its enthusiastic curator, Bruce Hanson, is transforming it into an excellent museum and country house. It now rivals the other Lake District big guns (Dove Cottage, Hill Top and Rydal Mount).

The house contains many of Ruskin's paintings and possessions. Look out for the Ruskin designed wallpaper in the downstairs rooms. Nice to see the political message of his writings coming across in a new video of his life and work, on constant show in one of the downstairs rooms. Ruskin fought hard against the worst aspects of Victorian society and values. Sobering to realise how much of his message is relevant today.

Next to the house is the Wainwright Room - a sort of shrine to the Blessed Wainwright. The room was chosen (or approved, rather) by AW himself and is in Brantwood's old printing room. It contains his desk, pipe and a pair of his boots, along with copies of the books, first editions and the original Gazette printing press which ran off the first editions, along with printing plates and original drawings. In need of a more professional touch, but a good idea.

A new landscape gardener, Sally Beamish, hopes to develop the 15 acre garden in the spirit of Ruskin (he abhorred 'fashionable' gardens). Brantwood stands in 250 acres of grounds and there's a good nature trail. There is now a new jetty to bring people across to Brantwood by the Gondola service, with the possibility of a privately-run launch operating from the Coniston Boating Centre in 1989.

Excellent tearooms, now called The Jumping Jenny (named after Ruskin's boat) and open to non-visitors to the house (the wood stove is very welcoming in winter). Upstairs is a craft gallery, called The Necessary Angel. Also a good book shop, in the house.

Open: Mid-March to mid-November, daily 11.00-5.30. November to March, Wednesday-Sunday 11.00-4.00. Admission - C.

There is a **Ruskin Museum** down in Coniston village, which is of interest, and a monument to him at Friar's Crag on Derwentwater, which bears the following quote from him: "the first thing I remember as an event in life was being taken by nurse to the brow at Friar's Crag on Derwentwater".

Beatrix Potter

Beatrix Potter was a Londoner, born there in 1866, but her family had connections with Lancashire cotton and she spent her holidays from the age of 16 in the Lake District, in rented, but rather grand houses, round Windermere and Derwentwater. Her parents were genteel, upper middle class Edwardians and she was educated at home and expected to devote her life to her parents, or get married. She found an outlet for artistic talents in drawing and painting "little books for children" and encouraged by the family's Lakeland friend, Canon Rawnsley, her first book, Peter Rabbit, was published in 1901.

The money she made with her books she used to buy Hill Top Farm at Near Sawrey in 1905. Over the next eight years, she wrote another 13 children's books, mostly while she was in the Lake District. In 1913, she married William Heelis, a local solicitor, and after that devoted her life to her farms and to the preservation of the countryside, doing a great deal to help the work of the National Trust, thanks again to the friendship and encouragement of Canon Rawnsley.

Beatrix Potter died in 1943. All her property, 15 farms

with their Herdwick flocks, many cottages and 4,000 acres of land, came to the National Trust. She asked that the Herdwicks, her favourite sheep, should continue to be bred, and that both farms and cottages should have local, reliable, tenants. Most of her original paintings eventually came to the Trust and can now be seen in the new Hawkshead Gallery -

☆☆ Beatrix Potter Gallery

Hawkshead. Tel: Ambleside 33883. For details see Chapter 10.

☆☆ Hill Top

Near Sawrey. Tel: Hawkshead 334.

Beatrix Potter built an extension on the house for her tenant farmer, but kept the original 17th century building for her own use. She wrote many of her books there and sometimes was able to stay for a few nights but at no time did she actually live there. Nearby Castle Cottage became her home after she married William Heelis.

Hill Top, which contains Beatrix Potter's furniture, is small and very popular, with 90,000 visitors going through it in the peak year of 1979. It is the duty of the National Trust to protect its properties, in this case against the fabric of the building being eroded by the sheer number of visitors, so restrictions have been introduced by limiting numbers allowed into the house at any one time, making no reductions for parties, not permitting coaches and shutting the house on Fridays. it must be one of the very few houses open to the public where they go to such lengths to restrict the public. Best to go mornings.

Open: Easter to October, 10.00-4.30, daily except Thursday and Friday. Admission - C.

☆☆ Mirehouse

Bassenthwaite Lake, Keswick. Tel: Keswick 72287.

The final major literary home in the Lakes which is open to the public is Mirehouse on the eastern shore of Bassenthwaite, four miles north of Keswick on the A591. It was once the home of James Spedding, a noted literary figure of the 19th century, the author of a 14-volume biography of Francis Bacon. One of his more notable visitors at Mirehouse was Tennyson, who stayed there whilst working on his vision of the Arthur Legend. He used Bassenthwaite in his description of Arthur's death - it was on this lake that the black barge bore away King Arthur's body in *Idylls of the King*.

Thomas Carlyle was a frequent visitor to Mirehouse.

He said that it was "beautiful and so were the ways of it . . . not to speak of Skiddaw and the finest mountains on earth". Not only was James Spedding the host for some of the literary notables of his day, his family also had literary connections. His father, John spent six years in the same class as Wordsworth at Hawkshead Grammar School. Some of Wordsworth's letters - along with those of Southey and Hartley Coleridge - can be seen at Mirehouse.

Still in the Spedding family, Mirehouse today is the epitome of the English country manor house. Very often a pianist is playing. The rooms are delightful, the house historic and the setting majestic. It has a nature trail in the grounds and Bassenthwaite Lake's only east-shore walk.

Mirehouse has only been recently opened to the general public and is still relatively unknown and uncrowded. The Speddings are likely to be on hand - if so, ask them to let you hear their Tennyson recording, reciting the Charge of the Light Brigade. Altogether a house not to miss.

Open: Easter to October, on Wednesdays, Sundays and Bank Holiday Mondays, 10.30-5.30. Admission - B. There is an excellent coffee shop nearby in the Old Sawmill, Dodd Wood, to which there is no admission charge.

Other Literary Connections in Lakeland

Most of the writers of the 19th century seem to have visited the Lake District and many took on holiday homes or even settled there.

Harriet Martineau, built the Knoll, at Ambleside, and lived there for 30 years. She wrote *The Complete Guide to the English Lakes* (but didn't give star ratings to anything). She was a friend of Wordsworth and her visitors included at various times Charlotte Bronte, George Elliot and Mathew Arnold.

Felicia Hemens also became a resident of Ambleside and lived at Doves Nest. Not very famous today, but she wrote *The Boy Stood on the Burning Deck* and spawned a host of parodies.

Charles Dickens and **Wilkie Collins** toured the area in 1857, describing their travels in *The Lazy Tour of Two Idle Apprentices*. They stayed at the Queen's Head Inn at Hesket Newmarket (now a private house) and went on an ill-advised expedition to climb Carrock Fell, getting caught in rain and mist.

Sir Hugh Walpole moved to Brackenburn in 1923, a house on the south-west shore of Derwentwater. His four famous *Herries* novels were set in Borrowdale. The home of Judith Parish can be seen at Watendlath, beside the tarn.

Arthur Ransome lived near Coniston and used settings from Windermere and Coniston for his *Swallows and Amazons.*

Literary Events

Winter Wonderland A winter service on Windermere, pointing out all the literary associations. Followed by coach to Grasmere and a visit to Dove Cottage, tea at the restaurant, and finally, a nice highlight to the trip, a candlelit wine reception and poetry reading at Rydal Mount. Runs Saturdays, November to March. Details from Bowness Bay Boating Company on Windermere 3360.

Wordsworth Winter School, and also Summer Conference and Book Collectors Weekend. Details from Dove Cottage.

Literary Lunch. An annual lunch, open to the public, in which prizes for the Lakeland Book of the Year are awarded. Details from Cumbria Tourist Board.

Samuel Taylor Coleridge

Chapter Twelve

Homes and Gardens

No, this is not a chapter about glossy magazines but a look at some of the more stately and historic delights of Cumbria. As elsewhere in Britain, many owners of grand homes have had to open up in recent years and let the rest of us come in and gape, or have handed them over to public or other bodies who now care for them. We also consider the Best Gardens, Castles, Old Mills. Then we end on Churches and Ancient Monuments.

Admission Charges

> **A** under £1
> **B** £1-£2
> **C** over £2.

Note well: Several of the big Stately Homes now close on Fridays and Saturdays, so check in advance.

☆☆ Belle Isle

Windermere. Tel: Windermere 3353.

A 38-acre island, right in the middle of Windermere. Has been in the ownership of the Curwen family for 220 years, a notable Cumbrian family. Wordsworth's son married a Curwen.

The house is circular, said to be the only truly circular house in the country. Of endless fascination to architects who try to work out where the sewage went, (in a pit under the house), what happened to the chimneys (hidden behind a dome on the roof) and what about the corridors (there aren't any - all rooms connect). Inside the 20 bedroomed house there are some good paintings, notably by Reynolds and Romney.

Open: Belle Isle is now a conference centre and has closed to the general public, which is very sad. The only way the ordinary visitor can now see it is from Cockshott Point or the passenger ferry. However, the house is open to booked parties of 20 or more, with coffees, lunches and teas offered. Also dinner parties can be arranged. Telephone for a detailed and attractive brochure if you're interested in a rather unique location for your next works conference.

Castle Dairy

Wildman Street, Kendal. Tel: Kendal 22170

Originally the dairy which served Kendal Castle and was in use when Katherine Parr lived there. It is now the oldest habitable stone-built house in the area. Of Tudor design, it was restored in 1564.

Open: Easter to September, Wednesdays only, 2.00-4.00. Admission - A (still only 5p).

☆☆☆ Dalemain

Penrith. Tel: Pooley Bridge 450

A large, Georgian-fronted house visible from the A592, with extensive grounds. The house itself is medieval, Elizabethan and early Georgian. Fascinating architecturally and contains family portraits of the Hasells, who have lived there since 1665. A magnificent garden and a fantastic tea shop in a baronial hall. Probably *the* best house to see in the northern lakes, if you've only time for one.

The garden is famous for its rare trees and shrubs. So is Mrs McCosh, the Lady of the House. Look out for her digging. Small museum of agricultural bits and pieces in the 16th century barn.

Open: Easter to mid-October, Sunday-Thursday 11.15-5.00. Admission - C.

☆ Holesfoot

Maulds Meaburn, Appleby. Tel: Appleby 51458

Just off the B6260, between Orton and Appleby. Parking on site.

Used to promote itself as Holesfoot Ancestral Research Centre, but now more a leisure park. A sort of smaller Lowther. The Research Centre is really a barn with interesting information about local ancient families, including portraits of the Clifford family, on loan from Abbot Hall and the National Portrait Gallery. The grounds are great for children; grass sledging, roller skating, assault course and BMX track - all with supervision and safety gear. Good place to lose the kids for a picnic. The latest attraction is a Victorian Bakehouse, where you can bake your own loaf in a genuine Victorian bread oven (one day we will compile a list of the ten oddest attractions in Cumbria ...)

Open: Easter, then late May Bank Holiday until mid-September, daily 10.30-5.00. Admission - B. (Good cafe on site with homemade fare.)

☆☆ Holker Hall

Cark-in-Cartmel, Grange-over-Sands. Tel: Flookburgh 328

An outstanding country house, dating back to the 17th century. Owned by the Cavendish family. The site itself used to belong to Cartmel Priory. Contains some beautiful examples of panelling and wood carving and some rare paintings. Including works by Van Dyke and Joshua Reynolds. It is a magnificent 'stately home' but without ropes and restrictions. The gardens are wonderful and contain what is said to be the oldest monkey puzzle tree in the country.

There's a lot going on at Holker, which can sometimes put you off as it sounds more like a country fair than a stately home. There are often model aircraft rallies, hot-air ballooning, vintage car rallies. If you want to see the house and grounds at their best, go when none of these wonders is on. The gardens are best in early summer. Cafeteria, playground, twee gift shop.

Open: Easter Sunday to October, daily (except Saturdays) 10.30-6.00. Last admission 4.30. Admission - B/C (very complicated). Also the site of the Lakeland Motor Museum (see Chapter 10) for which there is yet an additional fee.

☆☆ Hutton-in-the-Forest

Penrith. Tel: Skelton 500

Situated just off the B5305 between Penrith and Wigton, this was originally a 14th century pele tower with 17th, 18th and 19th century additions. It is the home of Lord Inglewood. It has a nice, amateur feel to it and you sense that the running of it isn't too severely professional. You get the distinct feeling that the occupants are around. Which they usually are. Very satisfying, architecturally, it is like visiting three stately homes in one.

Good gardens with some excellent tree specimens. Tea shop very good. Note the peculiar opening days. You have to be smart to catch it open.

Open: Easter Bank Holiday, then May to September, Thursday, Friday, Sunday and Bank Holidays; 1.00-4.00. Parties by arrangement at any time. Admission - C (children free).

☆☆☆ Levens Hall

Nr. Kendal. Tel: Sedgwick 60321.

Five miles south of Kendal, situated by Levens Bridge. Magnificent Elizabethan mansion, although it originally began as a Norman Pele Tower. Some fine paintings, furniture and plaster-work to be seen. Fascinating fireplace in the south drawing room with carvings depicting the four seasons, the four elements and the five senses. Very good topiary garden laid out in 1692.

Levens Hall is trying very hard to be a stately home on the southern model, providing lots of fun for kiddies, of all ages, such as their Steam Collection (in steam on Sunday afternoons and Bank Holidays). The House is run, owned and lived in by the Bagot family. It can be a bit too commercial for some tastes, but they are trying. Still rather more discreet and tasteful than Holker Hall. Look out for their special exhibition on Admiral Percy who started as a midshipman with Nelson on HMS Victory.

There are occasional guided tours of the garden, conducted by Chris Crowder (now the Blue Peter gardener). These are very good - informative and relaxed, and the gardens are improving all the time. Telephone for times and details.

Gift shop, of course, and licensed tearooms which do light lunches and ices.

Open: Easter Sunday to September; daily, except Friday and Saturday, 11.00-5.00. Admission - C (gardens only - B).

☆ Lowther Park
Hackthorpe, Penrith. Tel: Hackthorpe 523

Not exactly a stately home but in the tradition of some of the more modern commercial ones. Lowther Castle is now a facade, most of the interior having been pulled down. It was, in any case, an early 19th century Gothic mansion, rather than a true castle. Lowther Park now houses adventure playgrounds, assault course, mini race track and a resident circus, which is included in the admission price. A fun day out for all the family, so they say. Lowther connection apart, however, it's not unique and there are similar attractions farther south. Surely you aren't already bored with mountains and lakes?

Open: Easter Bank Holiday, then weekends only until late May. Late May to mid-September; daily, 10.00-6.00. Admission - C(+). Children under three years old, free (wow).

☆☆ Muncaster Castle
Ravenglass. Tel: Ravenglass 614

The Scots are indirectly responsible for the architecture of many of Cumbria's historic homes. Like many others, Muncaster Castle is based on a defensive pele tower, built in 1325, to keep them at bay. In the 1860s, the fourth Lord Muncaster had it rebuilt to make a tasteful mansion, still lived in by the Pennington family as their ancestral home since the 13th century. Contains furniture, tapestries and paintings, including some by Reynolds and Gainsborough.

The gardens are magnificent in early summer, when the rhododendrons and azaleas are at their best. Viewed against the background of the Lakeland fells, they are spectacular. One of the finest displays in Europe.

The bird garden also contains wallabies, the only chance to see wallabies in Lakeland. (Not wallies - they can be seen any time in Bowness during the summer.) Muncaster Castle is now the headquarters of the British Owl Breeding and Release Scheme, run by well-known local ornithologist Tony Warburton.

Tearooms, but rather poor. Plus a shop and small garden centre.

Open: Easter to September, Tuesday-Sunday (but open Bank Hol Mondays). Grounds 12.00-5.00; Castle 1.30-4.30. Admission - C (castle and grounds - half price for grounds only).

☆ Naworth Castle

Near Brampton, Carlisle. Tel: Brampton 2692.

A relative newcomer to the stately home stakes, Naworth has been the home of the Earls of Carlisle for the last 700 years. Present castle dates back to 1335. Rather dour, sandstone building, but fine courtyard and inside the Great Hall has some magnificent French tapestries and there's interesting alabaster by Burne-Jones in the Library. The Hall also houses the heraldic crests and family tree of the Howard family. Not as yet a great deal to do or see, though the family is trying hard. Lady Carlisle took the tickets the day I arrived while the Hon Philip Howard was the guide. (He was wearing a rather worn 'Lonsdale' sweatshirt, tut tut. The Howards, you see, have traditionally been the rival top Cumbrian family to the Lonsdales of Lowther Castle.)

Open: Easter Sunday and Monday; then May to September, Wednesday and Sunday only - plus Saturdays in July and August - 2.00-5.00. Admission - B.

☆☆ Sizergh Castle

Kendal. Tel: Sedgwick 60285

The home of the Strickland family for 700 years. There was an original house there, but this was replaced in 1340 with a pele tower. Those Scots again. Largest tower in Cumbria still standing. The great hall was added in 1450 and some very fine panelling and carving added in Elizabethan times - some of the finest in the country. A lovely house, the gardens date from the 18th century. Great on a warm, sunny day. Now owned and run by the National Trust. And there are teas available, at long last.

Open: Easter to October, Sunday, Monday, Wednesday and Thursday 2.00-6.00. Last admission 4.00. Closed Good Friday. Admission - C (castle and grounds; grounds only are half-price).

☆☆ Townend

Troutbeck, Windermere. Tel: Ambleside 32628

This is a 1626 statesman farmer's home - rather more prosperous than your average farmhouse - in an interesting, unspoilt hamlet.

Original and surprisingly elaborate furniture and panelling. A dark little place, it contrasts with all the stately homes, but it is very typical of its period. Run by the National Trust, who have recently opened three new rooms, once used by servants. The small garden is laid out to resemble a photograph of Townend from the late 19th century.

Open: Easter to end of Autumn Half-Term, Tuesday-Friday and Sunday (but open Bank Holiday Monday) 2.00-6.00. Last admission 5.30. Admission - B.

Note: No electric light, so it may close at dusk if this is earlier.

Gardens

Many of the above mentioned homes have fine gardens which are open to the public - notably Dalemain and Sizergh. If it is only the garden you wish to see, here are the ones already listed which let you in at a reduced rate:

> Holker Hall
> Levens Hall
> Muncaster Castle
> Mirehouse, Keswick (see 'Literary Lakes')
> Sizergh Castle.

There are also a few more worth seeing in their own right which are not part of a stately home or park -

☆☆ Acorn Bank

Temple Sowerby, near Penrith.
(Six miles east of Penrith)

An outstanding collection of over 140 types of herbs in this small, walled garden belonging to the manor-house of Acorn Bank. Now owned by the National Trust. Excellent spring display.

Open: Easter to end of Autumn Half-Term, daily 10.00-6.00. Admission - A.

☆☆ Graythwaite Hall

Newby Bridge. Tel: Newby Bridge 31248
(4 1/2 miles south of Hawkshead.)

Seven acres of garden, landscaped by Thomas Mawson. Marvellous for rhododendrons and azaleas.
Open: April to June, daily 10.00-6.00. Admission - B.

✰✰✰ Lakeland Horticultural Society Garden

Holehird, Troutbeck, near Windermere
(On A592, 3/4 mile north of mini-roundabout with A591.)

Extensive grounds with vast range of plants, alpines in glass houses, hundreds of heathers. A gardener's garden.
Open: 'at reasonable times'. Free admission (but there is a donation box).

✰✰✰ Lingholm Gardens

Keswick. Tel: Keswick 72003.
(shore of Derwentwater, near Portinscale).

Formal and natural gardens, with extensive rhododendrons and magnificent woodlands. A wonderful view over the lake to Borrowdale. Garden tour. (Just a short walk from the boat landing at Low Brandlehow.)

They now have a tearoom and small garden centre.
Open: April to October, daily 10.00-5.00. Admission - B.

✰✰✰ Nunnery Walks

Nunnery House, Staffield, Penrith. Tel: Lazonby 537.
(About nine miles north of Penrith, just off the Kirkoswald Road, in the Eden Valley)

Two miles of paths through wild woodlands on the banks of the River Eden, to one of the best waterfall displays in Cumbria. Go on a nice day after heavy rainfall and it's terrific.
Open: All year, daily 9.00-6.00. Admission - A. Tearooms.

✰✰ Rydal Hall

Rydal, Ambleside. Tel: Ambleside 32050.
(Between Ambleside and Grasmere, turn off the A591 at the sign for Rydal Mount)

The Hall itself is mainly Georgian, though parts go back to before 1600, and is owned by the Diocese of Carlisle. Used for conferences, holidays and retreats, the Hall itself is not open to the public, but it stands in 30 acres of grounds and the formal gardens have recently been opened up. The gardens were originally laid out by Thomas Mawson.

It means the public can once again visit the famous Lower Falls, much painted by the Early Tourists. Nearby is the Grotto, a summer house once regularly visited by Wordsworth. The gardens also have a nice fountain and splendid views over Rydal to Lake Windermere.
Open: Daily, all year. Admission - free, but donations welcome. Self-guiding leaflet available at the gate.

Halecat

Witherslack, nr. Grange-over-Sands. Tel: Witherslack 229.

A newcomer to the list of Cumbrian gardens. This was opened in 1988 and features a small garden, nicely laid out with shrubs and trees. Good views across Morcambe Bay.

Open: All year, Monday-Friday, 9.00-4.30; Sunday, 2.00-4.00. Admission free.

☆ Stagshaw Gardens
Ambleside. Tel: Ambleside 33265
(3/4 mile south of Ambleside on the A591)

Rhododendrons, azaleas, magnolias, all in eight acres of woodlands. Constantly developing as a memorial to the founder, Cuthbert Acland.
Open: April to June, daily 10.00-6.30. Admission - A.
Note: No tearooms and only a very small car park. Park at Waterhead and walk.

Other Gardens
Another method of seeing well laid-out formal gardens - which used to belong to the people that used to *live* in the Lakes - is to visit some of the larger ex-country houses, eg, Brockhole, which has 30 acres of grounds. Just up the road towards Ambleside is the Langdale Chase Hotel - go in for a bar lunch and then walk around the grounds. Great display and one of the best views over Windermere to the mountains from the hotel's terrace. The Storrs Hall Hotel, about three miles south of Bowness, has another good garden (and good bar lunches).

Each year the *National Gardens Scheme* publishes a list called **Gardens Open in Cumbria** - this lists a number of interesting gardens which are not normally open to the public on a regular basis, but open on selected dates during the year. Gives opening times, admission charge (if any) and who does teas. It is a free sheet, available from information centres, or send SAE to:

The National Gardens Scheme
57 Lower Belgrave Street
London SW1.

Finally, there is the **Three Gardens Package**, which is an excellent idea: Rydal Hall, Rydal Mount and Brockhole have got together to offer a package to booked groups of 10 or more. You get to tour three historic gardens (two of them laid out by Mawson) and coffees and lunches are part of the deal. The only snag is that you have to use your own transport. Details from Brockhole on Windermere 6601. (Brockhole also offers evening garden tours in summer, with Sue Tasker, their head gardener. Ring for dates.)

Castles
There are quite a few castles dotted about the fringes of the Lake District, a lot of them designed to repel the onslaughts of the marauding Scots. Some are little more than pele towers, others Neo-Gothic mansions, some simply follies, others romantic ruins.

☆☆☆ Carlisle Castle

Tel: Carlisle 31777.

Carlisle is the best by far and houses the Border Regiment Museum. Stirring history with Mary Queen of Scots and Bonny Prince Charlie connections. *Looks* like a real castle, dark and grim, not like your soft and fancy turreted Southern castles.

Open: All year. Summer, 9.30-6.30; winter and Sundays, 2.00-4.00. Admission - A.

☆ Appleby Castle

Tel: Appleby 51402.

At the top of the main street (opposite end to the church). Good car parking on site.

The castle dates from the 11th century though was largely restored by Lady Anne Clifford in 1653. The Norman keep and earthwork defences remain. Now listed as a Rare Breeds Survival Trust Centre with a wide range of unusual breeds on display - goats, cattle, sheep, ponies, chipmunks and wildfowl; plus bantams, heron, flamingos and ibis.

The Norman keep is open to the public with displays of medieval and 17th century furniture. There is also a collection of 19th century bicycles (not for breeding purposes) and you are allowed out onto the roof for wonderful views over the town. The great hall now houses a collection of Nan King porcelain. Cafe on site.

Open: Easter to October. Sunday-Thursday, 1.00-5.00. Admission - C.

Wray Castle

Low Wray, Ambleside. Tel: Ambleside 32320.

Two miles south of Ambleside, turn off the B5286 for Hawkshead at the sign for High Wray.

Not a real castle but a Victorian folly now owned by the National Trust and leased by the Wray Castle College of Marine Electronics (the only private college in the world training people for the merchant navy). Grounds have been open to the public for a number of years, but 1986 was the first year the public were allowed inside. Not a lot to see - just the hall and music room. They've really only opened it to satisfy everyone's curiosity. Beatrix Potter stayed here on her first visit to the LD at the age of 16 (her father rented it as a holiday home). Later she bought most of the land surrounding the building, though she never owned the castle itself. The grounds are very pleasant; look out for the mulberry tree planted by Wordsworth.

Open: In July and August, by arrangement only. Contact Ian Gordon at the above address.

Note: Muncaster Castle, Sizergh and Naworth Castles are covered in the Stately Homes section.

Ruined Castles

The following are ruins, open to the public or visible from the roadside:

☆☆ Brougham, Nr. Penrith

Well preserved ruin of an important castle built within the ramparts of a Roman fort. One of the castles restored by Lady Anne Clifford, and the place where she died. Best of the ruins. Run by English Heritage, with a shop on site. **Open:** 24 April to 30 September, daily. 1 October to 23 April, Tuesday to Sunday. Admission - A.

Cockermouth

Part ruined, part lived in and very rarely open to the public, except occasionally during Cockermouth Festival. Good view of the walls from beside the river.

Egremont, Nr. Whitehaven

In a public park at the south end of the town. It stands on a mound in a loop of the River Ehen. Some stylish herringbone masonry.

Kendal

An impressive stone-built affair which stands in a public park to the east of the town centre.

Kirkoswald, Nr. Penrith

A ruined tower in a farm field to the south east of the village. One of a group of castles built to deter the Scots from penetrating south and east through Mallerstang and Stainmore.

Penrith

In the public park, opposite the railway station. A favourite dwelling of Richard, Duke of Gloucester (later Richard III) when he was Warden of the West Marshes.

Piel (on Piel Island, off the coast by Barrow-in-Furness)

Built by the monks of Furness Abbey to protect their harbour from the Scots. Boats go out to it from Roa Island in summer.

Still in Cumbria, are **Brough,** also built within a Roman fort, and **Pendragon,** with its suggestion of Arthurian connections (they turn up all over Cumbria). Pendragon once guarded Mallerstang and Brough Stainmore. In the far north, uncomfortably exposed, is **Bewcastle** - you can see it when you go to see the stone cross.

Mills

There seems to be a little growth industry in Cumbrian Mills in the last few years with several being renovated and reopened, either as museums or as working mills, following centuries-old systems. Great to look at and listen to and, best of all for families, many of them do first class teas and cakes, often using their own products, made on the premises.

Here are a few of the best mills currently open to the public:

☆ Heron Corn Mill

Waterhouse Mills, Beetham, Nr Milnthorpe. Tel: Carnforth 734858

Hard to find, as you have to go through an untidy paper factory, but worth it. This was a working mill in a thriving farming community right up until 1955. There was a mill on this site as far back as 1220. Today, the mill is restored as a working museum, run as a charity, with fine displays and some old machinery grinding away. Newly opened from 1989, there is now a museum telling the history of paper making. Buy some stoneground flour before you leave.

Open: April to September, Tuesday-Sunday 11.00-5.00. Also open Bank Holidays. Admission - B. No teas - try the Wheatsheaf Hotel, just down the road.

Little Salkeld Mill

Penrith. Tel: Langwathby 523

Another water-powered corn mill, fully working and producing quite a famous range of stoneground flour. Only the shop is now open - mornings only. It's a family business - two of their children are called Snowdrop and Harvest. Ahh.

☆☆ Muncaster Mill

Ravenglass. Tel: Ravenglass 232

Yet another corn mill, with machinery dating back to the late 1700s, although there was probably a mill here before the 1400s. The watermill uses a millrace 3/4 mile long. It is in use as a working exhibition and flour is available for sale. It has a very homely, friendly atmosphere - especially when Ratty goes chugging past the door. Looks quite idyllic until you consider the amount of work which has gone into making it look that way.

Open: April, May and September, daily (except Saturdays) 11.00-5.00. June to August, 10.00-6.00.
Admission - A.

☆☆ Wythop Mill

Embleton. Tel: Bassenthwaite Lake 394.

(1/2 mile off the A66, 4 miles from Cockermouth)

An old woodworking mill which uses a working over-shot waterwheel. Originally a corn mill, it later became a sawmill around the mid-1800s. It has been fully restored and now contains a small exhibition of old woodworking machinery. The store has been converted into an excellent tea shop, serving light lunches and afternoon teas (it used to be called a coffee shop when they were open in the mornings as well). It also has a wine licence. There is a small car park.

Open: Easter to October, Sunday-Thursday, 1.00-5.00.

Churches

Cumbria has one Cathedral, several abbeys in various states of repair and a host of interesting churches. They tend not to be as ornate or rich, either outside or inside, as some southern churches. Many of them, especially near the Borders, were semi-fortified to repel raiders, but they are all rich in history and archaeological interest.

Impossible to list them all - it would take up most of the rest of the book - the Tourist Board do a leaflet *Christian Heritage Trails*, price 25p. Here are six of the most famous and interesting.

☆☆☆ Carlisle Cathedral

Began as an Augustinian church in early 12th century, promoted to cathedral in 1133 - the only Augustinian house in England to achieve this. Rather small, as cathedrals go, but has a magnificent east window, one of the best in England. The west end and transepts are the earliest parts. Most of the decorated features rebuilt following a great fire in 1292.

The Civil War took some toll on the structure and it had to wait for Victorian times for a decent restoration. Don't miss the 15th century paintings behind the choir stalls. A tour is available of the Prior's Tower - see 'museums' chapter. Next door is the very good Undercroft Buttery and a bookshop.

☆☆ Cartmel Priory

Cartmel, Nr Grange-over-Sands.

Founded by William Marshall, the Baron of Cartmel, in the late 12th century. Now nothing remaining of the original priory except the gatehouse (National Trust) and church. The gatehouse is open to the public, just off Cartmel Square (see 'museums'). The church has been restored several times and is now a collection of styles; the east window is 15th century. The best feature is the carved oak misericords, with some delightful mermaids, apes, elephants and unicorns. A very quiet, impressive church.

☆☆ Furness Abbey
Barrow-in-Furness.

Mentioned by Wordsworth, now a ruin in the care of English Heritage (the two facts are not connected). The remains are very impressive, some parts almost at their original height. It dates from around 1127 and the layout can be clearly seen - in sections, the walls rear overhead and you get the powerful feeling of the monastery's size and influence. Located in a small valley, midway between Barrow-in-Furness and Dalton, east of the A590.

☆ Holm Cultram Abbey
Abbey Town.

On the west coast, just east of Silloth, the little hamlet gets its name from the abbey, founded in 1150 (in fact, the houses, get their stone from the remains). Largely destroyed by the dreaded Scots, the remains now serve as the parish church. The west doorway is Norman and there are some good carvings.

☆☆ Lanercost Priory

Sandwiched between Brampton and Hadrian's Wall, this was an easy target for the Scots (more so than for the tourist). The nave is used as the parish church and the ruins are surprisingly intact almost as impressive as Furness, and now cared for by English Heritage. As at Furness, the admission is restricted to working hours (9.30-5.30).

☆ Shap Abbey

Set in a valley one mile west of Shap, it was founded in 1180. One of the few Premonstratensian abbeys standing. In a nice setting, you come upon in unexpectedly. The tower is the only part relatively intact, though you can still see the layout. If you want to see some of the stones that were once part of the Abbey, look closely at Lowther Castle.

☆ Quaker Meeting House
Mosedale

The Quakers have strong roots in Cumbria, dating back to George Fox's early years. (He married Margaret Fell of Swarthmoor Hall, Ulverston.) In 1653 he came to preach at Mosedale, a tiny hamlet south of Caldbeck, and later a Meeting House was built there which still stands today. It's been exquisitely restored and although small and humble, just one room, it's well worth stopping for, especially as in the summer, Tuesday to Saturday, they serve rather nice teas.

Other Churches

Almost every town or village in the Lakes has a church of some interest, although some are little more than a stone cabin (look at Wythburn). Some very remote, such as the ones in St John's-in-the-Vale and Wasdale.

In the towns, especially on busy days, they make a perfect escape from the noise and bustle and, apart from Grasmere Churchyard, where everyone is searching for the Wordsworth graves, their churchyards are usually completely ignored. Out favourite parish churches and churchyards are as follows:

St Martin's, Bowness. Excellent stained glass window.

St Michael's, Hawkshead. Brilliant views.

St John's, Keswick. More brilliant views.

St Kentigern's, Crosthwaite, Keswick. Late perpendicular.

St Anthony's, Cartmel Fell. Marvellous isolation.

All Saints, Cockermouth. Large, Victorian sandstone.

St Michael's, Isel. Perfect little Norman church.

St James's, Whitehaven. Spectacular Georgian interior.

St Andrew's, Dacre. Don't miss the four amazing bears, at each corner of the churchyard, but if the vicar sees you photographing them, there could be a fee . . .

St Mary's, Ambleside. Victorian built, but interesting memorabilia.

St Oswald's, Grasmere. Follow the crowds to THE grave.

Ancient Monuments

Loads of good archaeological sites, but for many of them you'd need a magnifying glass and a portable archaeologist. Here are the ones where you can actually see something.

☆☆☆ Bewcastle Stone Cross

One of the oldest and most magnificent crosses in Europe. In the churchyard of the village (north of Hadrian's Wall and only just in Cumbria), it is a beautifully carved sandstone cross, over 1,300 years old and over 13 foot high. Covered with incredible carvings. Amazing that it is still left outside, exposed to all weathers, and not indoors at the British Museum. (Let's hope the sneaks don't steal it, hoping for a swap . .). Both church and cross stand within the ramparts of a Roman fort.

☆☆ Gosforth Cross

Another sandstone cross, this one Viking and over 12 foot high. Tall and slender it looks frighteningly fragile and is covered with mythological heroes and Viking legends. Situated in the churchyard at Gosforth, on the west coast by Wasdale.

☆ Irton Cross

In Irton churchyard, just north of Ravenglass, near Santon Bridge a near perfect Anglian cross over 1000 years old. Intricately decorated with Runic inscriptions and patterns.

☆ Galava Roman Fort

The remains of a Roman fort at Waterhead, just south of Ambleside. Old local name is Borrans Fort. The foundations remain and the original fort probably dates from around AD79. The field in which it stands is owned by the National Trust. To get a really good view of the layout, climb Todd's Crag on Loughrigg and look down on it.

☆☆ Hardknott Roman Fort

Near the top of the pass, on the left as you go up from Eskdale. You can easily miss it from the road. One of the best Roman forts in Britain, set on a dramatic site guarding the road from Galava to Glannaventa (Ravenglass). The parade ground is fascinating and the views fantastic. The Roman name was Mediobogdum and the walls still stand, though not very high. Worth investigating.

Stone Circles

☆☆ Castlerigg

Just off the A66, before you get into Keswick from the south. It has a fantastic setting, surrounded by high fells, though the stones themselves are not very impressive; 38 of them in a circle, roughly 90 feet across. About 3 to 4,000 years old, its purpose is entirely unknown.

☆☆ Long Meg and her Daughters

Near Little Salkeld, just north of Penrith, the circle is huge, nearly 300 feet wide. Long Meg is the tallest of 27 stones, about 9 foot high and covered with mysterious symbols. The 'daughters' are the other stones and the circle probably dates from around 1,500 BC. Off the beaten track, but an incredible place.

Now for an oddity -
☆☆☆ The Bowder Stone

One of Lakeland's most famous features, this is a large, isolated rock, apparently in a state of delicate balance (30 feet high, 60 long and about 1,900 tons of it). Stands away from the rock face, overlooking the valley. How it got there, no one knows. A ladder allows you to climb to the top. It is perfectly safe, but just try walking under the overhanging sides of it - quite unnerving. Located in Borrowdale valley, with a nearby car park and well-marked footpath to it.

Chapter Thirteen

People, customs, phrases

Apart from all those Big Literary Names, from W. Wordsworth to B. Potter, who will for ever be associated with the Lake District, there are quite a few other more local people, from different walks of life, whose names you might come across when exploring Cumbria, or wonder at references to them which don't quite make sense, at least to outsiders. Here's a brief selection, plus some handy customs and curiosities, phrases and words which might be useful when talking to the locals.

People

Joe Bowman Huntsman of the Ullswater hounds from 1879 to 1924. Died in 1940, aged 90. Smart hunting folks maintain he was a better breeder than John Peel, though he is remembered only in local Cumbrian hunting circles.

Mary of Buttermere, or Maid of Buttermere. Mary Robinson, a beautiful innkeeper's daughter, was wronged by a blackguard who bigamously married her in 1802. Her case became the talk of the nation, was turned into a West End melodrama and mentioned by Wordsworth in the Prelude. She is buried in Caldbeck Church. Now recreated in a successful novel by Melvyn Bragg.

The Lowthers Cumbria's ruling family. For 400 years they have been the most dominant, wealthiest and most innovative family in the whole region. The present head of the family is the Seventh Earl of Lonsdale, James Lowther, who lives at Hackthorpe, near Penrith. A recent survey named him as the 19th richest man in the UK, worth £100 million. Their ancestral home, Lowther Castle, which is nearby, is now empty, a romantic ruin. At one time, they were like feudal kings in Cumbria, lords of all they surveyed. Wordsworth's father worked for them and

Wordsworth himself, having started off hating them, became very keen to have their patronage and friendship. They were behind the industrial mining and shipping development of West Cumbria from the 18th century. Throughout Cumbria today, you will still see references to the Lowther family, in street names, shops, cinemas, and now in horse trials and a country park. It was the fifth Earl, an eccentric spendthrift who was passionate about sport, and gave his name to the famous Lonsdale Belt for boxing. He was also passionate about the colour yellow, and made all his servants wear yellow livery. The Automobile Association, for whom he was first President, took their colour from him . . . To this day, Cumbrian Tories at election time always sport yellow, not blue as elsewhere in the land. All because of the Yellow Earl.

John Peel (1777-1854). Huntsman, born and lived in the Caldbeck area, a legend in his lifetime, if only a local one, for his passion for the hounds. He devoted all his energies to them, often at the expense of his own family. A much more selfish, unattractive figure than his legend might suggest. The famous song which commemorates him, now the Cumbrian national anthem and known throughout the English speaking world, was never heard by Peel himself. The words were put to the present tune fifteen years *after* his death. He died in 1854 and is buried in Caldbeck churchyard. His grave is well worth a visit, unless the anti-bloodsports supporters have vandalised it again.

St Kentigern - Better known as St Mungo. While the rest of England was still heathen, he came down from Scotland in 550 and established churches in Cumbria, notably at Keswick, Caldbeck, Mungrisdale and Crosthwaite.

Canon Rawnsley (1851-1920) of Crosthwaite Church, Keswick. A founder of the National Trust and one of Lakeland's great activists and preservationists.

Will Ritson (1808-1890). An innkeeper at Wasdale Head. He claimed to be a personal friend of Wordsworth and De Quincey. He also claimed that he was the biggest liar in England. An annual competition is still held in West Cumbria to find the biggest liar of the year. No politicians need apply.

Wonderful Walker Rev Robert Walker (1709-1802). Curate of Seathwaite in the Duddon Valley, known throughout Lakeland for his care and kindness. Despite living on a pittance all his life, gave endlessly to the poor. Written about by Wordsworth in his Duddon sonnets.

Famous Residents

People who were born, died or lived for some time in the Lake District.

Katherine Parr (wife of Henry VIII), lived Kendal 1512.

George Fox, founder of the Quakers, lived in Ulverston, 1670-75.

George Romney, artist, born Dalton-in-Furness 1734, died Kendal 1802. Buried Dalton.

Fletcher Christian, *Bounty* mutineer, born Cockermouth 1764.

John Dalton, atom theorist, born Eaglesfield, Cockermouth 1766.

William Wordsworth, poet, born Cockermouth 1770, died Rydal, 1850.

Samuel Taylor Coleridge, poet, lived Keswick, 1800-1810.

Robert Southey, poet, lived Keswick, 1803-1843.

Thomas De Quincey, writer, lived Grasmere, 1803-30.

William Wilberforce, lived Windermere, 1780-88.

John Peel, huntsman, born and died Caldbeck, 1776-1854.

John Wilson (alias Christopher North), writer, lived Windermere, 1807-15.

Percy Bysshe Shelley, lived Keswick 1811-12.

Dr Thomas Arnold, headmaster, retired to Ambleside 1834-42.

Matthew Arnold, poet, son of Thomas, lived Ambleside 1834-42.

Harriet Martineau, writer, lived Ambleside 1844-76.

W E Forster, educational reformer, lived Ambleside, 1850.

John Ruskin, writer, artist, lived Coniston 1871-1900, died Coniston, buried Coniston.

Stan Laurel (of Laurel and Hardy), born Ulverston 1890.

Canon Rawnsley, writer, preservationist, lived Keswick 1901-20.

Beatrix Potter, children's writer, lived Sawrey 1906-43, died Sawrey.

Arthur Ransome, children's writer, lived Coniston 1930-1967.

Sir Hugh Walpole, writer, lived Derwentwater 1932-41, died Derwentwater, buried Keswick.

Lord (Norman) Birkett, judge, born Ulverston, 1883, died 1962.

Kurt Schwitters, German artist, died Kendal 1948.

Kathleen Ferrier, singer, 1912-1953, lived Silloth and Carlisle.

Norman Nicholson, poet, born Millom 1914, died 1987.

George MacDonald Fraser, writer, born Carlisle 1925.

Lord (Willie) Whitelaw, lives near Penrith.

A Wainwright, the one and only, lived in Kendal since 1941.

Sir Fred Hoyle, scientist, lived Ullswater since 1970s.

Margaret Forster, writer, born Carlisle 1938.

Melvyn Bragg, author, broadcaster, born Wigton 1939.

Chris Bonington, mountaineer, lived Caldbeck since 1974.

Doug Scott, mountaineer, lived Hesket Newmarket since 1982.

Anna Ford, broadcaster, brought up in Wigton and Brampton.

Ken Russell, film director, has a home in Borrowdale.

Victoria Wood, comic, can sometimes be seen swimming in Kendal baths. Lives in Arnside.

Famous Visitors

Agricola, Roman governor, campaign in Cumbria AD79.

St Cuthbert, visited Carlisle and district 685.

David I, King of Scotland, died Carlisle 1153.

Edward I, Hammer of the Scots, died Burgh-by-Sands 1307.

Robert the Bruce, plundered Cumbria 1314.

Mary, Queen of Scots, imprisoned Carlisle Castle 1568.

Celia Fiennes, traveller, visited Lakes, 1698.

Bonnie Prince Charlie, captured Carlisle, 1745, marched through Cumbria.

John Wesley, evangelist, toured Lakes area, 1759.

Thomas Gray, poet, travel writer, toured Lakes 1767, 1769.

Benjamin Franklin, US statesman, stayed Derwentwater 1772.

Charles Lamb, writer, stayed Keswick 1802.

John Paul Jones, US sailor, raided Whitehaven, 1778.

William Hazlitt, writer, stayed Keswick 1803.

Sir Walter Scott, writer, regular visitor to Lakes 1805-25.

Sir Humphrey Davy, scientist, stayed Grasmere 1805.

John Constable, painter, two months in Lakes 1806.

George Canning, statesman, visited Lakes 1814, 1825.

Robert Owen, reformer, visited Lakes 1817.

William Wilberforce, philanthropist, stayed Rydal and Keswick 1818.

John Keats, poet, visited Lakes, climbed Skiddaw 1818.

Ralph Waldo Emerson, American essayist, visited Lakes 1833.

John Stuart Mill, philosopher, stayed Keswick 1833.

Lord Tennyson, poet, stayed Bassenthwaite 1835, honeymoon Coniston 1850.

Branwell Bronte, worked as tutor, Broughton-in-Furness 1840.

Thomas Carlyle, visited Bassenthwaite, 1840s-70s.

Charlotte Bronte, writer, stayed Ambleside 1849, 1850.

Mrs Gaskell, writer, stayed Ambleside 1850.

Charles Dickens, writer, toured Lakes, climbed Carrock Fell 1857.

Wilkie Collins, writer, toured with Dickens 1857.

Donald Campbell, racing driver, killed Coniston 1967.

Customs and Curiosities

Buttermere Round A coach trip in the olden days from Keswick down Borrowdale and over Honister to Buttermere then over Newlands back to Keswick. Passengers had to get off and walk up all the steep hills. References still seen in old Lakeland engravings and writings.

Char Windermere contains a unique species of fish called Char. It's a form of trout, a very ancient fish, thought to have been left behind after the Ice Age and got stuck, unable to migrate. Potted char and char pies were considered a great delicacy in the last century and were exported to London. Now only a few amateur char fishermen survive on Windermere.

Dry Stone Walls Walls without mortar or cement, put together by hand, from natural stones and slates. A much harder art than it appears. Between 1750-1850, most of the open fells were enclosed, or divided by these walls, even up to the mountain tops, an enormous undertaking, yet many of them still stand intact to this day.

You can have a go at doing it yourself at Brockhole or join a properly organised Dry Stone Walling Meet which the National Park people run. You spend a day with a Ranger, learning how to construct a dry stone wall. Most people turn up just to watch, then find themselves joining in. In 1985, an elderly American lady joined in, wearing a white suit.

Fell Ponies A distinctive feature of the Northern and Eastern Fells. Mostly black, brown or bay, they roam wild in groups round the open fellside and commons. In bad weather, they gather near villages or on minor roads. They appear to be *completely* wild, and are allowed to breed and wander freely, but they do have owners, so don't try to steal any. Formerly they pulled small farm carts or worked down the mines. Now very popular as children's ponies.

Gurning A traditional event, going back 700 years, which is held annually at the Egremont Crab Fair. Much loved by the British Tourist Authority and Americans. Competitors have to put on a horse collar and make the most ridiculous or ugly face.

Hodden grey A type of undyed, grey cloth, very hard wearing, mentioned in the John Peel song, 'coat so grey'. On no account make the mistake of singing in 'coat so gay'. Tut, tut.

Merry Neet A merry night, Cumbrian style, with singing and entertainment, traditionally after fox hunting.

Ratty Or La'al Ratty, meaning Little Ratty. Nickname for the preserved railway line at Ravenglass.

Rushbearing Annual ceremony at Grasmere Church, and elsewhere, to commemorate the renewal of rushes which were laid on the bare church floor every August, then taken up in the Spring.

Spinning galleries Wooden balconies on farm buildings where the wool was spun. Best known example, see all those post cards, is Yew Tree Farm near Coniston.

Statesman Ancient name for yeoman farmer, independent small farmers, with perhaps no more than 50-100 acres. They still make up most of the central farming community.

Words and Phrases

They all speak English, so in theory you should not have too many problems . . .

Norse Origins Their accents and place names often betray the influence of earlier settlers, especially Norse, and it is as well when map reading to know the meaning of the more common words which are peculiar to Cumbria.

Beck = stream
Blea = blue
Fell = mountain, open hill slopes
Force = waterfall
Garth = enclosure, field
Ghyll/gill = narrow ravine, usually with a stream
Grange = outlying farm belonging to a monastery
Hause = narrow pass
Holm = island
How = small hill, mound
Intake = land enclosed from waste
Kirk = church
Mere = lake, pool
Nab = projecting spur
Nes = headland, promontory
Pike = sharp summit, peak
Scree = loose stones, debris
Skarth = gap in a ridge
Tarn = small mountain lake
Thwaite = clearing in a forest

Sheep Names

The local names for ages and sex of sheep also betray their Norse origins and are still in common use. Yow means ewe, gimmer means a yearling, tup means a male, hogg is a last year's lamb, twinter is a two year-old, trinter a three year-old.

However, when Cumbrian farmers count their sheep they use an ancient Celtic form of counting. Even non farming Cumbrians, in the big smoke like Carlisle say yan for one and yance for once. Counting up to twenty sheep goes something like this:

Yan, tan, tether, mether, pimp, teezar, leezar, catterah, horna, dick, yan-dick, tan-dick, tether-dick, mether-dick, bumpit, yan-a-bumpit, tan-a-bumpit, tedera-bumpit, medera-bumpit, giggot . . .

Now you can go anywhere.

Chapter Fourteen

Sports and Entertainments

The native sports are what make Cumbrian gatherings so unusual. You will see sports which exist nowhere else in the world. They are fascinating to watch, even if you have no idea what is going on . . .

After the spectator events come the do-it-yourself activities, from fishing and riding to climbing and sailing.

Then finally entertainments for a more cultural type which are on offer in Cumbria, notably theatre, music and cinema. Yes, the National Park does boast cinemas. All two and a half of them . . .

Cumbria Sports

Cumberland and Westmorland Wrestling

The most famous of the Lake District's native sports and you can see it practised at all the main sporting events. It began with Norsemen and at one time was widespread across the country. Today it is almost exclusively Cumbrian and a feature of many of the sports and agricultural shows. It looks like a trial of strength but is actually quite technical. The best wrestlers usually follow in family tradition and seem to be practically bred for it. Just like the best animals.

Two men face each other in a small arena, watched by two judges and a referee. The wrestlers are usually dressed in costumes which resemble combinations and embroidered bathing trunks. After shaking hands, the two men 'tak hod', that is, lock arms behind each other's back. The aim is to try and topple the other fellow to the ground and break his hold. If both fall, the one on top is the winner. The secret lies in tempting your opponent into a position of apparent security and they quickly over-balancing him. To the casual spectator, the technical subtleties are often not very obvious, but the events usually have a sense of atmosphere and tradition which make them well worth attending.

Fell racing

One of the principal attractions of a Lake District sports day. It consists of a race to the top of the nearest fell, often a gruelling 1,500 foot struggle, round a flag at the summit, then a breakneck dash back down into the arena. A straightforward, though torturous race. The best of all is the Grasmere guides' race (nothing to do with boy scouts and brownies) which can be quite spectacular and very exciting to watch.

Sheep dog trials

Nowadays, these take place all over the country and are well known to everyone through television, but they began in the north of England. The first took place in Northumberland in 1876 and the following year sheep dog trials were being held on Belle Isle, Windermere. In 1891, the 'Lake District Sheep Dog Trials Association' was formed.

Five sheep are released at one end of the arena - up to a quarter of a mile away - and the shepherd has to remain at his post whilst his dog - usually a Border Collie - gathers the sheep and brings them towards the shepherd through a series of obstacles. The final and most difficult part is to coax the sheep into a pen and it is only at this stage that the shepherd is able to assist, other than by whistling and calling.

Towards the end, the tension can build up quite rapidly and there is often a sense of magic about the way the shepherds can control their dogs. These events are very popular and set against the Lakeland fells on a fine, summer day, you are seeing them at their best. They often form a part of an agricultural or sports show but it is best to see them at the Rydal or Patterdale Sheep Dog Trials for the greatest sense of atmosphere.

Fox hunting

Not unique to Lakeland, though the sport's most famous exponent - John Peel - is buried in Caldbeck churchyard. Cumbrian fox hunting on the fells is radically different from the 'polite' social occasions of the south. The Lakeland farmer hunts primarily to kill foxes and keep down their numbers - and does it on foot. The hunt followers no doubt have reasons of their own. There are no horses and red coats - all the members hunt on foot and only one, the huntsman, wears the red coat. Hunt followers can be seen parked beside the road at the foot of the fells, from whence comes the disembodied baying of the hounds. There are six main packs in Cumbria:

Blencathra - reckoned to be the premier pack. Established in 1840. Its territory includes the countryside around Thirlmere, Derwentwater, Skiddaw and Caldbeck.
Melbreak - concentrates on the north west fells and out to the coast.

Ullswater - including territory around Kentmere, Fairfield and out towards Penrith.
Eskdale and Ennerdale - south west Lakeland, Scafell and into Langdale and out to the coast.
Coniston - concentrates on the central Lakes and east of Windermere.
Lunesdale - operates out over the Pennines.

The fox hunting season extends from the beginning of October through until the end of April. Neither the time nor the sport is particularly convenient for the holiday maker to the Lakes. But should you winter in Lakeland, look out for it. Full details of all the fixtures for the fell packs are published in the October issue of *Lakescene* each year. Or watch the local newspapers.

Hound trailing

A favourite sport in Cumbria for more than a hundred years and probably originally derived from the method used by huntsmen to train fox-hounds. It is really fox hunting without the fox. It's done in the summer off-season, so it's perfect for visitors to watch. From a starting point, a trail is set down by dragging an aniseed-soaked cloth over the fellside, making the course as difficult as possible by including fences, hedges, walls and a variety of terrain. For a fully-grown dog, the trail can be up to 10 miles long and can take 25 to 45 minutes to complete.

After the scent has been laid, the hounds are released; they pick up the scent from the 'trailer', then the whole pack rushes off into the hills. They might be out of sight until the finish, when they follow the trail back and the owners shout, whistle and wave to coax their animals over the line. The end can be quite exciting, but for most 'serious' spectators the attraction lies in betting which hound will will. The local Cumbrian bookies, who appear at most big sports, are a feature in themselves.

Trailing is held throughout Cumbria from April to October and the *Whitehaven News* (published Fridays) carries details of venues and times for the area (though tracking down the locations can be a problem - ask your friendly TIC). Hound trailing is also an important part of many of the shows and sports days.

Sporting Shows

There are several dozen sporting and farming shows held every year in the various Cumbrian towns and villages, all worth going to, and most of them include native Cumbrian sports. Keep an eye out for the local papers or notice boards for the smaller village shows for they have a flavour of their own, but the two Big Sports Days are held at Grasmere and Ambleside. All visitors should try if possible to fit in one of them.

For more details and times nearer the day, contact the TIC nearest the show.

☆☆☆ Grasmere Sports
Third Thursday after the first Monday in August.

The major Lakeland sporting event and by far the most popular in the area with often up to 20,000 spectators. Held in the 'ring' - the field just outside Grasmere, across the A591 from Town End and Dove Cottage. A brilliant location with all the usual running, throwing and cycling events, attracting professionals from all over the country, along with the best of the traditional, local events, such as Cumberland and Westmorland wrestling (in addition, there is a contest for the best costume worn by the wrestlers). Also the famous guides' fell race and hound trailing. Gets very crowded, so go early, otherwise about the only place to park is Keswick. Full of atmosphere and excitement, despite its size and fame, this remains a local show, unique to the area and still administered mainly by Grasmere people.

☆☆☆ Ambleside Sports
Thursday before first Monday in August.

Held in Rydal Park, just north of Ambleside. Began before the first world war and was revived again about 30 years ago. Now one of the biggest events of its kind in the Lake District, with track events, fell races, Cumberland and Westmorland wrestling. An exciting event to go to in a lovely, fellside setting.

☆☆ Cartmel Races
Spring and late Summer Bank Holiday, Saturday and Monday.

Probably the smallest of the National Hunt courses, set at the opposite end of the village to the Priory. Apart from horse racing there is usually a small fairground, along with stalls and refreshment tents. Not worth families spending the whole day there as it can get very crowded, but perhaps worth using as a base for a day out exploring Cartmel itself and the surrounding area.

☆☆ Lowther Horse Driving Trials and Country Fair
Weekend in early August.

Held on the Lowther Estate, near Penrith, this is the largest established occasion of its kind and one of the country's leading sporting events. As well as the horse driving trials (in which Prince Philip has been known to take part) there are also supporting attractions and the country fair itself with a wide range of stalls and events.

Agricultural Shows

The distinction between an agricultural show and a sporting or field event tends to get a bit blurred in the Lake District, with many of the farming and country shows attracting people who have come to watch the sheep dog trails, hound trails or Cumberland and Westmorland wrestling. Nearly all the shows are intended for the general visitor, not just the farming community, so are worth seeking out if they coincide with your holiday. Here are some of the best:

☆☆ Cumberland Show

Next to last Thursday in July.

Held in Bitts Park, Carlisle, and for many years has been the largest of the agricultural shows in Cumbria. Lots of traditional and modern events staged to make it a whole day's entertainment.

☆☆ Skelton Show

Third Saturday in August.

Formerly a little local show, centred on a village north of Penrith, which in recent years has exploded in size and content and enterprise. They now claim to have more animals on show than their rivals.

☆☆ Ennerdale Show

Last Wednesday in August.

Held at Bowness Knott, Ennerdale. What began as a small flower show has evolved into a delightful little agricultural and horticultural show, with hound trails, fell racing , sheep dog trials and gymkhana. It all ends with a dance in the evening.

☆ Eskdale Show

Last Saturday in September.

Primarily a sheep show, but including fell races, children's sports and singing and horn-blowing competitions. The mountains providing a superb setting.

☆ Gosforth Show

Third Wednesday in August.

Another traditional Cumbrian agricultural show, with additional entertainments in the form of terrier racing and a gymkhana. Along with the Eskdale and Hawkshead shows, this tends to be a mainly agricultural affair which is probably more fun for the local than the visitor. Worth taking in, but only if you happen to be in the area at the time. Or you could plan a day's outing around it and explore the area.

☆ Hawkshead Show

Changeable.

On the lines of Gosforth, but this time with added hound trailing and horse jumping.

☆☆ Keswick Show

Late Summer Bank Holiday Monday.

An important agricultural show with a bit more of a general appeal in the form of hound trails and Cumberland and Westmorland wrestling.

☆☆ Loweswater Show

Third Thursday in September.

Thought by many to be the nicest small show of them all.

☆☆☆ Wasdale Show

Second Saturday in October.

Now this one is worth going out of your way for. A superb setting at Wasdale Head, this is one of the best sheep shows in Cumbria, with lots of judging of sheep, sheep dogs, shepherd's crooks and even their boots. There are also tug-of-war competitions, pillow fights, fell races, hound trails and the notorious Cumberland and Westmorland wrestling. Very good.

☆☆☆ Westmorland County Show

Second Thursday in September.

Held on the County Showfield, Kendal, and one of the best one-day shows in Cumbria. Better than the Cumberland Show, because Kendal's nicer than Carlisle (although you aren't supposed to say that if you live north of Dunmail Raise). All kinds of agricultural competitions and displays, dog shows, Cumberland and Westmorland wrestling, show jumping, horse drawn carriage driving and a 'welly' race. There is also usually a dance in the evening (you can always tell the best shows by this).

Note: Just to make things difficult, as this book was going to press came there were reports that the Showfield was to be flogged off to developers and the County Show held elsewhere. Kendal TIC will have details of the new location.

☆☆☆ Appleby Horse Fair

Second Wednesday in June.

Not really an agricultural show, but set up by a charter of 1685 as a fair for horse trading. Today it is world-famous, the largest of its kind in the world, and attracts a huge gypsy gathering. Well-worth going to if it coincides with your visit for the sheer spectacle and bustle. Great if the weather is good. People arrive and camp out in the area up to a week before the day of the sales.

Sheep Dog Trials

In addition to trials found at some of the agricultural shows, there are five main events held in the Lakes:

☆☆ Rydal
Second Thursday after first Monday in August. Held in Rydal Hall grounds, just outside Ambleside on the A591.

Lake District
First Thursday after the first Monday in August. Held at Ings, near Staveley.

Threlkeld
Third Wednesday after first Monday in August. In Burns Field, Threlkeld, near Keswick.

☆ Patterdale Dog Day
Late Summer Bank Holiday Saturday. Held in the King George V playing fields, Patterdale.

Kentmere
Last Thursday in September. Held at Millrigg, near Staveley (about three miles up the Kentmere valley).

The best of the sheep dog trials is definitely Rydal. An excellent show which is fun and doesn't take itself too seriously. (Even the announcements over the PA system are entertaining.)

Rushbearing Ceremonies

Rushbearing is the survival of the old custom of strewing the old, earth floors of churches with rushes. Today the 'rushbearing' is a cross made of rushes and flowers and carried by the children of the parish. A procession is led by a band, followed by the clergy and then the children of the village, carrying the bearings. The procession usually goes round the town or village and ends at the church with hymns and prayers. There are five rushbearing ceremonies remaining in the Lake District - any one of which is worth going along to watch. The children of Ambleside and Grasmere are traditionally given a piece of Grasmere gingerbread if they have carried one of the rushes.

Ambleside Rushbearing
First Saturday in July.

Grasmere
Saturday nearest St Oswald's Day (August 5).

Musgrave Rushbearing
First Saturday in July.

Urswick Rushbearing
Sunday nearest St Michael's Day (September 29).

☆☆ Warcop Rushbearing
St Peter's Day (June 29), unless it falls on a Sunday, in which case the previous Saturday (28th).

Warcop is the most interesting spectacle of the five and is accompanied by children's sports and a military band.

Miscellaneous Events

Things which aren't quite sports and aren't quite agricultural or traditional, but which are becoming a fixed part of the Lakeland calendar.

☆ Carlisle Great Fair

Third Saturday in August for about ten days.

A revived fair which was once old-established. The focal point is the open air market in the city centre and the fair begins with a charger, read out at 8.00am on the first day. Daily events are posted at the Tourist Information Centre. A sort of mini-Edinburgh Festival. In this case, very mini, but they are trying.

☆☆ Egremont Crab Fair

Third Saturday in September.

One of Cumbria's oldest and oddest annual events. Dating back to 1267, the fair begins when, at 12.30pm, about £40 worth of apples are thrown to the public. A greasy pole is erected at dawn in the main street and a pound note placed on top. Anyone who can climb the pole can have the money. (It used to be a half-sheep, but presumably that got too expensive.) There are track and field events and hound trails during the day. In the evening there is a pipe-smoking contest and an event for which the fair is famous; the World Gurning Championships. The entrants to this revered competition put their heads through a horse collar and grin or 'gurn' - the object being to pull the most revolting expression; the most grotesque wins. Entrants with dentures tend to have an advantage here, though it is said that one year the contest was won by a sympathetic onlooker who was just watching.

☆ Cumbria Steam Gathering

Last weekend in July.

An impressive gathering of old steam cars, traction engines and commercial vehicles. There is also a fairground and market. Held in Flookburgh.

☆☆ Lake Windermere Festival

Traditional Lakeland event, revived in 1982, which takes over Bowness and Waterhead for a week in early July. Events include helicopter rides, brass bands, water-ski displays, 'Miss Lakeland' beauty competition, triathlons, power boat racing and, of course, Cumberland and Westmorland wrestling. Most of the action takes place on or around the lake. Lots going on, aimed at visitors and locals alike. Good fun but can make accommodation at bit scarce - be warned.

☆ Lakeland Rose Show
Second weekend in July.

Taking place in Grange-over-Sands (but no longer at Holker Hall - contact Grange TIC for location), this two-day event is one of Cumbria's most trumpeted summer attractions. Opened by royalty, at the very least, it has become something of a showcase for horticulturists all over the country. Not only flowers, but also car shows, massed bands, parachute displays, the Red Arrows. (Sponsored by North West Water Authority in 1989 - ironic seeing that rain caused massive problems for the show in the past two years.) *The* flower show to go to in the north of England. Costs a bomb to get in.

☆☆ Kendal Gathering
Late August/beginning September.

This two-and-a-half week event occurs in and around Kendal. Not a show as such but a sort of mini-festival with a number of contrasting attractions, including show-biz personalities, shows, exhibitions, band contests, dances, ceilidhs. It usually incorporates the Westmorland County Fair (turning a traditional attraction into another tourist honey-pot). But undoubtedly the star of the Gathering is its culmination in the Torchlight Procession, when hundreds of people join in a procession route, lit by torches and candles, which winds throughout the town on the final evening of the Gathering. If going to the Procession, get there early as the police close the town to traffic early in the evening. Best times are given in the *Westmorland Gazette*. (People seem to come from all over for the Procession - two years running UFOs were spotted overhead, according to the local papers.)

The Biggest Liar in the World Competition
Third Thursday in November.

This eccentric little competition, administered by Copeland Borough Council, takes place every year at the Santon Bridge Inn. It dates back to Will Ritson, a 19th century publican who lived at the head of the Wasdale valley. 'Auld Will' was a genuine and sincere many who lied constantly; one tale was that turnips in Wasdale grew so big that the dalesfolk quarried into them for their Sunday lunch and then used them as sheds for the Herdwick sheep. (Nowadays, according to the contest-runners, people live in turnips because they are natural features of the landscape and they do not need planning permission from the LDSPB.) In 1974, Tom Purdham won the contest by telling a visiting BBC tv team - who had turned up to film the winner - that he wasn't taking part in the contest. The BBC were convinced and went home without filming him. A recent winner was Jos Naylor, the fell runner. The 1985 winner was John Reeves who works for British Nuclear Fuels at Sellafield. (Jolly useful chap, I'd have thought.) His Big Lie was some nonsense about Halley's Comet really being an everlasting carpet woven from Herdwick sheep wool. The contest is held strictly for amateurs - politicians, journalists and lawyers are barred from entry. Price of admission includes a tatie pot supper. Contact Copeland Council (see chapter 1 for address) and they will happily send you lots of lies about the contest.

Information on all Events

Information about all these events can be obtained from Tourist Information Centres, as well as local newspapers.

The Brewery Arts Centre, in Kendal, is another good source of information about events going on in and around South Cumbria, especially music and arts festivals. If in Kendal, it is worth popping in for a coffee and a browse amongst the leaflets.

Recreations

Having listed and described the spectator sports, and where you can go and see them happening, we now come to the do-it-yourself sports and activities; fishing, golf, riding, swimming, climbing, grass skiing, sailing and even parachuting.

Canoeing

Putting a canoe on a river in Cumbria can be a pain, with certain times when you can and other times when you can't; and some rivers where you can't do anything at all. Lake access is much better, with no restrictions on the major lakes as long as you don't go tramping across private land. For smaller lakes - e.g. Rydal Water - see Chapter Seven.

The British Canoe Union Regional Coaching Organiser is Barry Howell, on Grange-over-Sands 4172, and he can give advice on courses and access. Alternatively, ring the BCU access officer, Colin Lytton, on Barrow 89629, for advice about South Lakeland rivers.

Climbing

Rock climbing was virtually invented in the Lake District by a group of climbers basing themselves at Wasdale Head. Nowadays if you're out on any of the fells which has a suitable rock face nearby you'll probably see little figures moving slowly across it, strung together with their gaily coloured ropes. Not something for the novice to try without proper instruction or equipment (see *Instructors*). A number of guide books to the crags are available, but if you're coming to the area and want to get in touch with any of the climbing clubs or with climbing individuals, often the best approach is to contact the two main climbing shops:

George Fisher
Lake Road, Keswick. Tel: Keswick 72178.

Frank Davies (The Climber's Shop)
Compston Road, Ambleside. Tel: Ambleside 32297.

Climbing Clubs

Barrow Mountaineering and Ski Club
Avondale, Brow End, Great Urswick, Ulverston.

Carlisle Mountaineering Club
47 Balfour Road, Carlisle, CA2 7DU.

Eden Valley Mountaineering Club
5 Crown Terrace, Penrith, CA11 7XP.

Kendal Mountaineering Club
4 Chelsea Court, Milnthorpe, LA7 7DJ.

West Cumbria Mountaineering Club
60 Dalzell Street, Moor Row, Whitehaven, CA23 3JP.

In each case, address letters to the secretary and enclose a SAE.

Fishing

Every angler must hold a North West Water Authority Licence and will probably also need a permit, since most water seems to be either owned or let to clubs, associations or some other body. A complete list of licence distributors is available from any of the tourist information centres.

A couple of good Lakeland fishing books are available: *Angler's Guide to the Lake District* by James Holgate and Geoff Parkinson, 1987, £2.50, Westmorland Gazette (part of their *Castabout* series); and the cleverly titled *The Lure of the Lakes* by Angus Berry, 1986.

Fishing licences are administered by:

North West Water Authority
Rivers Division,
PO Box 12,
Warrington, Cheshire.

The NWWA can supply a licence if you write to them in advance, but permits should in most cases be obtained locally. They also do a useful guide *Fishing in the North West*, price 75p, which lists regulations and places where you can fish. The booklet is available from most TICs.

The following is a list of the major lakes and tarns, with details of what you can expect to catch and which require permits. If no address is given, consult the NWWA leaflet.

Blea Tarn, Langdale

Trout and freshwater fish. Permits available from Mrs Myers, Blea Tarn Farmhouse.

Bassenthwaite Lake
Perch, pike, brown trout and salmon. Permits from the LDSPB, Busher Walk, Kendal.

Brotherswater
Trout. No permit required.

Buttermere
Trout, char, pike and perch. Permits from Gatesgarth Farm, Buttermere, and The Gun Shop, Cockermouth.

Coniston Water
Trout, char, perch and eels. No permit required.

Crummock Water
Trout, char, pike and perch. Salmon and sea trout from July onwards. Permits from Rannerdale Farm, Buttermere, or The Gun Shop, Cockermouth.

Derwentwater
Perch, pike and brown trout. Permits from Temples, Station Road, Keswick.

Easedale
Freshwater fish. No permit required.

Elterwater
Brown trout, pike and perch. The lake is privately owned, so enquire at the local permit retailers, such as Hawkshead Post Office.

Esthwaite Water
Brown trout, pike and perch. Owned by Esthwaite Estates and permits available from T. W. Taylor, Esthwaite How Farm, Near Sawrey, Hawkshead.

Grasmere
Trout, perch and pike, but the fishing rights have been privately let so no permits available.

Haweswater
Schelly, char, brown trout. A limited number of bank permits available from the NWWA.

Loweswater
Trout, char, pike and perch. Permits available from the Kirkstile Inn, Loweswater, Scale Hill Hotel, Loweswater, and The Gun Shop, Cockermouth.

Rydal Water
Pike and perch with some brown trout. Permits from the Cycle Shop, Ambleside.

Tarn Hows
Permits and fishing rights in private hands.

Thirlmere
Pike, perch, brown trout. Permits from the NWWA.

Ullswater
Pike, perch, brown trout and schelly. No permits required but watch out that you are not on private shores (ask at Lake Leisure, Pooley Bridge, if you're unsure).

Wastwater
Trout, pike and perch. Permits from the warden at the National Trust campsite, Wasdale Head.

Windermere
Trout (noted for large fish of up to 8lbs), char, perch and pike. No permits required but additional information can be obtained from Windermere TIC.

Local Angling Associations

Local knowledge can be gleaned by chatting up the permit retailers, but angling associations can also provide good contacts (especially for river fishing). Here are a few of the main ones:

Cockermouth Angling Association
7 West End, Great Broughton, Cockermouth.

Kendal and District Angling Club
109 Milnthorpe Road, Kendal.

Keswick Angling Association
Springhaven, How Lane, Portinscale.

Windermere and District Angling Association
Rylstone, Limethwaite Road, Heathwaite, Windermere.

In all cases, when you write to them a stamped addressed envelope is appreciated.

Flying

Carlisle Flight Centre
Crosby-on-Eden, Carlisle. Tel: Crosby-on-Eden 333.

They undertake aircraft leasing, hire, sales, charter work and train people for private pilot's licence.

Also a much smaller organisation called *Furness Aviation*, based at Walney Island Aerodrome, Barrow-in-Furness do flying lessons, but on more of a part-time basis at present. Tel: Club House on Barrow 42404.

Gliding

Lakes Gliding Club, Walney Island, Barrow. Tel: Barrow 41458.

(Real gliding, by the way, see page 217 for hang gliding.)

They have a clubhouse and run weekly courses as well as day flights and lessons.

Golf

Golfing in the Lake District has its special attractions due to the scenery. The following five are amongst the best situated:

Kendal Golf Club
The Heights, Kendal. Tel: Kendal 24079.

Keswick Golf Club
Threlkeld Hall, Threlkeld. Tel: Threlkeld 324 or Keswick 72147.

Cockermouth Golf Club
Embleton. Tel: Bassenthwaite Lake 223.

Grange-over-Sands
Meathop. Tel: Grange 3180.

Windermere Golf Club
Cleabarrow, Windermere. Tel: Windermere 3123.

Grass Skiing

This is basically skiing without the snow. Most of the techniques are the same - you need similar boots, you can even use ski lifts. All you don't need are the funny suits and goggles. There is only one grass ski school in the Lakes - although there are one or two individual freelance instructors who have skis - and that is at Limefitt Park. They bill themselves as Britain's first and foremost school and have a good slope with their own ski lift and an instructor is available.

Limefitt Park
Windermere. Tel: Ambleside 32564.
(About 2 1/2 miles from Windermere on the A592 to Ullswater).

As for snow skiing there is a Lakeland Ski Club and Lakeland Cross Country Ski Club. Details from P. Storey, Keepers, 4 Greenbank Avenue, Storth, Milnthorpe.

Hang Gliding

Cumbria Hang Gliding Club, Mr. D. Foreman (Secretary), Roseneath, Church Road, Allithwaite, Grange-over-Sands. Tel: G-O-S 4074.

Land Yachting

Aha, bet you didn't expect to find this in Cumbria (there'll be a surfing club next ..). Contact the Cumbria Land Yacht Club, Mr M. Walker (Secretary), 33 Skelgate, Dalton-in-Furness.

Parachuting

For the really adventurous:
North West Parachute Centre
Cark Airfield, Flookburgh,
Grange-over-Sands. Tel: Flookburgh 672.

If you only want to spectate, Humphrey Head - the headland near Grange-over-Sands - has a grandstand view.

Riding and Pony Trekking

Anyone contemplating trekking and making extensive use of the various bridleways throughout Cumbria can contact the Cumbria Bridleways Society, who will help with route-planning and local knowledge.

Cumbria Bridleways Society
Secretary
2 Compston Villas, Ambleside.
Tel: Ambleside 33188.

Five recommended riding schools:

Side Farm Trekking Centre
Patterdale, Ullswater. Tel: Glenridding 337.

Limefitt Park
Troutbeck, Windermere. Tel: Ambleside 32564.

Bigland Hall
Backbarrow, near Ulverston. Tel: Newby Bridge 31728.

Hill Farm
Bassenthwaite, Keswick. Tel: Bassenthwaite Lake 498.

The Calvert Trust for the Disabled
Old Windebrowe, Brundholme Road, Keswick. Tel: Keswick 74395.

All are approved schools, catering for beginners as well as the more experienced and all provide riding hats. The Calvert Trust is one of several catering for the disabled and it specialises in small groups. It is primarily for disabled riders, but others are welcome.

Sailing and Windsurfing

The number of schools has decreased in recent years, with the loss of the Ullswater School and Lakeland Sailing Centre (the latter is still there but now only a chandlery). Plenty of opportunities for weekly courses and holidays, fewer for casual lessons on a daily or hourly basis. Your best bet for these is a local instructor (see *Instructors*, below). However, two recommended schools are:

Derwentwater Windsurfing School
Portinscale, Keswick.
Tel: Keswick 72912.

Glenridding Sailing School
Celleram Cottage, Tirril, Penrith.
Tel: Pooley Bridge 601 or Glenridding 575.

You could also try:

Talkin Tarn Country Park
Brampton. Tel: Brampton 3129.

Just east of Carlisle, small tarn with very good sailing, windsurfing fishing, rowing facilities. All much cheaper and less crowded than central Lakeland. And very clean showers. Resident warden.

Swimming

Until August and September, the lakes can be very cold, but if you are feeling cowardly there are number of indoor and outdoor pools around. (See Chapter Four for hotels with pools.)

Outdoor

Appleby
Church Street. Tel: Appleby 51212.

Askham (near Penrith)
Behind the Queen's Head Inn. Tel: Hackthorpe 570.

Grange-over-Sands
The Esplanade. Tel: Grange 3053.

The first two are heated. The Grange pool is an open-air, salt water pool with a splendid situation along the sea promenade, overlooking Morecambe Bay.

Indoor

A number of schools on the west coast of Cumbria and in the Eden valley are opening up their pools to visitors during the summer holidays and weekends. However, the following are purpose-built public swimming pools. All are indoor and all offer more than just a pool (usually training pools, saunas, etc):

Barrow-in-Furness
Abbey Baths, Abbey Road. Tel: Barrow-in-Furness 20706.

Bowness
Beech Hill Hotel, Bowness. Tel: Windermere 2137.
Open to public, 10.30-8.30pm.

Carlisle
Swimming Baths, James Street. Tel: Carlisle 22105.

Cockermouth
Sports Centre, Castlegate Drive. Tel: Cockermouth 823596.

Egremont
Wyndham Baths. Tel: Egremont 820465. Open to public in school holidays.

Kendal
South Lakeland Leisure Centre, Burton Road. Tel: Kendal 29511.

Keswick
Keswick Spa Leisure Pool, Station Road. Tel: Keswick 72760.

Not really for swimmers, this is really a souped-up kiddies' paddling pool, with waterchute, sloping 'beach' and a rather unpredictable wave machine. Great for kids, not so hot for adults (which seems a missed opportunity). Currently closed during winter months.

Penrith
Eden Swimming Baths, Southend Road. Tel: Penrith 63450.

Ulverston
Priory Road. Tel: Ulverston 54110.

Whitehaven
Cleator Moor Road Swimming Baths, Cleator Moor Road.
Tel: Whitehaven 5021.

Windermere
Troutbeck Bridge Swimming Pool, Troutbeck Bridge.
Tel: Windermere 3243.

Workington
Workington Sports Centre, Moorclose.
Tel: Workington 61771.

Waterskiing
Low Wood Waterski Centre
Low Wood Hotel, Ambleside. Tel: Ambleside 33338.
(Also run diving courses and now have a sailboarding school on site.)

Leisure Centres

Two big ones worth mentioning:

South Lakeland Leisure Centre
Burton Road, Kendal. Tel: Kendal 29511.
For sports bookings - telephone number as for swimming pools. For concert bookings, telephone Kendal 29702.
Has a range of facilities: squash, badminton, weight training, swimming. The centre houses the *Westmorland Hall*, where concerts, plays and performances are held. Also has a bar and cafe.

The Sands Centre
Carlisle. Tel: Carlisle 25222.
All the usual sports facilities, plus concerts and entertainments - especially during July and August.

Instructors
In addition to the specialist schools and centres, for those interested in climbing, canoeing, caving, orienteering or windsurfing, there are a number of individual instructors operating in the Lake District:

R & L Adventures
The Lodge, Bridge Lane, Troutbeck, Windermere.
Tel: Windermere 5104.
(Abseiling, canoeing, fell walking, map reading, orienteering, rock climbing and general mountaineering catered for.)

Lakeland Experience
Green Lodge, Eskdale Green.
Tel: Eskdale 228.
(Abseiling, canoeing, caving, fell walking, map reading, orienteering, rock climbing and mountaineering.)

Martin Clark
Banerigg, Grasmere.
Tel: Grasmere 204.
(Individual instruction holidays in canoeing, sailing and windsurfing.)

Summitreks
14 Yewdale Road, Coniston.
Tel: Coniston 41212.
(Abseiling, caving, fell walking, mountaineering, map reading, orienteering, rock climbing and windsurfing.)

Westmorland Watersports
Beech Hill Hotel, Bowness. Tel: Windermere 5756.
(Windsurfing, sailing, waterskiing - all operating out of the Beech Hill Hotel but run by local instructor, Geoff Kirton. Under the guise of Adventure Awareness, he also offers courses in caving, climbing, walking, abseiling, etc.)

Entertainment

Most people come to the Lakes for all that fresh air and scenery, but you never know, you might have an evening spare, for culture or amusement.

Theatre and Music

There are four main venues in or close to the Lake District (if we ignore Carlisle) which cater for music and drama. With the exception of the Century Theatre, they all host a variety of events - concerts, plays, lectures, recitals - and most tend to be one or two night occasions; the advantage is that these centres can sometimes attract some of the best touring companies in the country.

☆☆ Century Theatre, Lakeside Car Park, Keswick.
Tel: Keswick 74411.

The Century Theatre is the rather unsafe-looking collection of jacked-up portacabins that greets you as you walk to the lake shore from Keswick town centre. It used to be a touring theatre but has now put down roots and the resident company are now raising funds for a proper building. It's a lot nicer inside than the outside would have you believe.

The resident company operates during the summer months and put on three plays, running them in rotation so that you don't get the same play for more than three consecutive days. The plays are usually 'standards' and are well-performed. Well worth a visit. The Moot Hall Information Centre usually has leaflets telling you what they are putting on.

☆☆ **Theatre-in-the-Forest,** Grizedale Forest. Tel: Satterthwaite 291.

A nice little theatre in a unique position, tucked away miles from anywhere in the Grizedale Forest. (It is easy to find - just north of Satterthwaite on the Hawkshead road.) Provides a range of entertainment throughout the year, mainly concerts, talks and the odd theatrical production. BBC North tend to make a lot of use of it for folk concerts and the like. Programmes appear each week in the *Westmorland Gazette* - otherwise you often have a job finding out what is going on there without a visit. Hawkshead Tourist Information can usually help, though. A nice drive on a summer evening, but don't underestimate how long it takes to get there. It is easiest to find from the Hawkshead direction.

☆ **Rosehill Theatre,** Moresby, near Whitehaven. Tel: Whitehaven 2422.

Rather a trek from the central Lakes, but another very good arts centre which puts on a range of concerts and productions throughout the year. They also have workshops regularly and there is an adjoining restaurant. Events listed in the *Whitehaven News* and sometimes at Whitehaven, Keswick and other Tourist Information Centres.

☆☆ **Brewery Arts Centre,** 122a Highgate, Kendal. Tel: Kendal 25133.

An active little arts centre in a restored Brewery building. It has become the cultural heart of Kendal and puts on a very good range of plays, concerts, films and special events throughout the year. There is a good bar and it has a photographic gallery and a number of workshops. Very good on mime and folk. This is really a community arts centre run on very professional lines. The Centre sponsors two very good music festivals each year:

Kendal Jazz Festival - around the end of summer, with some big names often appearing.
Kendal Folk Festival - in late August, featuring a wide range of events over a week or more, from concerts and ceilidhs to workshops, displays and competitions.

The Centre itself always has a wide range of information on display about arts activities generally in and around the Lakes.

Renaissance Theatre Trust, 17 Fountain Street, Ulverston. Tel: Ulverston 52299.

Not a theatre as such, but a small coffee shop and arts centre which houses the Trust itself. They are responsible for promoting and organising concerts and shows throughout South Cumbria and the Furness area. They book other venues (such as Civic Halls) and bring in outside artists.

The Centre has rooms for a small-scale concert or lecture and a very good cafe. It also operates at the Ulverston Tourist Information Centre.

West Walls Theatre, West Walls, Carlisle.
Tel: Carlisle 33233.

☆☆ Lake District Summer Musical Festival

This is staged every year, around mid-summer, and consists of music and arts events and exhibitions staged at various venues throughout the Lakes. The emphasis is on 'serious' music and arts and the Festival attracts many international names. One of the regular venues is Kendal Leisure Centre, which has an excellent Concert Hall facility (and a rather expensive Steinway piano). Details appear well ahead of time in the *Gazette*, or ring Witherslack 222. Of its kind, this has been one of the north of England's premier events. Needs revitalised.

☆ Wordsworth Summer Conference

Residential conference for poetry lovers, usually in July or August. (Winter Conference as well.) Details from Dove Cottage, Grasmere.

Grizedale Piano Festival

Held every year in early summer. Contact Theatre in the Forest.

Cinemas

The National Park contains only three public cinemas (or two and a half if you take into account that one is closed during the winter). Just as well that two of them are pretty good.

Bowness
☆ Royalty Cinema, Lake Road. Tel: W'mere 3364.

A small, but quite good cinema which can sometimes get big feature releases surprisingly quickly, especially during the summer. It tends to spoil this by repeating blockbusters throughout the height of the season - during the summer of '88, it looked as though *Crocodile Dundee* 2 must have jammed in the projector. Okay for visitors, but a bit boring for the locals. **Warning:** they have a vile habit of breaking films halfway through so they can flog ice creams; if this is liable to cause apoplexy, wait and see it at Zeffirelli's.

Ambleside
☆☆ **Zeffirelli's Cinema**, Compston Road. Tel: Ambleside 33845.

Very good, with some nice decorative touches, such as fan lighting and old projectors as ornaments in the foyer. Doesn't get the blockbusters as quickly as Bowness, but amply compensates for this by putting on interesting films slightly out of the crowd-pulling mainstream. This is definitely a cinema run by an enthusiast and a rather classier affair than the Royalty.

Programmes for these two usually change Friday and details appear in *The Westmorland Gazette*.

Keswick
Alhambra Theatre. Tel: Keswick 72195.

A small cinema tucked away in St. John's Street. A bit like Derwentwater's floating island, it seems to come and go. Closed in winter. What makes you think they're only interested in the tourist trade?

Other Cinemas
There are of course a lot more cinemas around the outskirts of the Lakes, especially in the larger Cumbrian towns. They include:

Barrow
Astra 1, 2 and 3, Abbey Road. Tel: Barrow 25354.

Carlisle
Lonsdale Cinema, Warwick Road. Tel: Carlisle 25586.

Carlisle has lost one of its cinemas in the past three years - does everyone in Cumbria's capital now have a video?

Kendal
Brewery Arts Centre, Highgate. Tel: Kendal 25133.

Run in conjunction with Zeff's in Ambleside, and now a much more professional venture than formerly. Screen still a bit titchy, though.

Penrith
Cosy Alhambra Picture House, Middlegate.   Recently revamped. Tel: Penrith 62400.

Ulverston
Roxy Cinema, Brogden Street. Tel: Ulverston 52340.

Whitehaven
Gaiety Cinema. Tel: Whitehaven 3012.

Chapter Fifteen

Shopping

Yes, we know you haven't come to the Lakes to shop, or so you think. But just look at all those crowds on the pavements of Bowness and Keswick. Where do they all come from. There does come a stage in the life of any holiday maker when you end up wanting to find a shop, even if it's only to buy a present. So we have surveyed five types of shops which visitors, and residents, might well want to use at some time.

Finally, we contemplate that biggest fantasy purchase of all - Buying a House in the Lake District and Settling Down. Start counting the pennies now . . .

Antique Shops

Ambleside
Alladin's Cave
Zeffirelli's Arcade, Compston Road.
Tel: Ambleside 33722.

Cockermouth
☆☆ Antique Market
Old Courthouse, Cocker Bridge, Main Street.
Tel: Cockermouth 824346.

☆☆ Cockermouth Antiques
Station Street. Tel: Cockermouth 826746.

High Newton
Shire Antiques
The Post House, Near Grange-over-Sands.
Tel: Newby Bridge 31431.

Kendal
Cottage Antiques
151 Highgate. Tel: Kendal 22683.

☆ Highgate Antiques
Tudor House, 181 Highgate. Tel: Kendal 24527.

Keswick
John Young & Son
12 Main Street. Tel: Keswick 73434.

Kirkby Stephen
Haughey Antiques
28-30 Market Street.Tel: Kirkby Stephen 71302.

Newby Bridge
☆☆ Townhead Antiques
Townhead, Newby Bridge Road. Tel: Newby Bridge 31321.

Windermere
Joseph Thornton Antiques
4 Victoria Street. Tel: Windermere 2930.

Bird Cage Antiques
College Road. Tel: Windermere 5063.

Book Shops
Well, you might want to buy more copies of *The Good Guide to the Lakes* - go on, spoil the friends back home.

Lakeland book shops are terribly good on Lakeland books and maps - not so hot on the latest sensitive novel from London. All Lakeland book shops which stock this book are of course excellent, but here's a small selection:

Ambleside
Fred Holdsworth
Central Buildings. Tel: Ambleside 33388.

Wearing's Bookshop
Lake Road. Tel: Ambleside 32312

Bowness
Lakes Bookshop
Quarry Rigg, Lake Road. Tel: Windermere 5780.

Cockermouth
The New Bookshop
102 Main Street. Tel: Cockermouth 822062.

Grasmere
Sam Read
Broadgate House. Tel: Grasmere 374.

Hawkshead
Ideas
The Square. Tel: Hawkshead 650.

Kendal
Bookworm
93 Highgate. Tel: Kendal 24419.

. Henry Roberts
7 Stramongate. Tel: Kendal 20425.

Keswick
Lake Road Bookshop
Lake Road. Tel: Keswick 72910.

Chaplin's
19 Station Road. Tel: Keswick 72440.

There is also a good selection of books upstairs at Mayson's, in Lake Road.

Millom
Duddon Books
2 St George's Road. Tel: Millom 4307.

Penrith
Bluebell Bookshop
Angel Square. Tel: Penrith 66660.

Ulverston
James Atkinson
6 King Street. Tel: Ulverston 53097.

Whitehaven
Cribbs Bookshop
6 College Street. Tel: Whitehaven 5111.

No ratings this time for bookshops - they get terribly jealous of each other. However, in our personal opinion, the two most interesting are probably Fred Holdsworth's, in Ambleside, and The Bluebell, in Penrith. Fred Holdsworth's stocks more of the out-of-the-way books and it is amazing what he has got hidden in the crowded shelves of his little shop. The Bluebell, by contrast, now in new posh premises, boasts that it is the biggest bookshop in all Cumbria, with 3,500 square feet. Certainly the nicest to use, as they also do wholesome light lunches and teas.

For anything on Wordsworth or the Lake Poets, try:
The Wordsworth Bookshop
Town End, Grasmere.
Tel: Grasmere 464.
This is next to - and run by - Dove Cottage.
Even better, because they carry less of the souvenir stuff, is the bookshop at Brantwood, Ruskin's house in Coniston. The National Park Visitor Centre, Brockhole, also has a good selection of books on the area, but you first have to pay to enter the grounds. The larger tourist information centres (especially the National Park TICs) also have books on the area.

Secondhand Book Shops
Ambleside
The Little Bookshop
1 Cheapside. Tel: Ambleside 32094.

Barrow
The Mostly Bookshop
247 Rowlinson Street. Tel: Barrow 36808.

Braithwaite
Book Cottage. Tel: Braithwaite 275.

Caldbeck
Book End
Priests Mill. Tel: (home) Raughton Head 431.

Carlisle
☆☆ Bookcase
17 Castle Street. Tel: Carlisle 44560.

Carnforth
☆☆ The Carnforth Bookshop
38-42 Market Street. Tel: Carnforth 734588.

Cartmel
Peter Bain Smith
Bank Court, Market Square. Tel: Cartmel 36369.

Cockermouth
☆ Winkworth Antiquarian Books
102 Main Street. Tel: Cockermouth 824984.

☆ Old Storyteller's Bookshop
10 Old King's Arms Lane. Tel: Cockermouth 823751.

Keswick
Appleby's Books
5 St John's Street.

Penrith
St Andrew's Bookshop
St Andrew's View. Tel: Penrith 64453.

Sedbergh
☆☆ F R & G Hollett
6 Finkle Street Tel: Sedbergh 20298.

Whitehaven
☆☆☆ Michael Moon
41-42 Roper Street. Tel: Whitehaven 62936.
A huge place, great for browsing. As a rule, he knows what he has got in stock, but he's not sure exactly where to find it. However, he'll tend to keep you amused whilst you're both looking for it. One mile of shelves. Boasts he can accommodate two full coach loads on a wet day, especially now he has opened up his new Art Gallery.

Craft Shops and Galleries
There's a vast number of gift shops in the Lakes, far too many to mention, or even give a second glance to, but

there's a growing number of more up market art galleries and workshops. Yes, they're still hoping you'll buy something to take home, but at least you have a fair chance of the produce being home-made. Some are small, one person operations, often the results of someone's desire to escape the rat race of a Big City (for the rat race of a small village). Others have been going for centuries and continue to use traditional working methods.

The best present is something unique to the area so, if you've already stocked up with Kendal Mint Cake and want to find something smarter, you might try these:

Ambleside

☆ Kirkstone Slate Gallery

Skelwith Bridge, Ambleside. Tel: Ambleside 33296.
A wide range of green slate ornaments and objects, produced on site and ranging from slate ashtrays to table lamps. Becoming very commercial in its range of products.

☆☆ Adrian Sankey Glass

Rothay Road. Tel: Ambleside 33039.
Glass sculptures and glass ware. You can visit the workshop and see the finished products being made.

Barrow-in-Furness

☆ Cumbria Crystal

Tel: Ulverston 54400.
Factory in which you can watch glass blowing and see all the stages of production of crystal glass, with a showroom selling seconds too. Small admission charge. No address, unfortunately, as they were finalising plans to move at the time of writing. Ring their old Ulverston number and calls will be passed through.

Bowness

Craftsmen of Cumbria

3 St. Martin's Parade, Low Side. Tel: Windermere 2959.
Wide range of crafts, including pottery and gemstone jewellery. All locally produced. Good place to have a go yourself at a variety of crafts.

Elterwater

Fibrecrafts at Barnhowe

Elterwater. Tel: Langdale 346.
Spinning and weaving demonstrations.

Grasmere

The Heaton Cooper Studio

Tel: Grasmere 280.
(Also at Quarry Rigg, Bowness. Tel: Windermere 4766.)
The paintings of W. Heaton Cooper have become a major industry in the Lake District, on postcards and greetings cards everywhere. These two studios specialise in prints and reproductions but also have one or two originals on

display. To some people, Heaton Cooper's paintings *are* the Lake District.

Chris Reekie
The Old Coach House, Stock Lane. Tel: Grasmere 221.
Excellent for woollens and clothing, much of the weaving taking place on the premises.

Haverthwaite
Clock Tower Buildings
Low Wood, Haverthwaite. Tel: Newby Bridge 31155.
Two galleries in one. Artcrystal and C. E. Studio.

Kendal
☆ Susan Foster
9 Windermere Road. Tel: Kendal 26494.
A weaving and spinning workshop with rugs, cushions, bags and a small range of clothing for sale.

Kendal Glass Engravers
177 Highgate. Tel: Kendal 33800.
Hand-produced glass engravings, displayed in the adjacent gallery, all individually signed and dated.

Keswick
☆ Thornthwaite Galleries
Thornthwaite. Tel: Braithwaite 248.
(Off the A66, between Keswick and Cockermouth.)
Fascinating - if rather up market - art gallery with a range of work for sale by local artists. Recently undergone a change of ownership, so let's hope the standard is kept up.

☆☆ Lakeland Guild Craft Gallery
Lake Road. Tel: Keswick 73636.
Run by Lakeland Guild of Craftsmen. Very wide range.

Kirkby Stephen
☆ Heredities
Crossfield Mill. Tel: Kirkby Stephen 71543.
A firm producing cold cast bronze sculptures; the world's largest producer of its kind. Showrooms and exhibition, and the bronzes are made on site. Unusual and potentially expensive, though very often seconds are available at much reduced prices.

Penrith
☆ Wetheriggs Country Pottery
Clifton Dykes.
Tel: Penrith 62946.
Gallery, showroom and exhibition offering a range of pottery made on site. They use traditional techniques and you can visit the workshop and see the work taking place. Also a very good cafe and they claim there has been a pottery on this site for nearly a thousand years.

Sedbergh
Dent Crafts Centre
Helmside, Dent. Tel: Dent 400.
Spinning, pottery, printing and hand-frame knitting.

Silverdale
☆☆ Wolf House Gallery
Gibraltar. Tel: Silverdale 701405.
A bit off the beaten track, but an excellent art gallery. There are three galleries, displaying national as well as local work. They specialise in original paintings, rather than prints. There is also a textile workshop and there is the added bonus of an excellent little tea shop.

Staveley
Wedge Hall Gallery
Windermere Road. Tel: Staveley 821130.
Not a lot of stock but trying to support a range of small, local crafts producers. Also a nice tea room.

Windermere
John Kershaw Pottery
40a Main Road. Tel: Windermere 4844.
Stoneware pottery, made on the premises.

The NP people have Craft Days at Seatoller Barn in Borrowdale. Can be quite jolly as craftspersons come from all over to sell or demonstrate.

Food Shops
If you're self-catering, or just feeling peckish, you will need to stock up. Beware. There are some places in the Lake District where you might starve to death, unless you can live off Kendal mint cake and leather Lakeland key fobs. Bowness is rather like that - great for gifts and souvenirs, not so hot for food (though it does have a couple of shops and one of them - McClure's, Lake Road, tel: Windermere 2667 - stays open until 10pm in the summer). Windermere is better for food shopping. Very few of the smaller Lake District villages have shops, you have to trek to the larger towns. In general, if you're in the northern Lakes, head for Cockermouth or Penrith, if you're in the south, go to Ambleside, Kendal or Ulverston to stock up. The following is a summary:

Good for Food
Ambleside - good grocers, butchers and greengrocers. Especially good on market day (Wednesday).
Kendal - lots of supermarkets and smaller food shops. Late opening in most of them on Friday nights. Also a good food market on Saturday.
Penrith - lots of food shops and one or two good supermarkets.

Cockermouth - also good for food shops, with a nice little market on Monday plus the new Walter Wilson supermarket.

Towns round the fringes of the Lakes, where tourism is less important, are also quite good if you're stocking up for a holiday. These include Whitehaven, Workington, Ulverston and Grange-over-Sands. Carlisle, of course, being the largest town, has the biggest shops and supermarkets. They have an excellent Marks and Spencer Foodstore and the Lanes Shopping Complex.

Poor for food:

In the main, these are the places where there are few good food shops, where competition is limited or where there are no good shops at all, having been driven out by the tourist traffic. If you have the choice, go to one of the towns listed under 'Good'.

Hawkshead
Coniston
Bowness
Grasmere.

They are, however, excellent if you want gifts and presents, rather than food. Coincidence?

For specialised food shops, see Chapter Five.

Walkers' Shops

Shops which specialise in the great outdoors, supplying gear for walkers and climbers, are a feature of the landscape in the Lake District. Invaluable for guide books, maps, wet-weather and walking clothes as well as general advice. The two biggest - Fisher's and Frank Davies - are good sources of information on walking and climbing activities generally and frequently have notices displayed in the windows giving details of talks, lectures and local instructors. Some will also hire out specialised equipment. Keswick Mountain Sports, Fisher's and Frank Davies all hire boots, Frank Davies hires waterproofs too.

Ambleside is becoming *the* centre for walking and outdoor shops; there were five and a half at the last count (see below for explanation). Keswick isn't far behind, though.

For this type of shopping, it is best to stick to the specialist shops (such as those listed here) and ignore the ordinary sports shops and gift shops selling cheap rucksacks.

Ambleside
☆☆ Frank Davies
(The Climber's Shop), Compston Road. Tel: A'side 32297.

Stewart Cunningham
Outdoor Centre, 12 Rydal Road. Tel: Ambleside 32636.

Miniwalkers
Rydal Road.
Not really an outdoor shop, more a window display opposite Cunningham's. It features waterproofs and walking gear for children.

Rock and Run
4 Cheapside. Tel: Ambleside 33660.
Now with a cheap, pleasant cafe upstairs.

John Gaynor's
Market Cross. Tel: Ambleside 33305.
   Not really a specialist, but a good range of outdoor clothing and tents.

Wilf. Nicholson
Central Buildings. Tel: Ambleside 32235.

Bowness
☆ Stuart's Sports
Lake Road. Tel: Windermere 3001.

Broughton-in-Furness
Mountain Centre Sports
Market Street. Tel: Broughton 461.

Kendal
Lakeland Mountain Centre
3 Kirkland. Tel: Kendal 28356.

Peter Bland Sports
42a Kirkland. Tel: Kendal 31012.
   Good on footwear for the fells, but only if you plan to run up them.

Kendal Sports
30 Stramongate.
Tel: Kendal 21554.

Moor & Mountain/Survival Aids
Waterside. Tel: Kendal 29699.

Keswick
☆☆ George Fisher
Lake Road. Tel: Keswick 72178.

Mountain World
28 Lake Road. Tel: Keswick 73524.

Rathbone's Outdoor Sports
26 Main Street. Tel: Keswick 72700.

Keswick Mountain Sports
73 Main Street. Tel: Keswick 73845.

Penrith

Survival Aids
Morland, Nr. Penrith. Tel: Morland 444.

The most specialised of the lot, perhaps. A wide range of outdoor and travelling gear, some of it rather militaristic. And yes, this is the same firm that sits rather strangely in London, among the shops beside Euston Station .

Wasdale

A neat little climbing shop, right beside the Inn:
Barn Door Shop
Wasdale Head. Tel: Wasdale 229.

Windermere

☆ The Fellsman
2 Victoria Street. Tel: Windermere 4876.
Especially good for skiing equipment.

Buying a House in the Lake District

For the last 200 years, millions of people who have visited the Lakes have come away with the same fantasy - why can't we find a nice little cottage and settle down here for good. Today, such things are harder to achieve than they have ever been, either finding a cottage or getting a local job. Wordsworth himself had a hell of a problem. He never ended up in his own house, as both Dove Cottage and Rydal Mount were rented, and it took him years of begging letters to influential friends to get himself a nice local job, Distributor of Stamps for Westmorland. But it can be done, even for complete outsiders.

It is possible, if you look hard and stick to the West Cumbrian fringes, to find something around the £30,000 mark. It won't be all that desirable and will need work, but they do exist. And if you have a good idea, plus a bit of talent and energy, you could even start your own business in Lakeland. Those two at Sharrow Bay, who now run England's nicest hotel, started from scratch. The Mountain Goat Bus Company, that's another recent development, begun by an offcomer. It is very often the outsiders who do bring new life and new vitality, but there are problems peculiar to the Lake District, due to the fact that it's a National Park. Your chances of opening a hamburger haven on the top of Skiddaw are a bit slim. The National Park people are not frightfully keen on that sort of thing. But, you never know. Your particular dream might be the one to succeed.

First of all, there are a few basic guidelines . . .

Which area?

It is vital to decide as quickly as possible on the particular area you want to look at, choosing a lake, a town or valley you like the best. On the map, the National Park looks pretty small, but you just can't look through all of it. There's the travelling around for one thing and secondly, the local newspapers and estate agents strictly divide up Lakeland along that north-south divide.

National Park

As a general rule, the south is more expensive than the north, thanks to the better road and rail communications. Folks from Liverpool and Manchester tend to settle round the southern Lakes. People from Newcastle aim for the northern bits.

Grasmere, despite the crowds, is still considered a very desirable place to live, especially near the lake. Ambleside and Coniston are also expensive. Windermere and Bowness are equally expensive, but thought a bit flash. Borrowdale is smart but Keswick is bourgeois. Furness has some discriminating fans while the Caldbeck fells are an acquired taste.

Cumbria

Just outside the NP boundaries, there are some smart fringes and not so smart fringes.

No one wants to live amidst the industrial deadliness of West Cumbria, unless they have no alternative, so avoid Workington, Cleator Moor, Frizington, Distington. Barrow has few fans, outside Barrow. But Maryport is quite nice and Whitehaven is coming up. Nicest of all, along that western fringe, is to look for something near Cockermouth.

Incidentally, the *real* landed-gentry of Cumbria neither live in central Lakeland nor on those western fringes - they tend to live just to the east, well away from either industry or the holiday hordes. The Lowthers are near Penrith and so are several other of Cumbria's landed nobs. Some of the biggest and nicest houses of all are in the Eden Valley.

Estate Agents

Having decided on your area, even if it's only north as opposed to south, contact the estate agents covering that section and get put on their mailing list. They will send you a copy of their property newspaper (most bigger agents have them and they are free) and details of any individual properties as they come on to the market. Have a firm idea of what you want and how much you can spend. The best agents will get in touch after you have viewed the property to see how it matched up to your expectations - this help them to narrow it down and only send you details of properties you might be interested in.

Estate Agents

The main local ones are - Thompson & Matthews and Hackney & Leigh for the south and central Lake District; Tiffen, King, Nicholson and Gibbins & Thornbarrow for the north and west coast. See Yellow Pages for local offices.

Newspapers

Always buy all the local papers when house hunting. Though few people in Cumbria sell their properties privately, you will see all the agents' adverts.

For the south and central Lakes - the best is *The Westmorland Gazette*.

For northern Lakes - *Cumberland News* or *Keswick Reminder*.

The West Coast papers (see Chapter One for addresses) can also be useful. You can get a local newspaper by post, if you get on their circulation list, as this is the best way of keeping in touch with the market from outside.

House Prices

Now we come to the tough bit - tough to generalise about and tough when you realise just how much you will have to spend to get that really desirable cottage, the one everyone wants, with the cosy porch and the nice view of the lake and the pretty fell behind. Starting from the fringes and the most cheapest, this is what you might expect to pay in 1989.

Cumbria

For an undesirable terrace house, in a place like Workington or the slummer parts of Carlisle . . . 20,000.

For a remote cottage, in rotten condition, miles away near the Scottish Borders or on the Pennines . . . £30,000.

For a better situated though unconverted cottage, on the pleasant fringes of the National Park, such as near Cockermouth or Penrith, Kendal or Furness . . . £50,000.

National Park

Small terraced house in one of the Lakeland towns, such as Windermere . . . from £60,000.

Unconverted cottage on the fringes, such as Caldbeck . . . £50,000.

Village house without views . . . £85,000 plus.

Dream cottage, in a desirable situation and fully modernised . . . from £110,000.

Detached house, with lake frontage . . . from £300,000.

Also Note:

There is usually an annual increase of up to 10% on the above prices but things went mad in 1988, with increases of 25 to 35% in that year alone. Demand far outsrips supply. Smaller houses, 2-4 bedrooms, are expensive because everyone wants them. Larger houses - unless guest houses - can be less expensive, in ratio terms, because demand is less.

It is worth noting that if you have cash available (this tends to apply more to people after holiday homes) then most agents will put you on their 'hot list' and will notify you immediately (usually by telephone) if the type of property you are seeking comes onto the market. As an idea of the competition, one of the larger estate agents currently has a 1,000 names on his 'hot list' (although not all are after the same type of property). For each house there can be as many as 75 people on the 'hot list' waiting for it.

In addition to people looking for holiday homes, or even some who actually intend to live and work in the area, the LD is very popular as a retirement area, so demand for a two or three bedroom bungalow in a good location is phenomenal, if the price is right.

Flats

These are well-worth considering for holiday homes and have a number of advantages. For a start, they aren't isolated, so security is far better. They have no garden to look after, are cheaper to maintain and there's often a management company which will look after the property in your absence.

There are some splendid flats available; manor houses were built in the last century specifically to take advantage of position and views. Many have now been converted into flats. Expect to pay about £90,000 for a two-bedroom flat with good lake views in one of these houses.

Sheltered housing

No longer the preserve of council owned properties, the upmarket, full maintained sheltered retirement home is a booming market in the LD at present (it is difficult to avoid the feeling that one day the LD will be all timeshares and sheltered housing). With these, you buy a flat in an exclusive purpose-built or redeveloped property. There's a warden on site and you get security and maintenance provided for a weekly charge by the company holding the leasehold, but the flat is yours, to keep or sell as you wish. The only restriction is that occupants have to be over a certain age, usually around 55.

Can be very handy if you'd like to retire to the area but don't want to be too tied down by property worries. Locals moving into these kind of properties has resulted in the release of a lot of larger houses coming onto the market.

Prices vary a great deal, even within an individual development. Expect a starting price of around £50,000 for a one-bedroom flat in the central Lakes, £40-45,000 in somewhere like Kendal. They are usually available through local estate agents.

Building a House

So what about building a new house? Well, for a start you are likely to be restricted to existing settlements. Nobody wants the fells cluttered up with expensive condominiums. One of the functions of the Lake District Special

Planning Board is to try and control the amount and type of new building that goes on within the National Park. If you build a house in the NP, for example, it must have a local slate roof - both to blend in with existing buildings and to maintain local industry. The LDSPB is a Good Thing, though the amount of control it exercises has been undermined in recent years by successive Secretaries of State. However, political gripes aside, being in a NP does mean that building plots are comparatively rare and expensive - a small plot in or near Windermere, for example, would fetch in excess of £50,000.

For a while the Board had a Section 52 agreement, whereby it tried to impose occupancy agreements on new housing in favour of local people (who are gradually being forced out of the market by the increasing number of holiday homes). That was overruled and the current position is that there will be no occupancy restrictions on *new* dwellings erected within a settlement. Outside settlements, strict planning control is exercised so that it is unlikely that anyone without an essential need (eg, a farm or forestry worker) will get consent.

Barn conversions are a separate area altogether and the Board provides a free leaflet as a useful starting point.

One final point - if you are buying a house, particularly in a rural area, get your solicitor to check carefully that there is not an existing occupancy restriction in force (eg for agricultural workers). The Board *is* able to enforce these and is keen to do so.

Time Sharing

Lakeland's biggest growth area. Basically, you are buying a share in a property for up to 80 years ahead, buying only the week or weeks of the year in which you take your holiday. For those weeks, the place is yours to do with as you like - you can rent it, lend it to friends, holiday in it yourself or even swap it with timeshare places elsewhere in the world. The advantage is that for the rest of the year, you have no worries about the property or its maintenance - and the standard of these places can be very high indeed, with plenty of facilities on site (swimming pools, bars, saunas, etc). The disadvantage is that you can only use the place for the week or weeks you have bought (unless you do a swap). There is never the feeling of it being 'your' holiday home. There can also be hefty maintenance expenses which can go up all the time.

Prices vary according to which part of the year you prefer, higher in the summer and Christmas period, lower in January and the tail end of the year. School holidays are always expensive, so October is best value.

The Lake District currently has eleven true timeshare developments, with more at the planning stage. The developments range from estates, offering a very high standard of accommodation and services, to simple apartments or cottages on their own, with fewer facilities.

We have rated the best of the estates:

☆☆☆ The Langdale Partnership, Great Langdale, Ambleside. Tel: Langdale 391.

This was the first of the Lake District's timeshare establishments, opened in 1982, and remains the most successful. Built at the old Langdale gunpowder works, they now offer a range of accommodation based around a large, landscaped estate near Elterwater. The original Swiss-style chalets are still there, but now there are also apartments in Chapel Stile and very plush (some might say flash) apartments in Elterwater Hall. All very up-market and a little cut off from the locals, though the Partnership is responsible for sponsoring several arts events locally. Facilities include a hotel, an excellent leisure centre, with swimming pool, sauna, squash court, solarium and gymnasium. There are also bars and a restaurant on site, some of which are also open to the general public (the leisure centre is restricted to timeshare or hotel residents, or to locals buying a yearly club membership).

Since the last edition the Partnership has swallowed up the Langdale Hotel, done it up and relaunched it as The Wainwright. (A bit cheeky, but they really mean the local name for a wheelwright. Of course they do.)

You can buy from one to ten weeks; a two-bedroom lodge will cost from £3,800 to £11,000 per week, depending on time of year. This price is for an 80 year ownership. On top, there is a management charge (which can go up each year), covering rates, maintenance, insurance of the house and contents and domestic services (cleaning, provision of towels, etc - they boast that you don't have to lift a finger to see that your property is well looked after). Each lodge has central heating, is furnished to a high standard and telephones are available. A Chapel Stile apartment costs between £3,150 and £8,000 and an apartment in Elterwater Hall is between £4,000 and £12,000.

☆☆☆ The Lakeland Village, Newby Bridge, near Ulverston. Tel: Newby Bridge 31144.

This is a prestigious development built jointly by Douglas and Kenning on the banks of the River Leven. Centrepiece is the Whitewater Hotel which provides luxury hotel accommodation, plus restaurant, bar and conference facilities, in what was originally an old textile mill. Timeshare accommodation consists of traditionally-built Lakeland stone cottages, all finished to a very high standard and rather more homely than Swiss chalets. Pride and joy of the development is the leisure centre (called Cascades - they all have to have their twee names); it provides swimming pool, jacuzzi, squash court, gym and dance studio, and on the top floor they provide specialised health and beauty treatment on an appointment basis, available to timeshare owners and members of the outside world alike (for a fee). Used to be run by Champneys, the health farm people, but now run by the Lakeland Village themselves. Use of the leisure centre comes with timeshare ownership or staying at the hotel and is also available on a club membership basis to locals. Prices from £5,520 to £10,350.

The Lakeland Village has less of a Tropicana Club atmosphere than the Langdales and the air of luxury is more discreet, but some people belong to both so they obviously couldn't make up their minds either.

☆ The Lakelands, Lower Gale, Ambleside.
Tel: Ambleside 33777.

Substantial buildings, done in local stone by a local builder, which offers indoor pool, sauna and bistro. Much smaller than the first two developments; by the end of 1988, they only had 100 weeks left for sale. Price range is £4,200 to £8,500. The lease is for an initial 25 years, after which it becomes the property of the timeshare owners themselves, to sell or keep as they wish.

The same lot are also responsible for **The Quaysiders Club** at Waterhead (Ambleside 33969). Self-catering apartments on a much-smaller site (though they make up for it with huge and garish signs at the roadside). Usual 80 year lease; prices £2,900 to £6,500.

☆ Keswick Bridge, Old Station, Station Road, Keswick.
Tel: Keswick 74649.

Don't be confused by Keswick Spa, the public leisure pool complex, put up by the same developers. Or put off. The timeshare bit is behind, carefully hidden, beside the river, on what was once a field used for archery. Attractive Swedish style lodges, with high quality furnishing and fittings (well up to Langdales standards) but so far the other facilities are not in the same league, such as the restaurant. They will always have Keswick Spa to contend with, and the setting is cramped, despite that pretty bit of river. Hard to forget you are so near the town, though of course some might consider that an advantage. They promise more, and better, but they will have to work hard. Prices still reasonable, considering the lush lodges, so could be a good investment, if it all takes off. Cheapest lodge, to sleep four, £3,000 in 1989. Best, sleeping eight, £7,300.

☆ Windermere Marina Village, Nabwood, Bowness-on-Windermere. Tel: Windermere 6551.

One of the newest timeshares, opened in 1987. Built on the site of a privately owned marina and it's all frightfully nautical. Purpose-built cottages and a £1.5m leisure centre, called the Spinnaker Club, overlook a busy yacht marina. The cottages are neat and homely, and if you own a boat you can moor it alongside for the duration of your stay. In the evening, you can sit out on your balcony and watch the sun go down over a forest of masts. Could be deafening if they don't all tie their halyards down.

The Spinnaker is very new and plush, but rather cramped. Everything is built practically on top of the swimming pool, which can make it stifling. In addition to the pool, there are jacuzzis, a sauna, the Commodore Bistro and a games room, featuring space invader machines. Membership of the club is restricted to timeshare owners and berth-holders on the marina.

Prices are from £2,900 to £10,950. Leases run to 2040, after which the whole place will be updated and offered for resale (original owners get first choice).

Setting up in Business

Tourism and farming apart, there are few large industries within the National Park boundary. Most of it is clustered on the fringes - Carlisle, the West Cumbrian coast, Barrow-in-Furness, Penrith and Kendal.

Assistance for business has changed considerably since the last edition and, in general, anyone with a good idea for a small business will find more help in outer Cumbria, where the higher unemployment leads to more grants.

Cumbria County Council. Recommended as the first contact for anyone thinking of setting up. The Economic Development and Corporate Policy Dept. will give advice about what opportunities are available, even down to detailed information about premises and training staff.

They are also keen to look after existing businesses and are promoting a 'Made in Cumbria' scheme. For information packs, contact:

> Industrial Promotions Officer
> Cumbria County Council
> The Courts, Carlisle
> Tel: Carlisle 23456.

Other Useful Contacts: There are a number of other contacts which can be of help to smaller businesses.

The Rural Development Commission is a consultant service for small firms; lots of useful information about how to expand, develop or market your firm. Address from Cumbria County Council.

There are also a number of Enterprise Agencies which

offer a free service for new starters. Contact the relevant area office:

Furness Business Initiatives, Project Office, Walney Road, Barrow-in-Furness. Tel: Barrow 22132.

Cumbria Rural Enterprise Agency, 44/46 Lound Road, Kendal. Tel: Kendal 26624.

Business Initiatives Carlisle, Carlisle Enterprise Centre, James Street, Carlisle. Tel: Carlisle 34120.

Anyone on the West Coast is advised to apply direct to:
The West Cumbria Development Agency
(Address from Cumbria County Council.)

The local councils are involved in Enterprise schemes, depending on the needs of their particular area. It is also worth looking out for Training Advice Points (TAPs) in local libraries, and the Cumbria Information Service, in Carlisle library.

Finally, there is a **Small Business Club** at Kendal and there are a number of useful courses at colleges throughout the area (again, the Economic Development Department at Cumbria County Council can provide details).

Chapter Sixteen

Surveys and Fascinating Facts

Tourism

Number of visitors per year - around 10 million (day visitors) plus 3 million (staying).

90% of all visitors to the Park come by private car.

14.5 million people live within 3 hours drive of the Lake District.

Where they come from

Great Britain

North	16%
Yorkshire/Humberside	11%
North West	31%
East Midlands	5%
West Midlands	3%
East Anglia	3%
South East	20%
South West	3%
Wales	1%
Scotland	9%

(NB These figures taken from ETB research; it is possible that they may need a new battery in their calculator.)

Overseas visitors

USA/ Canada	41%
France	3%
West Germany	16%
Netherlands	2%
Other EEC countries	7%
Australia/New Zealand	11%
All Others	20%

Purpose of visit

Holidays	75%
Visiting friends or relations	7%
Business/conference	15%
Other	3%

Purpose of day trips

Visiting heritage attractions (sic)	5%
Visiting commercial outdoor attractions	3%
Informal outdoor recreation	38%
Sport	28%
Indoor entertainment	11%
Bathing/sunbathing	2%
Visiting friends/relatives	10%
Other	3%

It is interesting to note that general moving around and doing things (climbing a fell, sailing a boat or riding a horse) accounts for 66% of the figures. So much for needing more indoor visitor attractions in the Lakes. In July and August 1975, the National Park people went round 77 car parks and asked people what they planned to do:

Picnicking/sitting	34%
Admiring the view	32%
Walking - over 1 mile	28%
over 4 miles	11%
fell walking	10%
Visiting shops/cafeterias	20%

Still hanging around the car parks, the NPA asked people if there were any parts of the Lake District they no longer enjoyed, and if so why? Bowness and Windermere came top of the table, as the place people no longer enjoyed most. Some way behind came Keswick, Ambleside and Coniston. In all cases, the overriding reason was that they were too crowded (and not because they lacked facilities - interesting).

Employment

In 1986, 25 350 people were employed in the Cumbrian tourist industry - around 13% of the total workforce.

Who Comes to the Lakes:

age	
16-24	19%
25-35	17%
35-44	18%
45-54	14%
55-64	21%
65+	10%

Occupation of Head of Household:

AB Senior & Middle Managers	43%
C1 Junior Managers, Clerical	24%
C2 Skilled Manual	21%
DE Semi & Unskilled, Pensioners	12%

Preferred Time of Year for Trips to Cumbria

Jan, Feb, March	7%
April, May, June	30%
July	12%
August	18%
September	17%
Oct, Nov, December	16%

In 1974 on an August Sunday, 60,000 vehicles entered the Lake District National Park, adding 180,000 people to the 50,000 or more already on holiday in the area on that day.

On a Spring Bank Holiday there may be as many as 7,000 tents in the National Park. (And there are about 1,800 holiday or second homes.)

Peers

Has Penrith got more hereditary peers associated with it than any other town of its size in the country? Well there's the Earl of Lonsdale (Head of the Lowther family), then Viscount Ullswater, Lord Howard of Penrith, Lord Inglewood of Hutton-in-the-Forest, and Viscount Whitelaw, Willie Whitelaw as was. So that's five. Beat that, any town.

Population

The Lake District National Park has 40,674 people, according to the 1981 figures. Almost 24% of these were retired folks. The number of young children (under 14 years) had fallen from 21% in 1971 to 17% in 1981.

The total population figure has in fact hardly changed at all in the last 30 years - in 1951 it was 40,500. But it is pretty obvious what's happening - we're all getting older. There are now 10% more elderly people than 10 years ago. Will the Lake District become a Museum - the people and not just the exhibits?

In the county of Cumbria as a whole, there are 478,000 persons in an area of 2,629 square miles. In 1983, there were 39,500 pupils attending 340 primary schools and 38,800 pupils attending 51 secondary schools. There were seven colleges of Further Education with 12,5000 students. Roads, I'm glad you asked about roads, because I have the figure here which is 4,796 miles of roads, including 273 Motorway and Trunk Roads. Thank you.

Cumbria's Top Twenty Five Tourist Attractions: 1988

1.	Windermere Iron Steamboat Company	520,060
2.	Ravenglass & Eskdale Railway	250,000
3.	Sellafield	148,000
4.	Brockhole, National Park Visitor Centre	98,000
5.	Hill Top	90,000
6.	Lakeside & Haverthwaite Railway	85,000
7.	Lowther Park	84,000
8.	Dove Cottage	80,400
9.	Holker Hall	80,100
10.	Cumberland Pencil Museum	75,000
11.	Whinlatter Visitor Centre	74,500
12.	Border Regiment Museum, Carlisle	58,621
13.	Carlisle Castle	57,495
14.	Carlisle Museum & Art Gallery	55,000
15.	Wetheriggs Pottery, Penrith	50,000
16.	Levens Hall	47,701
17.	Lakeland Motor Museum	43,209
18.	Windermere Steamboat Museum	40,236
19.	Sizergh	40,000
20.	Muncaster Castle	39,553
21.	Rydal Mount	39,500
22.	Brantwood	33,014
23.	Mirehouse	31,200
24.	Townend, Troutbeck	25,000
25.	Beatrix Potter Gallery	21,000

Some surprising changes, in our regular and terribly exciting survey of the Top Attractions. As usual, like is not always being compared with like, such as our Number One. It's not fair on a little literary home to be put up against the hordes who like to take a boat down Windermere. So let's forget that and look at the Number Three. Wow. Sellafield has come from practically nowhere, but then so it should, with all that costly TV and media promotion, plus all the children they bus in. It's also free. Brockhole, alas, is going down, by almost 50,000 since our 1986 edition. Hill Top and Dove Cottage have both gone up, with Hill Top still just ahead. The Cumberland Pencil Museum in Keswick has shot up. Levens Hall is also doing well. Of the Visitor Centres, we have only allowed the figures for Whinlatter to appear on our list, as they have a little beam which counts bodies, whereas Grizedale offered a figure of 100,000, which turned out to be the number of cars. Cheaters. Look out though for the new Beatrix Potter Gallery in Hawkshead. They were open for only four months in 1988, but didn't they do well, creeping in at number 25.

Things People Have Asked

Some of the questions which have been put to the various Tourist Information Centres in the Lake District. Now that you know so much about Lakeland, you will of course know all the correct answers.

Can you direct me to the Beatrix Potteries?
How do you fill up the lakes?
Does it ever stop raining?
What time do the Windermere boats leave for the Isle of Man?
When is high tide on the lakes?
Can we visit the glass factory at Ravenglass?
Where's the rhinoceros pass?
Which mine does all the mint cake come from?
Have you got this week's Dorothy's journals?
Where are the Mountain Goats?
Where are the Kilt Factories?
Where can I see dryrot fencing?

The guide at Dove Cottage was explaining that Scott had come to the Lakes to visit Wordsworth. "Was that before or after", asked a visitor, "that he went to the South Pole?"

`During the 1985 season a notice began to appear around Bowness and Ambleside which read as follows:
Submarine Trips beneath Belle Isle.
See the 300-year old mooring platform
holding the island in place. Also
marine life and wrecks. £5.

People began to ask TICs for details of departure times, and were genuinely disappointed when they were told it was all a hoax. A similar stunt was pulled in 1984 when the National Park Treacle Mines in Borrowdale held an open day. The NPA was not amused.

The Great Wheeze of 1986 occurred when Windermere Civic Society arranged for a pair of road signs to stand on the outskirts of the village, on the A591. These should have read "Windermere welcomes tidy visitors", but some miscreant changed the second "d" into "n". It kept happening, so the signs were taken down.

Index

Acknowledgements

I am grateful to the following people for their help, interest, information and enthusiasm during the compiling of this edition: Lorna Shelbourn, Bobbie Nunn, Angela Borrowdale and Jim Morley at the Cumbria Tourist Board; Barry Tullett at the National Park Authority (and best wishes for early 'retirement'); Richard Knowles at Cumbria County Council Economic Development and Corporate Policy Department; Robin Higham at Thompson & Matthews; Abbot Hall Gallery for use of photographs and to those long gone photographers and artists responsible for the 19th century illustrations we have used in the book but been unable to name, Thanks, whoever you were. Oliver Turnbull and staff at Titus Wilson, for knocking the book into shape. And thanks to Joyce Blake for proof-reading and indexing and providing additional information (especially on castles and cooking...). Lastly, without the enormous work done by chief researcher Colin Shelbourn and assistant researchers, Marjorie Dodds and Pam Williamson, the book would never have been possible.

To All Readers

It is hoped that this book will be reprinted every two years, for ever and ever, and we plan to update almost everything in due course. It is meant to help everyone who loves the Lakes, either residents or visitors, so if you have any good news, new restaurants or new amenities, or bad news, places which you think we should not recommend any more, then do let us know. The more opinions that come in the better. And if you are in the book, or your firm or services, please let us know of any changes, any improvements, excitements. You can't expect us to find out everything. And if you're not in, but think you should be, tell us. We might give a nice mensh, all for free. Thanks. You've been a lovely audience. Now start writing your own comments and information. Post them to Hunter Davies, Titus Wilson & Son Ltd, Redmayne's Yard, 10 Stricklandgate, Kendal, Cumbria, LA9 4TB

Chief Researcher Colin Shelbourn lives in Windermere and is a freelance writer and cartoonist. He was educated at York University where he read psychology. Cartoonist for *The Westmorland Gazette* and *Lakes Leader* and author of *Great Walks in the Lake District* and *Lakeland Towns and Villages*.

Author Hunter Davies comes from Carlisle, was educated at University College, Durham, and is a well-known author and broadcaster. He lives part of every year at Loweswater. He is married with three children and is the author of many books, including *A Walk Around the Lakes, Beatrix Potter's Lakeland* and a biography of Wordsworth.